PEOPLE WHO DO THINGS TO EACH OTHER

Essays in Analytical Psychology

Judith Hubback

CHIRON PUBLICATIONS

Wilmette, Illinois

Chapters 1, 4, 5, 6, 7, 8, 9, 10, 11, 12, 14 of this book are reprinted from *The Journal of Analytical Psychology* with permission.

Chapter 3 is reprinted from *Harvest* with the permission of the Harvest Committee of the Analytical Psychology Club, London.

Printed in the United States of America

Book design by Kirk George Panikis

Library of Congress Cataloging-in-Publication Data

Hubback, Judith.
  People who do things to each other.

  Includes index.
    1. Psychotherapist and patient.   2. Psychotherapy
3. Jung, C. G. (Carl Gustav), 1875-1961.   I. Title.
RC480.8.H93 1988   616.89'14   87-18236
ISBN 0-933029-27-6
ISBN 0-933029-21-7 (pbk.)

Contents

Preface

Most introductions are written, I believe, after the book, and most readers quite rightly treat them for what they are—postscripts. If read at all, introductions are probably read after the book. I learned at school a dull-sounding but eminently useful precept: say what you are going to say, say it, then say you have said it. As a communicator, I have tried to be on the reader's side, whatever his or her interest. To satisfy valid narcissism, writers are expressionists: in relating to others, writers take them into account as equals and allies.

For those who are neither practitioners nor have ever embarked on therapy, it is worth saying at the outset that I use the word "psychotherapy" in the way I believe Jung used it. It is the larger general term which includes the specialty of analysis. It means here the treatment or therapy of the patient and his or her psyche by a qualified analytical psychologist, taking as full account as possible of the unconscious forces at work, both individual and collective (personal and archetypal), forces which are distorting the patient's conscious life and relationships, but which most likely contain elements offering possibilities of fruitful development in the direction of that person's fullest potential, leading towards individuation. The analytic element in a thorough analysis is an essential one, and the therapeutic process involves the total psyche of the psychotherapist-analyst. The concept of the wounded healer is at the center of the work.

This book of collected papers on analysis and psychotherapy will, I hope, be easy on the busy reader. It can be read in a protracted way, interspersed with other activities: there is no need to attend immediately to chapters which seem from their titles to have little appeal; they can be read in more or less any order. All the same, quite a lot of thought went into arranging their sequence, once I had taken two decisions.

First, I discarded the idea of putting them in the chronological order of their first publication, which would mainly have reflected how my observations and ideas developed through the gradual accumulation of clinical experience. I decided that was not especially significant since, in the course of rereading them, it appeared that my present major interests— the relation of the self to the other, symbols, and change—were already present when I first qualified as a member of the London Society of Analytical Psychology: "ordinary" life had alerted me to the importance of matters about which I wanted to find out more, and which are still of great concern.

The second decision was of necessity to pay less rather than more attention to the classification of the chapters: the conventional distinction is between papers on theory and those of a clinical nature, but only two (Chapters 6 and 7) in this book contain no clinical matter or examples. There are no new major contributions to the theory of analytical psychology. I offer descriptions of attempts to come to terms with the vicissitudes of personal life and the human condition, to reflect on them, and to apply as much lucid thought as possible in the circumstances.

The first five chapters offer a number of observations on the art, craft, and technique of analytical therapy. In their texture they each contain the warp of examining the elements of the patient's trouble—analysis —and the woof of attending to healing—therapy. The concept of cure is not featured, since the nature of the work of an analytical psychologist is very different from that of the physician. The feeling of having been cured is one that probably most of us wish to attain when we enter treatment, psychological as well as physical; few of us ever find that wish granted, and we come to accept that the most we achieve are scars where there had once been open wounds. But the psychotherapist's craft is all-important, so the book opens with a discussion of what I consider to be the basic nature of the work, the symbolic attitude that it asks of practitioners. That is what differentiates it from counselling. Chapter 1 was my first clinical paper and it was specifically about analytical psychotherapy. I have paired it with one of the latest, "Reflections on Concepts and Experience" (Chapter 2) in order to offer help to those who are training to be analysts: they will see that the work of an analytical psychologist consists in the constant interaction between the patient and the analyst, and between what happens (when that can be established) and what is thought about it. There is a mysterious marriage between the two, which is yet not so singularly mysterious as to be unfathomable. Then follow three further descriptions of what comes about—or does not—when two people project varying amounts of unconscious contents, attitudes, and preconceptions into each other (transference and countertransference) and into the space and the relation between them.

That concept of *people* who do things to each other (Chapter 3) together with the one of some of the *things* they do (Chapter 4) develops further the theme of interaction. And it is taken up in Chapter 5, on acting out. That originally psychoanalytic term and its applications in contemporary Jungian practice are studied there with archetypes in mind, and that provides a fruitful way of reappraising it. It demonstrates how the patient's anxieties lead to acting out as well as to attempts to manipulate, and the understanding of both of them improves when symbols with an archetypal dimension are taken into account. The underlying notion in that set of chapters is the well-known one of being and doing. And the in-forming essential factors are the influence of unconscious actions and reactions, and the archetypal components of them.

The next section, Chapters 6 and 7, offers two somewhat contrasted approaches to the study of the theory of analytical psychology. In "Uses and Abuses of Analogy" I explore the topic of image-making as the background to conscious thinking, glance briefly at other contemporary disciplines which evidence analogous processes and concepts, and offer an opening on the theme of the unitary world idea in so far as it applies to a theory of transference projections. The *"VII Sermones ad Mortuos"* (Chapter 7) is a partner to the one on analogy; it is, in a sense, my eldest analytic-literary child, the offspring of two ways of studying: Jung's strange document would only yield its meanings (or at least some of them) to a combination of the academic and the poetic approaches. I enjoyed writing it, and I hope some of the pleasure it gave me is still there for later generations of Jungians.

Chapters 8, 9 and 10 constitute the clinical center of the book. In all three the dynamics of the transference/countertransference are demonstrated in action and each patient's need to have the early structures worked over as deeply as possible and reconstituted with the analyst. Having recognized the great value of Melanie Klein's writings, it had to be admitted openly that a certain emulation—as of that of a younger sister—was pushing me towards exploring the viciousness of envy, to see if there was some element carrying a different charge of energy, which could be found to have heuristic and developmental value. The linking of Kleinian and Jungian concepts has been of use to many contemporary psychotherapists, particularly where unconscious fantasies and archetypal imagery are concerned. And in Chapter 9, "Depressed Patients and the *Coniunctio*," I explore the ever-important theme of the *coniunctio* within the psyche of the analyst with special attention given to how his or her reasonably viable sense of self is used by the patient who is in search of an improved, less depression-prone, sixth sense.

"Reflections on the Psychology of Women" is thus titled in order to convey that it is a small contribution to an enormous subject. It was, to a great extent, various experiences and observations during the first half of my life that led me, before analysis, to study some aspects of socio-psychology where highly educated married women were concerned. In the wider world members of the women's liberation movements in many countries were, a little later, making it possible for women to examine their faulty sense of identity as well as encouraging them perhaps simplistically to react to unfavorable cultural and economic conditions. The dynamism behind that offensive-defensive reactivity is now, in the main, being channelled more constructively, but I think most analysts would concur that both the men and the women they encounter professionally have a long way to go before the contrasexual archetypes of anima and animus are lived with consciously and positively.

The short chapter about a small piece of research on the occasion of the assassination of Senator Robert Kennedy has been included for a dual reason: it seemed a good example of how an enterprise of limited size can be mounted among cooperative colleagues, and therefore of how a similar one might be attempted some time in the future, but it also illustrates how a violent event in the public arena of one country—the USA—made an impact in the small world of analysts in London. It shows how news of exterior aggression can act, in some instances, as a catalyst for analyzing yet once more transference and countertransference; and how some patients identified with the victim while others could acknowledge the potential aggressor within themselves. Everything is grist for the analyst's mill.

Chapter 12 is one London analyst's view in 1980 of how analytical psychology had developed and changed since Jung's visit to London in 1935, when he gave what came to be known as the Tavistock Lectures, and the way in which we are still using many of his concepts and attitudes. It contains one particular sentence to which I would like to draw attention: "We go on asking: what brings about change for a particular person, and for different types of people? When we take time to step back from daily pressures we can ask fundamental questions" (towards the end of paragraph one of the section headed "Research").

That leads me to just a few comments on Chapters 13 and 14. I am grateful to Murray Stein and Nathan Schwartz-Salant, editors of the Chiron Clinical Series and conveners of the annual conferences held at Ghost Ranch in New Mexico, for inviting me to give a paper there in 1985, when the topic was "The Body in Analysis." With their permission, Chapter 13 of this book is reproduced from the Chiron Clinical

Series, vol. 1986. Writing it gave me the opportunity to link certain clinical events with one of the essential features of analytical psychology, the analyst's imperfections and, therefore, humanness. The next and last chapter on change is built round a theme which has been waiting in my mind for some time. It is, as its title shows, not about full transformation, which is an impressive achievement, when it occurs, carrying with it perhaps even the marvellous quality of metamorphosis, which the *Oxford English Dictionary* defines as "a complete change in the appearance, condition, character of a person." But when there is the amount of alteration that can be qualified as "real change," it is, in the observation and experience of analysis, irreversible: it does belong to the self. This is not the place for a further addition to the numerous writings on the self in analytical psychology. I wish only to record my experience that we need the self in the other, and the self of the other, to bring about positive changes in each of ourselves.

Chapter 1

The Symbolic Attitude in Psychotherapy

The intention in this paper is to study some aspects of psychotherapy, as distinct from analysis, with a view to finding out what happens; to examine the value of the therapist's having an active attitude to the developmental possibilities inherent in various kinds of symbols and symbolic occurrences; and to show that the nature of effective interaction is the same whether the treatment is labelled analysis or psychotherapy.

The analyst pays attention to what he or she is doing, to what the patient is doing, and to the psychodynamics of what is happening. In this work, actions and interactions are of even greater interest than are concepts. Concepts distract from actions through turning them into things; concepts can be used defensively against experiencing and understanding the patient as a person. Without neglecting the careful consideration of nouns we must be even more closely acquainted with verbs.

Over the years interest has gradually deepened in the theoretical bases of the various types of treatment. Jung in "Problems of Modern Psychotherapy," says: "The doctor is as much in the analysis as the patient" (1929). In "Medicine and Psychotherapy" he says: "The real point is the treatment of the whole psychic human being" (1945). In "Fundamental Questions of Psychotherapy" he says: "The intelligent psychotherapist has known for years that any complicated treatment is an individual, *dialectical*, process" (1951, p.123), and, later in the same paper, "I therefore consider it my main task to examine the manifestations of the unconscious . . . but . . . the symbols produced by the unconscious derive from archaic modes of psychic functioning" (p.123). These considerations are theoretical statements arrived at through clinical experience. They apply in brief as well as in long therapy.

In the paper "Analytical Psychology and Psychotherapy," originally

Originally published in *The Journal of Analytical Psychology* 14:1 (1969), pp.36–47. Also in *Technique in Jungian Analysis*, Library of Analytical Psychology, London: Heinemann 1974.

published in 1949, Fordham writes: "In stating that analytical psychology can contribute to the theory of psychotherapy it is necessary to point out that analytic concepts can be applied whether the procedure under consideration be long or short. Therapy is basically not a question of time, but of how the needs of a patient can best be met" (1958, p.169). The psychoanalyst Szurek, in attempting to differentiate between analysis and therapy, discusses the question of whether the similarities between the two are the factors which account for improvements in the patient, and asks whether the differences are matters of nature or of degree. He also wonders whether psychotherapy is a special application of the same basic theory as psychoanalysis and queries whether an analytic situation is possible with fewer than five sessions each week. He comes perhaps a little closer to Fordham's view, quoted above, when he makes use of Freud's discovery that the question "How can, must, or shall I treat the patient?" was the wrong one, and that a better one to ask is "What can I do *with* the patient?" (1958).

Another psychoanalyst, Edward Glover, reviewing the theory of psychotherapy in the United States and in Great Britain, comes to the conclusion that "it is doubtful whether the principles of general psychotherapy have changed much since the period following the First World War," but he is willing to add that "the move towards character analysis" and "the complications of ego-analysis" do not alter the "fundamental factor of transference" and "the approaches to the unconscious." He writes, moreover, that "the prerequisite of a coherent theory of psychotherapy is a theory of mind that will account for both normal and abnormal manifestations" (1960, p.75).

The increasing attention given to symbols, to symbol formation, to object relations, to transference and to countertransference in their totality is gradually contributing to the understanding of what happens in all personal relationships, of which therapy is one, and to the theory of minds in action. The constituent theories, and the possible general theory, have to be seen against the background of various current social facts. An important one for the purposes of this chapter is that there is a rising demand for therapy, as compared with full analysis, which analytical psychologists are trying to meet in a variety of settings.

Where a theory of mind is concerned, there are distinctions but there are no hard and fast lines either between normal and abnormal, or between therapist and patient, or between analysis and psychotherapy. Therapists use the same tool—themselves—whenever they meet a patient (or try to meet a patient who is frightened of meeting) even though they use this tool in varying ways with different people, in different settings, and at different times. In his *Study of Brief Psychotherapy*, Malan shows most convincingly what others have discovered independently for themselves, that it is necessary to tackle the patient's negative feelings and the mourning and separation problems inherent in the end of even brief treatment. The other finding of importance is the influence of enthusiasm: "Perhaps the intense interest of any worker new to this field engenders a corresponding heightened excitement in the patient, with the result that repressed feelings come easily to the surface and are experienced with such intensity and completeness that no further working through is necessary. Subsequently this excitement can never quite be recaptured, nor can its effects" (1963, p.13).

The study of work which has been done in long analyses on the integrating aspects of the functioning of symbols "has much to offer if it can be related to current knowledge of how symbol formation comes about" (Jackson 1963, p.156). And more recently Plaut, being concerned with ego development, linked transference preparedness, and the lack of it, with trust and with the inability to trust, and with the capacity to make and to use images (1966).

Psychotherapy

The term psychotherapy will be used here to denote what is commonly thought of as brief work: a matter of months, not usually years. The experiences of sixteen particular patients in therapy, and mine with them, provide the background individually and cumulatively. Three are presented in detail to substantiate some of the processes I want to describe. Nine came once a week only: they were university students. Seven used to come, or are at present coming, twice a week; fourteen of the sixteen are under thirty years old; ten are under twenty-five. Of those who pay for their therapy themselves only one could at present afford to come frequently. They are a group of patients who, by and large, come to the number of sessions which are considered sufficient for psychotherapy, but not analysis; they are in this position for reasons of age, and geographical reasons, or because they are students earning nothing, or people with very small incomes.

Therapy once or twice a week is not miniature analysis, in the sense of frequent sessions over a long period, dependency, and a very considerable investment of libido on the part of analyst and patient. There are many features in a long intensive contact which can only rarely be discerned in the work described here, but a strongly experienced involvement can occur in the therapist which, if well understood, contributes

greatly to the patient's development and to the integration of previously
damaging unconsciousness.

When I think of the course of treatment with each of these patients,
and try to discern which factor was crucially important, it seems to me
that it was the patient's use of a symbol or of a symbolic event which on
each occasion led to ego development. The patients were people who
were amenable to therapy, meaning that their personalities predisposed
them to being able to make use of it, and most particularly of its symbolizing component. Certainly many people who are referred for therapy
turn out not to have this.

Symbols and the Symbolic Attitude

In spite of the great amount of work done, and the consequential vast
literature written, on the subject of symbols, there is as yet no consensus
of opinion which satisfies a variety of analysts on how to use the word.
In the present state of the controversy, and for the present purpose, symbol is being used as a descriptive word for any idea, thing, action or
event representing in the present any such item which existed previously. The item in the past is, as a result of repression, relatively unknown in the present; the symbol is, at the time of its occurrence, the
best possible representation. "Whether a thing is a symbol or not depends chiefly upon the attitude of the consciousness considering it . . . it
is quite possible for a man to produce a fact which does not appear in the
least symbolic to himself, although profoundly so to another" (Jung
1921, p.603). A symbol "manifests itself spontaneously in a symbolical
effect upon the regarding subject" (ibid). And the therapist's symbolic
attitude (still following Jung) "is the outcome of a definite view of life
endowing the occurrence, whether great or small, with a meaning to
which a certain deeper value is given than to pure actuality" (ibid.
p.604).

The therapist is responsible for discerning the prospective meaning of
the phenomenon being used as a symbol by the patient. On the basis of
his greater consciousness he can, with a symbolic attitude, make possible
an experience of transition from lesser to greater awareness of the previously unconscious forces at work, which are distorting current events and
behavior. It follows that in even brief therapy the patient can be seen to
be using unconsciously a wide range of possible ways of conveying to the
therapist essential information about pathogenic facts in his earlier life.
The particular activity of the symbol which is used in therapy is its activation of ego development, as a result of unintegrated past experiences

being brought together with present ones, in the transference, so that something happens.

In the popular world outside most consulting rooms there are a number of new terms which have entered my orbit in the last year (they have probably been around much longer) and one of them is "a happening." This is not necessarily the same as a "love-in"; a "happening" is a generic term, of which a "love-in" is one instance. Unless a therapy hour has at least some of the same essence as a "happening," the loss of tempo, impetus, interest, and libido will be serious. And this is of greater importance in once or twice a week therapy than when the contacts are more frequent.

In considering happenings in therapy, it is worth being thoroughly acquainted with what "attitude" is, and the power it exerts. Jung defined it as "a readiness of the psyche to act in a certain direction . . . an attitude always has an objective; this can be either conscious or unconscious" (1921, p.526). "Attitude" also includes the concepts of aptitude, fitness, a posture, and a gesture adapted to some purpose. In cases where, for whatever reason, less frequent rather than more frequent therapy is undertaken, the first basic attitude must be of accepting the limitations imposed by the reality, and deciding to adapt oneself to the maximum within that frame.

In treating those who can come only once or twice a week, I find it essential to try to keep in mind that if I can manage to adapt to them, this is more than likely to foster in them the growth of a capacity to adapt in the various ways that each individual is going to need. In so far as "attitude" is a synonym for readiness, the analogy of the mother being ready for a particular baby to give her indications of its individuality from the earliest possible moment, and her readiness to respond partly as *a* mother but also as *the* mother that *that* baby requires—this is the sort of thing which happens in the less frequent just as much as in the more frequent therapies.

It is necessary to be ready for almost anything to become an image representing, in therapy, earlier events, experiences or attitudes to others and to the patient himself; and to be ready to bring out the symbolic potential in such images. If they are left, rather than picked up, there is some likelihood in once-a-week or twice-a-week therapy that they will not recur. When I am reflecting on the course of a particular hour with a patient who comes infrequently and find that I failed to notice something which had an image and a symbol potential, then I think more has been lost than when this occurs with a patient in full analysis. This is inherent in the conditions of work, although it may also be an example of excessive super-ego domination within me.

The Illusional Transference

Images, illusions, and delusions can be examined in conjunction with each other. An image, in therapy, is a more straightforward presentation or representation of material than is an illusion or a delusion. The root word in "image" is the Latin *imitor*, meaning "I imitate." The root in "illusion" and in "delusion" is *ludo*, "I play." In "illusion," the image plays in with the subject; in "delusion," the image plays him down and mocks at him.

The important happening in therapy is the interplay between therapist and patient, on the basis of the fact that play and interplay between the mother and the infant set the tone of the infant's later interplay and interaction with other people. In a deep analysis there may well be a long stage, or a short phase, in which the patient's transference onto the analyst takes on a delusional quality, particularly when it has become essential for paranoid anxieties to be worked through.

I have not yet found that a situation of that depth or quality has developed in once-a-week or twice-a-week therapy. It is tantalizing to have patients who would quite likely be able to benefit by such a difficult experience, who most likely need it if they are to be enabled to achieve a hopeful amount of healing, but who, at the current stage of their lives are financially debarred from the possibility. Short of the fully experienced delusional transference and the regression to symbolic equivalence, which is what happens then, the rather less extreme illusional transference develops, and the therapist plays in with this.

A small example may illustrate what I have in mind. One of my twice-a-week patients, who uses the couch, is very knowledgeable and leads an active and full life; in therapy, also, he uses almost every available instant of his time. He is decidedly observant. His dreams, as well as being vivid, accurately recalled and physical in content, also contain jokes. On occasions he has thought that I will not believe him, that I will think he has invented them, cleverly, and perhaps especially for me. For weeks on end he needs to have the illusion of feeding me, which he does in many other ways as well as the dreams with jokes.

He can easily tell me about his overt envy of me, but the unconscious envy (which is what he defends himself against in reversing the roles and trying so often to feed me) only emerges through an actual and startling experience of an illusion. This happened after he had been coming for some months, a few sessions after he had told me that his friend's analyst supplies *his* patients with a coverlet. The friend had been in analysis nearly six years, going five times a week. I just managed not to fall into what looked like a trap set to catch me out in not feeding him adequately, in which case he would have continued in his fantasy of always being the feeding one: I made no comment on the fact that there was, and always had been, a coverlet on the couch. It seemed better to wait until he had noticed it himself. Over the weekend his envy of the friend and also of myself dropped in intensity and at the next session the moment he arrived he saw the coverlet, and the illusion was dropped to the tune of much amusement on his part.

Unfortunately, I felt, the side effect of the incident was to reinforce his idealization of my powers and his conviction of my being "a clever one." But it is possible that he still needed that illusion, and that in time it will come within reach of experience and interpretation. The coverlet incident made it possible for him to start getting over his very considerable deprivation in childhood with two fussily obsessional and anxious parents, who apparently never joked at all; the patient thought he had to impress them with cleverness so that he became excessively keen to be "bright" and to succeed intellectually. In therapy he grew able to allow himself to make unintellectual punning jokes. It seemed important not to be heavy-handed in commenting on jokes, which would have represented, within the transference, a pompous parent's status-conscious frown, or an irritable mother's slap. So I took up the act of joking, with the element of playful attack, rather than the content of the jokes.

With patients who can come only once a week and who are, many of them, very much aware of their frustrated wishes to come more often, the particular feature of their earlier lives which they find it most difficult to tolerate, and which was perhaps most potent in inhibiting normal development, may have to be discovered in just as actual a way, and just as much enacted in the transference, as would be the case with those who are in full analysis.

In this connection I think of a very uncheerful young man whose presenting symptom was an apathetic inability to work. Among the first things he told me about himself were: how he could not get up in the morning, how he fell asleep when working, and how much he enjoyed being sarcastic. He had enjoyed friendships with a small group of rather clever boys at school but his teachers had labelled him lazy. He had failed the first part of his university course, and had been demoted from working for an honors degree to doing the general one. His manner was in some ways passive and yet, already in the first session there were, I felt, cutting attacks going on somewhere, so that it looked as though there might be a serious risk of unmasking a depression of a kind which could not be properly treated in once-a-week sessions.

I decided not to try to fit him into a morning appointment, even though that might perhaps have resulted in his getting up, so that he might then have attended his college for at least the remainder of one day a week, and then possibly it would have helped him to reacquire the taste for work. This would have been a practical approach, but I thought it would be less therapeutic than an afternoon session. He held the view that he could not get up in the morning merely because he stayed up so late with friends. After a few weeks it emerged that from the age of about seven onwards, his mother being out at work, he stayed in bed every Saturday until she came back in the afternoon, and also much of Sunday, because neither she nor his father ever did anything with him. On weekdays, when he had to go to school, she used to bring him his breakfast in bed (he told me this consisted solely of bread and marga-rine—he did not want anything else) and he never said "thank you" (his mother never required this of him, and she did not mind).

This régime continued until he was sixteen, when his mother had to be hospitalized, where she died, after an operation for cancer. He re-membered sitting by her bed during the visiting hour, with nothing to say at all. He was, of course, very often silent in therapy; but this went with an ability surprising in the circumstances, to express himself well and accurately when he felt comfortable. He gradually became able to make good use of his time, when he had worked through the fantasy that during these silences I was having scathing and sarcastic thoughts about him, and then another alternative fantasy, that I was not thinking about him at all, but using the time to think of something else.

When I pointed out that these fantasies contained considerable at-tacks on me, he said he preferred to imagine that I was being critical, as that would make me more like him, and less like his mother, who never had anything to say to him and did not seem to mind that he had noth-ing to say to her. Another fantasy was connected with his stepmother (his father had remarried): breaking one of the silences, he said he had been fearing that I was thinking up an attacking kind of remark, as the stepmother, who invariably reproached him for never saying "thank you." Fairly soon after this he said that he hid from people, in silence or in bed, in order to try to force them to fetch him, but that he hoped at the same time that they would leave him in peace.

This revealing information did not come about as a result of verbal in-teraction, but through an incident in which, instead of coming first to my door as usual to see if it was open at the time for a session, he had gone off to the waiting room. I was waiting for him and he was waiting to be fetched. But it turned out that there was another routine, dating from earlier in life, that he knew in a different way. After a bit, I went to look for him, to fetch him; and I left it to him to start.

He said: "My grandmother once told me that my mother believed in feeding by the clock. If I cried before the right time, she wouldn't fetch me. I've spent all these weeks trying not to tell you that, because I want to be different from other people: I didn't want you to use your textbook knowledge with me, and tell me everything that goes wrong is due to what happened in the cradle; I want to be able to do things I decide on, rather than always have things happen to me, as a result of other people's actions." Then he added: "To be honest, I must say, too, that I've been spinning out therapy by not telling important things, because you seem to care, and I like coming."

After this session the amount of work he did increased (although it did not become exactly impressive); he had the sense to seek advice from his academic tutor, which he had until then avoided doing because, in the same way as he had needed to treat me in fantasy as a noncommunicating and noncaring mother, so the tutor was being forced into the role of the semiabsent father. Not long after, he completed his final examinations and obtained a degree. He wrote to tell me that he had done so, and also described his future plans. He ended the letter by saying: "Anyway, I keep so cheerful it amazes me, for which I thank you (or me, or psychotherapy, or luck)."

I suggest that in a case such as that, the improvement factor lies in the therapist's holding the attitude that, within the transference, there was growth potential. The waiting incident had the characteristics of a symbol and it was fully within the transference, so that ego growth resulted. The interaction in the transference-countertransference projections was representative of the archetypal mother-infant relationship, and it was also individual and specific to that patient.

His behavior had some of the quality of acting out (avoiding verbal or nonverbal experiences with the therapist and interacting unsuitably with members of the environment) but what is more important is that it did the work of a symbol. The patient had to work through the illusion, which developed an almost actual quality, of me being like a mother who decides by the clock when to pick him up, and then to discover me as more like one who waits until he is ready, or goes to fetch him when he is. The imagery and the illusion were in the silences and then in the waiting; the transcendent or developing quality of the experience was in the fact that imagery occurred as a result of factors in him and in me; there was, I think, communication at an unconscious level; his sarcasm turned out not to be too destructive, nor his skepticism too strong, for him to pick up and to use just enough of my view that libido could be reached and set free from the "laziness" which had held it captive.

Adolescent Depression and the Illusional Transference

Patients who are depressed, or whose symptoms are very clearly defensive substitutes for admitting to being depressed, can present very considerable difficulties in psychotherapy. One way of tackling the work with them is to aim first at trying to find out which aspect of feeling depressed is the one around which the others cluster. If there is improvement in that limited area, the ego may be strengthened, and in late adolescence enough growth may be set going for the therapist to retire from the situation and leave the patient to do the rest.

In this connection one of Ernest Jones' remarks in "The Theory of Symbolism" is a useful one: "The order of development seems to be: concrete, general, abstract" (1948). Marion Milner's work on the role of illusion in symbol formation, with the key idea that "this word (illusion) does imply that there is a relation to an external object of feeling" (1955, p.86) is also helpful in experiences with a depressed patient between, say, eighteen and twenty-five years old, even if it only shows why treatment failed. Such a patient, when an infant or a child, had certain experiences which were concrete in the sense of actual. Therapists have learned how to derive the general from the particular concrete experience; they abstract and select from their generalized knowledge what is of immediate use to the individual patient. The therapist becomes the new external object who can represent the parent symbolically, the parent who should have been there enough, and who steps out of the way when not needed. That applies particularly to adolescents. There must, if possible, be real happenings within the transference, experienced with feeling, by the therapist as well as the patient. Patients learn from the concrete experience with the therapist to generalize in their experiences with other people, and can abstract from therapy what they need in the rest of their lives.

The treatment of a certain depressed young man illustrates the value of a constructive illusion, although it has only an outline quality to it, both here and also as therapy. The patient looked saturnine, gauche, and fierce. I had been told that he hated his parents, particularly his father, who was withdrawn and hostile, and that he had been quarrelling with his flat-mates. He objected to being referred for therapy, saying that it would do him more harm than good, but that he had no alternative than to comply. In manner he was cynical and aggressive. He was obviously frightened. The persecutory element behind the depression seemed very pronounced. He had very dark eyes, and thick eyebrows. He had a harelip. On first meeting him I assumed that, whatever were the hidden roots of his depression, the harelip would feature in therapy.

But in the twenty sessions which he allowed himself before deciding to carry on independently, he mentioned it only once. The occasion for this was when he had given me an opening for pointing out that his mind, which he talked about most intelligently, was in his body, and he responded with saying that *perhaps* his harelip was *partly* a cause of his difficulties. This remark rang true; it became clear to me that it was not the lip by itself but the interpersonal aspects of it which provided the persecutory basis of the current depression. It is tenable that the worst aspect of early persecutory fears is the terror of annihilation, death just at the beginning of life. He seemed to be having, at the crisis of growing up, entering adult life, a recurrence of such persecutory fears.

He started therapy one January, and he told me of a fateful experience he had had in the recent Christmas vacation, in which he had had a terrifying feeling of being senile. He had days in therapy when his fear of me was quite patent: he spoke with his mouth almost shut, but just managed to say that he was certain I was going to open him up. During most sessions his arms would gradually stiffen, and most of his body followed. I pointed out that this was happening, and each time that I interpreted the stiffness in terms of his preventing himself from in any way attacking me, improvement followed in the form of greater ease, and he reported better contacts with his workmates.

The crucial session was one in which he finally allowed personal feelings to emerge naturally: he said that I did not like him personally, and that I knew that he was afraid of intimacy but, because this was my work, I would try to get him out of his hermitlike defensive retreats. If this had been analysis I would have thought of the transference projection behind his statement that I did not like him as delusional in quality and I would have assumed it would take quite a time to resolve. But in this instance I treated it as if it were an illusion on the grounds that he had shown he had enough ego strength to tolerate the fact that I had never given him any overt indication of liking, as it is usually conveyed in ordinary social contacts, and it looked as if I could trust to his being able to discover that, in effect, I did.

So in the session referred to just now, all it was necessary to do, in response to the remark I have reported, was to keep looking at him. He gradually opened his eyes a little wider, the scared, suspicious, and saturnine expression altered very slowly, and he ended up with a look which I can only describe as amused. He concluded the session saying that he could not expect people to like him unless he was likable. That may sound too crudely logical to be a felt remark, but at the time it was said there was an impressive and convincing simplicity about it. The simplicity became an interesting event to me, as I felt that its truth was crucially connected with his having had to experience the illusion of my having had an essentially nonpersonal attitude in work, and then discovering that the facts were different.

The illusion which had gripped him earlier in life (and revived in the crisis of late adolescence) seemed to be of himself as basically unlikable, damaged, quarrelsome, defensively aggressive, irrevocably set on the path towards becoming an objectionable old man like his father.

As therapist I was "the external object of feeling" (in Milner's words) which had temporarily been fused with that illusion. In the transference, the past where this had originated was brought together with a present quite opposite in quality. There was in this instance no idea or single event which could be called a symbol, but he benefited by experience in therapy as a direct result of being able to use the symbolic attitude with which I was functioning. I think that symbolization occurred in this case, in the fact of discovering he was liked: this disposed of his current version of the original persecutory terror and made it possible for him to make the remark with which he opened the next session: "Now that I've found out my main problem, it's up to me to do something about it, and this means I've decided to make definite efforts to become more likable."

Conclusion

With the patients described here, the issue often focused around the need each of them had to attack in safety. This sometimes involved a need to feel, within the transference illusion, that he or she was counterattacking defensively, and to discover that the incidents which brought this impulse to light were actual and present-day, concrete events, which could perhaps be made into something else.

In attempting to convey the feel of some psychotherapy sessions, I have given material from three patients, with the intention of showing in action the influence and effect of the symbolic attitude: the experience of constructive illusions from which ego development may proceed.

The commonly perceptible themes in the process by which an image develops into a transforming symbol emerge in a more sketchy form if patients can only be seen once, or, better, twice a week, than they do in analysis. But to use some of Milner's words again, "The creative illusion which analysts call the transference" is just as necessary, usable and creative in psychotherapy as in analysis. In relation to brief psychotherapy perhaps the straightforward words "to make" should be substituted for "to create." Making it possible for these three patients to make something better of themselves than heretofore happens through the patients' making use of the symbolic nature of the transference. It is action of a particular sort made possible by a particular attitude of mind.

Detecting the presence of transference projections and of potential symbols and symbolic events seems to me to have to be done in a very similar way in both therapy and analysis and, of course, this way can only be one's personal way of working. With some patients it seems preferable to wait, rather than to press on; with others it is better to take more active steps. The temptations in this work are to hasten rather than to hold back, to get anxious when the working-through process is skimped, as it often is, and to form opinions too quickly, and therefore with the risk of forming them in a forceful rather than a receptive way.

References

Fordham, M. 1958. Analytical Psychology and Psychotherapy. In *The Objective Psyche*. London: Routledge & Kegan Paul.

Glover, E. 1960. Psychoanalysis and Psychotherapy. *British Journal of Medical Psychology*, 33:1.

Jackson, M. 1963. Symbol Formation and the Delusional Transference. *Journal of Analytical Psychology*, 8:2.

Jones, E. 1948. The Theory of Symbolism. In *Papers on Psychoanalysis*, 5th ed. London: Baillière, Tindall & Cox.

Jung, C.G. 1921. *Psychological Types* (trans. 1923). London: Routledge & Kegan Paul.

———. 1929. Problems of Modern Psychotherapy. In *Collected Works*, 16.

———. 1945. Medicine and Psychotherapy. In *Collected Works*, 16.

———. 1951. Fundamental Questions of Psychotherapy. In *Collected Works*, 16.

Malan, D.H. 1963. A *Study of Brief Psychotherapy*. London: Tavistock.

Milner, M. 1955. The Role of Illusion in Symbol Formation. In *New Directions in Psychoanalysis*. London: Tavistock.

Plaut, A. 1966. Reflections About Not Being Able To Imagine. *Journal of Analytical Psychology*, 11:2.

Szurek, S.A. 1958. *The Roots of Psychoanalysis and Psychotherapy*. Oxford: Blackwell.

Chapter **2**

Reflections on Concepts and Experience

In the course of the training program at the London Society of Analytical Psychology it is frequent for candidates to confront those who are already in practice, such as seminar leaders and supervisors (a term which corresponds to that of control analysts in some other places), with their difficulty in linking what they are taught in the program with what they learn by experience. There seems to the candidates to be, at times, an unbridgeable gap between ideas offered them in seminars and books, and the process they are in, first in their own analyses and then with their training patients—their control cases. Trying to understand the concepts that can be abstracted from a particular piece of clinical interaction is an essential part of teaching and learning during analytic training, especially in the course of supervision. It is in work with patients in full analytical therapy that we can study the many aspects of analytical psychology: images and symbols, dreams, transference projections, and countertransference in all its variants, archetypal and developmental phenomena. It is as though, in analysis, we are using a psychological spotlight, or a microscope. We study the elements of theory when we are living them in clinical actuality.

Among the many possible manifestations of archetypal configurations which illustrate how clinical descriptions are developed into formulations and theoretical terms, I am concentrating here on the anima and the animus.

I will cite just two patients at this point, Charles and Anna, whose adult personalities had been very seriously distorted by the early malfunctioning of animus in the family setting. I want to emphasize that in working with them it had to be the close interplay between background theory and the day-to-day meetings in the analytical sessions that made possible such change as did take place in those people.

Adapted from a lecture delivered in Chicago, May 30, 1986.

Charles's emotional development had been held up by the negative mother-image—the root of negative anima for him—which he projected onto his depressed personal mother who had lost her first baby son about a year before my patient was born. At the same time as I was treating him, it was necessary for me to deepen my study of the two contrasexual archetypes and the workings of envy, both as demonstrated in his actual life with his wife and daughters, and the transference and countertransference interactions in his four times a week analysis. I tried to study how in reacting to me he used his internalized figures, and how projections operated when they showed in dreams and fantasies, and that was the background of theory about those matters which had to be kept in mind as well as living the process itself.

With Charles, to whom I will return later, the envy of me in the transference was not really very blatant. It only showed in subtle ways, or very indirectly in dreams. With Anna the envy mushroomed up at intervals phenomenally: it was always as a result of my functioning, as it seemed to me, fairly well, that is, in such a way as to foster mutative growth. To her, a good interpretation was sometimes agonizingly enviable, and at such times, in the following session she would launch into a snide, denigratory attack. What was particularly interesting from the point of view of theory (in that it illustrates the interface between analytical psychology and psychoanalysis) was an occasion when her access of envy led her to project, with tremendous animosity, her negative emotions about me onto another woman, one who she considered "brilliant": she was temporarily protecting me from attack. The envy she was experiencing spread over into scorn and persecutory anxiety. For a time during the session she became paranoid, making out that the other woman had bested her in arguments and had made her feel hopelessly small. It was necessary to get her to see first that it was not so much that other women whose "brilliance" had put her in the shade and brought about this attacking and self-denigratory mood, but her envy that the day before I had pointed out to her something which had emerged during the analysis of a dream. It was an interpretation which she had felt at the time was most remarkable; she had in fact thought it far more amazing that it really was and she had gone away beaming with happiness. She had exaggerated my supposed brilliance; but this was followed by her imagining that I was blaming her for having yet once more "fallen into the trap" as she put it, of idealizing and overadmiring and then envying and attacking. Anna needs many times to work through the regression to persecutory anxiety and to recognize, through what happens between her and me, that it will go on being to some extent unconscious until it yields to the process set in motion by the developmental and healing forces in her, by means of which the power of the regressive ones will decrease. During the time when the process is still unconscious, she cannot be held responsible and cannot be blamed.

When I consider and reflect on the interactions between that particular woman patient and myself, I find she is a good example of how the negative animus is connected with the unconscious workings of the two basic impulses, that of loving and that of attacking. She had a strong wish that I should love her and comfort her, praise her, strengthen her defective primary narcissism, and also a desire to force me, if necessary, to do all the things she wanted, which included agreeing with her, and, when forcing did not turn out to be successful, she resorted to asserting that what she believed had happened, really had happened. She had what we call "a good mind," she was intelligent but overused her thinking function to the detriment of her feeling function; she became tense and cold, both physically and emotionally, because her positive use of the animus gave way when her unconscious omnipotence was threatened. We can assume that the fantasy of being all-powerful, together with its opposite of being tiny and therefore having no power at all, dates in all of us from very early in life, namely earlier than the constellation of either of the contrasexual archetypes.

In describing Anna, who at intervals had a phase of acute envious attack, I have used observations and reflections from a number of incidents over the years. What happened between her and me showed how close are immediate experiences to their psychological correlates. She resisted accepting that what she had assumed or deduced is not necessarily the same as the objective facts. She made categorical statements, for example, at the very beginning of a session, but it was gradually possible to get her to see that they were assumptions. Misperceptions, or partial perceptions, contribute to persecutory delusions and paranoid reactions. The way this happened with Anna shows how the negative use of the animus, in a woman prone to convert her intellectual ability into envious attacks on her analyst, who in the main she regarded as a good object, can interfere dangerously with interpersonal relationships. The situation between Anna and me was a therapeutic one, in which I aimed not to react in an overpersonal way when she attacked, but rather to try to find out, by whatever means were possible, first, precisely how the attack had built up, and second, what were the unconscious anxieties in operation which damaged a potentially positive or constructive atmosphere between us. Gradually, it became possible for Anna to discover the effect she was having. That leads to ego development. From what happened between Anna and me, she could then draw the analogy with how it was in her marriage, in her other personal relationships, and in situations where collective factors were the operative ones. The transference/countertransference projections in her analysis acted as miniature versions of the outer world, and there was more chance of altering what went on within her relationship to me than there was in other places and with other people, since I was not too bothered by the immediacy of her animus attacks. The two aspects, of concepts and interactions, were equally essential if both Anna and I were to understand in a way which would be mutative. The theory and concepts on their own would have been sterile and too intellectual, too cold, perhaps; there had to be a raising of temperature caused by her doing things (psychological ones) and me feeling them happen, for a "marriage" to take place, within which a new version of her could be born.

Regression

Within therapy, it is frequent, or even usual, for change to be desired. But change often involves painful regression. Regression can seem to be like a nasty dirt road beset with rough patches and potholes. There are tears, distress, and depression. But analytical therapy cannot be all smooth, like driving on a well-maintained highway. There are times of misery, real or fantasied persecution, and destructiveness. Analysis can be likened to many modern countries; there are badlands, erosion, polluted rivers, and lakes. But there are also fertile farms and worthwhile businesses. For the patient to get to know himself or herself thoroughly and to go forward into life with greater insight and more flexibility, the earlier layers of psychological geology have to be explored, and it is often in them that misery lies.

Those early layers of conscious and unconscious life do not emerge as a result of a program or a routine, nor are they in any sense demanded or required. Exploring them is not "supposed" to take place: I say "supposed" because I have a patient, Kathy, who was particularly blocked and resistant to talking freely, and it emerged, almost incidentally, one day, that she felt she was not doing anything she was "supposed" to do. That fantasy or belief had been acting in a most persecutory manner and was based on a web of miscellaneous information she had collected from various acquaintances and she scorned people who were (in her view) naive about analysis. Kathy thought there was a "theory" of how patients and analysts should operate, but had kept very quiet about it. It had been one of her secrets.

Regression is, effectively, progress in reverse. It is reversing in order to be able to go forward after some previous maladaptation has been attended to, some split healed, and after some pathological defense has been more healthily integrated. It can take the form of a return to an earlier stage of personal life, or to an earlier archetypal position. Descriptively, someone who is regressed probably arrives looking pale, tired, sulky, silent (a resentful, bottled-up kind of silence, not a comfortable one); perhaps in a state of shock from some unexpected loss; depressed, aggressive, in a schizoid state or full of persecutory anxieties or even paranoid delusions, or launching into envious attacks. Sometimes it is not clear what the patient wants or tries to say, or what he or she means; the patient is confused but may be using confusion as a defense against insight. Fantasies may be unrealistic to a great degree, or there may be none at all. A very frequent feature of regression is extreme sensitivity, irrational hate of the analyst may develop, or persecutory self-hate.

Among the patients I can remember vividly who have been particularly prone to regress, the majority are those who get depressed for quite a long time. In them the narcissistic wounds which distorted healthy infantile and childhood development date from too close contact with a pathologically depressed mother who had not come to terms with love and hate within herself or towards others. In infancy such a mother could not be an adequate receiver, or container, of projections of feelings of either good or bad. So goodness and badness, or love and coldness, would have frequently been experienced by the infant in their extreme forms. The child then would have been likely to grow into adulthood with the tendency to absolutes; the moment something goes wrong, such a person believes all is lost. The other unfortunate result of a small child being too much in the shadow of a very depressed mother is that ordinary curiosity about life develops isolated from feelings. Trying to find out what mother is like is a natural desire: if discoveries about her, and experiences of her moods, yield anxiety-provoking experiences, the child's searches will tend to become fear-laden inquisitiveness. Emotions will then seem frightening, the child may even hate emotions as the years go by, and that can slip over into hatred of life itself. Patients who fit more or less into that kind of pattern try, in the transference relationship, to keep emotions at bay. They report about themselves, discuss themselves, but find it difficult to *be* themselves. Friendly or constructive feelings, warmth or appreciation, are sometimes fended off or denied, usually not explicitly, because that would be too dangerous: the analyst does after all incarnate the possibility of a lifeline to better things. When I think of a particular woman patient, Gerda, who fits that description (she was clinging onto the pessimism acquired very early in life), I can reexperience my feelings at her wordless tears when, unable to conceal her previously hidden appreciation of her analysis, she was suffused with distress, and could do nothing except suddenly leave, choking and sobbing something almost inaudible about not being able to come back. It was dreadful. She did come for her next session and found that something better than what she was used to, far from being unacceptable, was in fact just what she wanted. The gradual building up of trust may take a long time if infancy and childhood were passed in a very destructive atmosphere, but I think it is worth persevering, provided analysts can rely on themselves to be containers, as compared to refusers, of emotions.

If all goes reasonably well during emergence from serious regression, the patient finds it in himself (or herself) to express desires which had previously been clamped down. If basic needs are met in the transference, those desires can evolve and be expressed without an unbearable amount of guilt, within the safety offered in therapy. That safety provides a space within which the natural healing potential of the psyche is set in motion. If we see the self, as written about by Jung, as both the totality and the center of the psyche, we can see that the safe container of therapy enables the self to be actualized when it had been overlaid by false ego development. The many descriptions of the self in Jung's works may seem abstract unless we can bring them to life in the reality and actuality of what happens between therapist and patient. For many months Gerda spoke very little, and when she did it was mainly to complain that she was, as she put it, "in a bad space." It took quite a long time for me to understand what she meant, as she seemed bent on concealing from me what the "bad space" referred to: was it her material daily life, or was it her inner life, or something else? Then she divulged that the "bad space" started when she came into the room where I was waiting for her. It became clear that badness of archetypal proportions was immediately generated by the sight of me and my presence. That woman had had a deeply traumatic childhood, in a cold and largely pathological family, living in one of the occupied European countries during the Second World War. Her phrase, "a bad space," in fact meant the totality of her sense of herself and of the world. Analysis includes a certain amount of ritual, one obvious aspect of which is the arrival in the analyst's room. For her that was much the same as arriving in the world, and every time she came (at that stage of her analysis) I "became" the bad world for her: she projected the negative mother archetype on to me. Fortunately, it was possible to tell her that in the split second when I opened the door to her I could see warmth in her eyes. Before the closure and regression to bad days and a bad space had set in there was a moment when a better potential was evident. So I made sure of telling her each time I saw anything of that sort. She was very surprised, and tried to deny it. It was necessary to wait, to go slowly, to allow the regressive process its full action, not to despair, to keep on holding to my knowledge that Jung's concepts and formulations of the self and of the healing potential hidden within the pathology of such a negative transference would help me to *be with* that woman in such a way as would perhaps some time enable her to see the world with different eyes. The phrase of Jung's from old alchemical texts, *Deo concedente* (with God's help), became almost an amulet for me, a charm I used to protect me from impatience. It was only by looking back over the work of many months that I could discern very slow change: there was no single event, or dream, which could be selected as the turning point. But she did change.

There is a passage in a relatively early work of Jung's which throws some light on that brief vignette from a contemporary analysis. He wrote in 1912, ". . . [regressive] fantasies have a double character . . . on the one hand a pathological tendency to resist, on the other a helpful and preparatory tendency. With a normal person the libido, when it is blocked by an obstacle, forces him into a state of introversion and makes him reflect. So, too, with a neurotic under the same conditions: an introversion ensues, with increased fantasy activity. But he gets stuck there because he prefers the infantile mode of adaptation as being the easier one" (1912, paras. 404–406).

I suppose that today not many therapists refer to their patients as neurotics in the slightly derogatory tone that Jung sometimes conveys, as in that passage. Patients in regression may be classified as neurotic, but they are usually very distressed. With some, distress becomes serious when and because they begin to unfreeze: those are the ones whose cold state is due to an excess of early personal and interpersonal failures. If the analyst had in any way comparable life experiences, he or she may be in danger of a countertransference in which there is a tendency to identify with the patient. If that happens, it is essential for the sake of the analysis—which means for the patient's and the analyst's sakes—to return to, and to sustain, a position and an attitude in which objectivity and sensitivity are combined. The best valid protection or necessary defense against a countertransference identification is to base oneself solidly in knowledge and understanding of analytical theory, woven in with experience in personal and professional life.

The analyst needs ego strength of a flexible kind, based on training and experience, in order to be able to gauge how much regression the patient can stand. It can sometimes be necessary to intervene in a situation where he or she is operating in the transference in a delusional as compared with an illusional way. Gerda was in a state of delusion with her reiterated assertion about the "bad place," and it enabled her to begin to emerge from that state when I pointed out to her a small piece of her reality, the expression in her eyes. As there is danger in an omnipotent attitude in the analyst who thinks he or she knows it all, so there is also danger in the opposite, which is of forgetting the natural possibilities of recovery in the psyche. In the case of a delusional transference, the patient is in fact concretizing, as yet unable to appreciate the symbolic quality of the relationship with the analyst. When the "as if" dimension is still too difficult for a deeply regressed patient, that has to be tolerated, while the mysterious process of the conjunction between the analyst's more developed psyche and the patient's more primitive one develops in the dark.

Art and Craft in Analysis

When the craft of therapy is being studied, it is important to learn to distinguish between images and symbols. I feel inclined to lay down a basic starting proposition: it is wise to proceed gradually in this matter, to begin by way of the image, to see it first and foremost as probably personal rather than archetypal, to make sure that its individual significance has been taken seriously before jumping to the exciting supposition that it carries a greater or even a numinous quality. When it is an image which occurs universally, for instance, the baby, the child, water, wild or domestic animals, et cetera, it is very tempting to assume, without a proper examination of all the surrounding affects, that its universality is what is being experienced and communicated. Then the therapist may conclude too quickly that universality is the same as collectivity, and therefore the presence of an archetype is perhaps mistakenly detected. And big things are worked on in the analysis too soon. The concept of the archetype is almost archetypal itself! As Jungians we can fairly easily perceive the workings of archetypes, indeed the researches of Jung are now widely known and increasingly studied, so that the general educated public also is well able to see them. This is particularly true, I think, in the arts, but also in the cinema, the theatre and on television, in sport and in politics. Those "hidden persuaders," the advertisers, use them, or perhaps I could say abuse them, since they are such powerful forces. A great force seems impressive. Yet it is worth remembering the catch phrase, "small is beautiful." The image may seem less prestigious and smaller than the symbol or the archetype, but both it and the handling of it can be really beautiful.

I am particularly interested in the art and craft of analytical therapy and in how to link concepts and experience. I can get as excited as anyone by fascinating studies in mythology and anthropology, literature and history, but I have observed that all too often there are significant aspects of the immediate interplay between patient and analyst which are in danger of being overlooked if we go off into those areas unadvisedly. If the subtleties of the interplay are time and again not noticed, not consciously experienced, they can activate a dangerous negativity between the two people, dangerous for the future of the therapy if they are not brought out into the open. The book ideas and the theories taught in seminars fade into insignificance when there is real life in the analytical session. Suppose a small instance, which is offered unconsciously by the patient, perhaps in the form of an incidental remark as he arrives, or soon after: if it is not picked up and treated as a picture of how he is feeling that day about his analysis, which is a microcosm of his life outside, an opportunity can be lost which may not present itself again for some time. What we call, in technical language, an image may take the form of a gesture or an action: there are other images than pictures in dreams and fantasies.

Here is an example: some years ago Charles, whom I mentioned earlier, was starting to recount a dispute with his somewhat dominant wife. He was successful in his professional work, where he operated independently, if perhaps somewhat aggressively, but at home he was under her influence. As he spoke he put his hand up to his necktie. I said, "You are reminding yourself that you are a man." He answered: "That's it! She can't see I'm trying to tell her that. I've got a woman analyst, there's my wife at home, and both of you remind me of my mother, who tried to be the boss, and all my father could do about it was to keep the family waiting for meals—which she had cooked—while he was hitting little white balls around with his friends at the golf course." Then he laughed and said, "That's it! If I can manage to link up how impotent I sometimes feel here with how it is at home, and how it was when I was a child, then I feel better." He paused, and said, "I feel more myself now." The necktie meant to him that he was a man: it was an image for him of his penis. A small boy, when anxious about what is going on between himself and one or the other parent, may instinctively clutch his genitals. Within the session, the touching of the necktie was an indication that it was being used unconsciously as an image of maleness. As Charles and

I talked it took on the character of being symbolically equivalent to that essential part of the male body. When by means of the necktie he touched and felt himself physically, he also felt more himself psychologically. Reminding himself put body and mind together. The transcendent function was at work.

The process of therapy activates the production of imagery which at times acquires the stature of symbolism. For Anna, early in her analysis, the image of the baby was a frequently occurring one. It is indeed found in many people. There was a time when month after month her dreams were almost exclusively about a baby: usually it was a miserable one, undersized, underfed, neglected, lost, alone, abandoned, or left among the lost property at a railway terminus. Her view of herself was deeply negative, as also was her view of how the human environment had been when she was a child. It was the slow buildup of confidence in me and in the relationship with me that over time began to alter the images and symbols in her dreams.

I have referred to the art and craft of therapy and have tended to avoid the term technique. Among Jungians there is apt to be a lot of heat generated by that word. It suggests, some people think, using a tool or an instrument. That criticism is understandable. But some psychoanalyst, whose name I cannot now remember, once wrote a paper entitled, "Myself as Instrument." There is also the more medical phrase which was coined, I think, in the process of seminars for general practitioners organized in London by Michael Balint: it was "the drug [named] doctor," they were to use themselves, instead of writing a prescription for a medicinal drug. It seems to me possible to see the analyst's accumulated experiences as a constantly well-honed tool. A self-respecting craftsman, carpenter, sculptor, cook or whoever keeps tools in good order, rust-free, and finely tuned. I think the analogy holds with work done in the analyst's room. The lines between craft, art, technique, skill, style, and ways of being, are not easy to draw. It is possible to use the word technique pejoratively as a term of abuse to shoot at some therapist who is, in an overall way, uncongenial: it is a little less aggressive to criticize technique than personality, though most people in the therapy world know that they go together.

One aspect of technique, or I could say craft, which is worth discussing is that of the number of sessions per week. The theory and concept and practice of psychoanalysis in the early days of Freud conspired to lay it down that no analysis, in what he considered the proper sense, could take place unless the patient attended every day, which then meant six days a week. It seems to many present-day Jungians that that is not only rigid and doctrinaire, but also not in the patient's best interests. I am leaving aside for the moment the economic impossibility of it for most people. It became a matter of conceptual difference between Freudians and Jungians, and fairly well known among potential patients, in the same way as the question of chair or couch seemed to represent a major difference between the two best-known kinds of depth psychologists. The particular Freudians I know say that less than four times a week is psychotherapy, not analysis. I try to use the word therapy as a general one, if I do not want to specify whether or not it is deep analysis. But I certainly find that patients whose difficulties or pathology go back to very early days make a great deal more progress if they are able and willing to come more, rather than less, often. In England, also, the usual fee for a session is far lower than it is in the USA, so that there is not the same objection to an analyst's making a strong recommendation for several sessions. From the point of view of the art, craft and technique of deep therapy it is possible to go back to Jung himself, who, in the chapter entitled "General Problems of Psychotherapy" (1935) in Volume 16 of the *Collected Works*, wrote:

> All methods of influence including the analytical, require that the patient be seen as often as possible. I content myself with a maximum of four consultations a week. With the beginning of synthetic treatment it is of advantage to spread out the consultations. I then generally reduce them to one or two hours a week, for the patient must learn to go his own way (par. 25).

The advantage of frequent sessions is that the analyst does not have to be so cautious about the patient getting very anxious and perhaps acting out, because the working through which is not completed by the end of the fifty minutes can be taken up again very soon without the defenses having had time to reestablish themselves. The patients referred to in this chapter had, at various times, during their analyses, four or five sessions, decreasing to three towards the end.

Conclusion

In order to do adequate and effective work with patients whose infancy and childhood presented them with more interactional difficulties than they could integrate, it has been found that the imagery that wells up spontaneously in the transference is closely connected with their body experiences. There is symbolic potential for change and growth for such people as Anna, Charles, and Gerda, when their images, or actions, can put them in touch with early sensations and feelings. The transcendent function, which came into play very clearly with Charles, made it possible for him to use actual incidents or gestures as a way of moving from experiencing his world concretely to appreciating it meaningfully and symbolically. That is the great change that we must work for in analysis. Patients who live well in their bodies produce images which develop into symbols much more readily than those who do not appreciate themselves as physical beings. And that characteristic is irrespective of whether or not they have a well-developed sensation function. Typologically they may even be sensation types, but their bodily experiences in infancy and childhood, in the relationship with significant parents, are what will have set the tone for a capacity to integrate body imagery.

The transcendent function, which links the strange to the familiar, the unconscious to the conscious, is activated in an analysis where the analyst responds intuitively and intelligently to the patient's imagery so that the interaction and interplay of their two separate ways of being results in the patient experiencing life much more intensively than had been possible earlier. The analyst who is, at least most of the time, in touch with his or her own potential for change, activates that potential in the patient. The study of normal infants as well as the study of our patients' infancies confirms time and again that sensing and perceiving even small signs and then giving them validity helps those signs to become images and to lead on to symbolization. Each time an image, during analysis, is offered the chance of developing to the full, the analyst is fostering the strengthening of the transcendent function.

Observing and partaking—the day to day activities of an analyst—have to be linked with accepting that other analysts before us have had similar even if not identical experiences and have extracted concepts to explain happenings. Their concepts and models then act as guides to those who follow. Conceptual thinking is necessary for differentiation between generations of analysts so that there can be reasonably healthy respect without slavish copying. The tenacity of identification with analytic "parents" is sometimes painfully obvious to colleagues, and probably the best antidote is to try to keep on reassessing our own clinical work, listening with the third ear to our inner voices, and learning to interpret what we hear.

Chapter **3**

People Who Do Things to Each Other: Therapists and Patients

An invitation to speak about transference and countertransference led me to realize what a great deal has been written on those subjects over the past seventy years or so by well-known analysts such as Freud, Jung, L. Stein, Moody, Little, Plaut, Winnicott, Heimann, Kraemer, M. Fordham, Searles, Menninger, Racker, Erikson, Milner, Dieckmann and Gordon. There are no doubt many others.

The thought that probably everything on the subject had already been said touched on the two major complexes connected with the symbolic relationships I have to those people: some of them are parent figures, others more like siblings. That goes to show that incest fantasies are at the heart of the matter—that was Jung's view as well as Freud's. I also had a memory of a slogan from the Second World War which was displayed particularly in public houses: "Careless talk costs lives"; and in the context of therapy that meant to me that our patients' lives are in our hands, so we should not act or talk carelessly; we must be as conscious as possible with them, but we should also let ourselves be spontaneous, which may involve speaking from unconscious layers in ourselves that the patient has touched—layers from which symbolism may come, for the patient and for ourselves.

Those reflections and considerations were behind my choice of title. Actually, I did not choose it consciously: I was reading, before going to sleep one evening, some new poems by R. S. Thomas—that depressed Welsh poet who has been wrestling with God for fifty years or so—and I "heard" the title. R. S. Thomas and God both do things to each other, and each is patient with the other; both are getting slightly less fierce, if the recent poems are anything to go by.

The reader may have sensed what I am probably doing to him (I may not be succeeding): to disarm his criticism, skepticism and capacity to

Originally published in *Harvest*, Number 31 (1985), pp. 77–84.

think clearly, to undermine his powers of attack like the wolves that
ethologists describe who lie on their backs, exposing their vulnerable
underbellies, to inhibit the attacks of their intraspecific enemies—the
wolves from the neighboring territory.

Of course the people in my title have only a little in common with
wolves—or with our stereotyped and anthropomorphizing view of those
animals. But that little is that we as patients or therapists are often in
the grip of patterns, patterns of behavior insofar as we are animals, patterns of affect insofar as we are psychological beings, deep archetypal
instinctlike forces which may play havoc with our conscious intentions.
Those forces can feel to be reincarnations of people with whom we
related earlier in our lives—grandparents or parents, siblings or teachers—or with whom we interact at present, the next generation, our
children perhaps. The central thing is that we are both what we are and
what we do. Actions are not just physical things, and we do things even
when what we do is to choose to remain silent. I want to avoid the abstract words, transference and countertransference, as much as I can, because they easily become reifications of what is happening in our minds
and of what we are doing. In one of my early papers I stated:

> The analyst pays attention to what he is doing, to what the patient
> is doing, and to the psychodynamics of what is happening. In this
> work, actions and interactions are of even greater interest than are
> concepts. Concepts distract from actions through turning them
> into things; they can be used defensively against experiencing and
> understanding the patient as a person. Without neglecting the
> careful consideration of nouns we have to be even more closely
> acquainted with verbs (1974, p. 3).

The great questions, from the very first time the patient comes into
the consulting room and on each succeeding occasion are: "What are
this person and I going to do *to* each other? What can I do *with* this
person?"

A psychologically unsophisticated acquaintance of mine who had
been quite seriously depressed for several months (and on several previous occasions in his life), was in the care of his general practitioner and
was referred after a while to a consultant for, as he thought, psychotherapy, since the antidepressant medication was having almost no effect,
certainly not producing mutative insight. He trusted his doctor and went
along to the consultation with moderately hopeful intentions. I met him
not long after and he told me nothing had come of it except a prescrip-

tion for a different drug, and he added that the consultant was somehow not as much a person as he had expected. Whether he could have coped with really meeting another person, I do not know, but it sounded as though the consultant had very quickly decided all he could do was to keep that man at arm's length with drugs.

From what I wrote earlier, and from that incident about psychotherapy which did not begin, it will be clear what my theme is: who and how we are and what we do constantly interact and interplay in creative or frustrating or destructive ways. That applies both to therapists and to those who come to meet them. If a meeting takes place, the "creative illusion which analysts call the transference" (Milner 1955), or "that peculiar mixture of overestimation and mistrust" (Erikson 1964), will begin to occur and operate in both directions. It will constitute a number of projections which it will take some time, or a long time, to perceive and to work through. I am going to offer three examples of those illusions and interactions that illustrate three aspects of the incest problem, which is at the heart of all therapies. The first example is of a male analyst and a female patient: Jung and Sabina Spielrein. The second is of an analyst and a patient of the same sex, namely myself and a woman. And the third is of a woman analyst, myself, and a man patient. The sexual theme was overt in the first of those, implicit but undeveloped in the second, and psychological in the third. All three clinical examples illustrate several aspects of what people do to each other in psychotherapy and analysis: our unconscious reactions to our patients seen first as interferences to good therapy; second, as indicators of what is happening; third, as potential mediators of the necessary movement from the concrete to the symbolic, from regressive-destructive incest to developmental *coniunctio*.

Clinical Examples

Jung & Spielrein: Presymbolic Transference/Countertransference

Both Freud and Jung discovered early on that transference projections which become very binding ties have the intrinsic nature and quality of "the relation between father and child." "The tie is the result of an unconscious process . . . the unmistakable outward sign of the situation is that the 'feeling-toned' memory-image of the father is transferred to the doctor" (Jung 1954, p. 61). The oedipal phase, in psychoanalytic terminology, and the incest archetype, in analytical psychology, were the two resulting formulations of concepts derived from the experience of what the female patients were doing to, and with, those male therapists. Early in his career, from 1904 to about 1909, before he had made his many often-quoted remarks about chemical combinations and other aspects of transference and countertransference, Jung had a protracted difficult time with a young woman patient, Sabina Spielrein. That part of the story which shows very clearly what delusional and eroticized fantasies Sabina projected onto him can be read in her published diaries and her letters to Jung (Carotenuto 1982). He consulted Freud about the difficulties he was having, possibly before they had reached their peak, but the evidence as to how much detail he divulged to Freud and how thoroughly Freud helped him to work on them is unfortunately far from adequate. There has been much discussion among very competent analysts since the diaries and letters were published in 1982, focusing rather less on the almost prurient desire to know whether they did make love physically and rather more on the psychology of what they did to each other. She idealized Jung to a colossal extent and conveyed in what she wrote that there was a realistic possibility of their having a beautiful blond son together, whom she named Siegfried. It looks as though, at that stage of his life, Jung understood transference and countertransference only inadequately. The archetypal projections that had probably been made onto him were those of the saviour—she was recovering, thanks to him, from very severe, almost crippling, illness—and of the father in the oedipal or incest stage of the daughter's love for him. To allow that to be understood as adult love was a distortion and a failure to see that the movement from the concrete to the symbolic is the necessary one in therapy as well as in ordinary life.

Comment on Jung & Spielrein

There is now no doubt but that with Sabina, Jung acted out, to a greater or lesser extent, unassimilated aspects, shadow features and erotic needs which only a few years later he was able to describe in measured terms in the course of his many writings. That was after he had lived creatively through the agonies brought on by the break from Freud, and had found out how to use figures produced from inside himself in active imagination, in a similar way to how patients who have a personal analyst discover the extraordinary combination of subjective and objective experiences through projecting onto him or her. So in 1921, Jung wrote: "One could say that in the same measure as the doctor assimilates the intimate psychic contents of the patient into himself, he is in turn assimilated as a figure into the patient's psyche" (1954, p. 136). Notice that he puts countertransference before transference in that passage. He also wrote, in the same paper, "Analysis makes far higher demands on the mental and moral stature of the doctor than the mere application of a routine technique, and also his therapeutic influence lies primarily in the more personal direction" (p.138). In another passage he wrote, "Twist and turn the matter as we may, the relation between doctor and patient remains the personal one, within the impersonal framework of professional treatment" (p.71). When we go into detail as to what is meant by *personal* we come to all the subtleties of what happens subliminally and at a deeper unconscious level every time we see a patient. Jung wrote, "One cannot treat the psyche without regard to the totality of its functions—or rather, as a few representatives of modern medicine maintain, the totality of the sick man himself" (p.76).

It should be added, by those of us who try to do adequate therapy, our own sickness is part of our personal totality, which includes, among other things, our unresolved shadow, anima and animus conflicts, our ever-recurrent and originally incestuous desire to be loved, our difficulty in offering unpossessive love to the other, the protection of our inner sanctum, our need to hold together and not to lose our boundaries. My impression is that, as therapists, we are doing well when we act, in sessions with our patients, on a genuine working belief that sickness and shadow, integrity and integration, are parts of a continuous spectrum. The as-yet-unconscious countertransference can be at first an interference, so to speak a sickness, as it was with Jung and Spielrein; when we examine it, it can become an indicator of what the patient needed to evoke in us psychologically in order to take back into himself what he had projected; then the combination of what he does to us and we do to him can move on to the next phase, presymbolic incestuous longings of all sorts may become a genuine, even if mysterious, *coniunctio*.

Myself and Deborah: Power Only Half Understood

My contact with Deborah was short: she came to see me only four times. I suspect that I experienced those few sessions as far more mortifying than she did. I would have liked to go on seeing her. From her point of view too little trust developed for her to be able to use me as a therapist; what I think I learned was that if in the first session the patient asks for physical action from me I may not be good at managing the consequent psychological problem. The same practical situation (namely, the request for an ash tray) happened to the analyst William Goodheart, who examined, in a long paper, the results of the opening interchanges with a pa-

tient. He describes first how he had "recently decided not to allow smok-
ing in his office and had put his ashtrays into a drawer. The patient [was]
an aggressive, fifty-year-old, forceful man." After a bit of talk, there was
tenseness; then a bit more talk; then more tenseness. The patient asked
if he could smoke. Goodheart reports that he found himself "reaching
over and anxiously . . . taking out an ashtray from the drawer." Then he
goes on to show how the countertransference anxiety hindered the patient from discovering a way of relating to his therapist which would
have fostered the growth of the symbolic attitude. It is clear that he
believes that process should and can get going in a well-conducted first
session (1984). Goodheart and I agree that we learn more from our
mistakes than from our successes, if we are willing to devote time to examine them thoroughly.

My reaction to Deborah, at the physical level, was the opposite one,
of *not* giving her an ashtray and attempting to discuss with her what I
thought was probably going on between her and me. She, incidentally,
like Goodheart's patient, was an aggressive and forceful person, though
much younger. She had recently made two suicide attempts; she was a
gifted and energetic woman who seemed a worthwhile if challenging
patient.

The details are that when she had told me a little about herself, her
past and her present, her early family, her marriage, her career hopes,
she suddenly broke off, looked rather fiercely round the room and said,
"I can't see an ashtray. I want to smoke." She took a cigarette out of her
handbag and was going to light it. I forget my exact words, but I think I
conveyed something of the "not so fast" kind. So the cigarette did not
actually get lit. I pointed out that it was after giving me an outline picture of herself and her life that she had felt she must have a cigarette—I
said: "Something between your lips, and the wish for a smoke-screen between you and me." That was two interpretations in one: I should probably have chosen the one or the other; and I ran a risk in interpreting at
that moment. A power struggle developed during which I believe she decided she did not *like* me. She wanted to smoke each of the four times
she came.

Comment on the Deborah Case

For my part, I do not like the smell of cigarette smoke and even more
strongly do I dislike the left-over smell in my consulting room for the rest
of the day. I don't want to subject those who come later to the staleness
of it and the physical reminder of other people who come to see me. Per-

haps, I found as I reflected on the incident, I am at times overprotective of my patients. I am using the word "overprotective" to mean something different from providing a setting which is suitably protective or containing. I was able to discover that "overprotective of the patient" is a defensive cover-up way of referring to protecting myself from their possible angry attacks. I might be depriving them of an opportunity of getting into their persecutory fantasy of being less loved than others in my life, or their splitting defense of not telling me when they are envious or anxious. But there was another series of transference/countertransference projections occurring, as I came to see more clearly later: Deborah had described her mother in a way that I think possibly one or other of my own offspring might have pictured me (at times of acute adolescent stress), the familial interactions sounded all to familiar, and I felt a sharp jab of anxiety. As she had tried twice to kill herself, she must have a dangerous tendency to act out, and to avoid working on the inner and archetypal conflict. Was I angry with her mother/me for not being a good-enough mother? Was I in the grip of the omnipotent fantasy that mothers and analysts can invariably prevent acting out—suicide? So I was anxious, and one of my usual responses to anxiety is to rely on previous experience, learned with patients who have been with me for longer than ten minutes, and to try to sense the nature of the interaction: what is she doing to me and what am I doing to her? Just like Goodheart who responded physically in the other way than I, I am keen to establish with psychological actions that the symbolic attitude is what I hope to engender. Neither he nor I, although we reacted apparently differently, succeeded in getting our forceful patients to accept what we intended to offer. Deborah projected the overfirm mother-image onto me, and I suspect that I reacted with a version of "mother knows best": I too quickly decided not to fetch an ashtray because I was anxious to experience yet once more the benefit of keeping it all psychological, whereas to her, in her first session, it seemed merely another instance of conflict.

Myself and Leo: Anima and Animus as Mediators of Development

This patient had been seeing me for rather more than two years when the session occurred which illustrates the discovery of long-buried projections. Leo was tall, well-built and strikingly handsome. When I opened the door to him the first time he came, I thought he had a commanding, very adult look, almost aristocratic into the bargain, so I was surprised by noticing how small his feet were, like a boy's, and how short each footstep he took into the room, like a child. He asked on that occasion,

"Which chair do you want me to sit in?" but added at once, "I can see which is yours." I looked questioningly at him and he said, "I want to be told which to sit in." Given his appearance, the story he told me of childhood with both parents doing heavy manual jobs, was quite surprising. As the therapy developed, slowly but surely he first worked on memories of the miserable years after his mother died, suddenly, from heart failure, when he was twelve. She had been very hard on him all through childhood, but she was beginning to soften. He had felt abandoned by her dying but he had no words for it at the time, and no one took any notice of his needing help to be openly upset and to mourn. During that part of the therapy I seemed to be carrying the image of the good mother with whom things are not too harsh, life goes on, and feeling and talking are both encouraged. I found that kind of "good mother" singularly unsatisfactory to me as an analyst, it was a feeling of being only partially used—and I was shockingly bored. The boredom used to worry me a lot, seeing that I liked him as a person and found him very attractive as a man, who was not far off my age. In summer afternoon sessions I got drowsy quite often. From time to time he asked me if I was bored (I usually do not answer questions, but interpret the anxiety behind them). The next stage of his therapy was many months of complaints about the father who was nothing but crude, unimaginative, violent, and totally uninterested in Leo. During this phase he treated me as the "good father" with whom—according to him—real contact was possible. Not long after the mother had died, the father had contracted a serious disease and refused to stay in the hospital; he gave it to Leo and to his sister. The father died of it, the sister nearly died and was left with permanently impaired health, but Leo recovered very well. It was a dramatic story, but I had heard the details, both material and psychological, so many times that the periods of boredom continued. It seemed to be no good when I tried to interpret his repetitions of the painful stories. They anesthetized me. The next time he speculated about whether I was bored, I answered, "Yes," and that was more helpful than interpreting had been.

One day, just before he arrived, I said to myself: "I wonder if I should raise the question of whether he feels he's getting anywhere, and should I try to discuss terminating?" though I knew that that had a lot to do with my feeling underused by him. He walked in looking particularly smart and indeed attractive; he lay down on the couch in an energetic and determined way and started at once to tell me he really appreciated my masculine side, but he knows he resists the woman part of me. He went on to describe how he feels my femaleness is dangerous: by the time I have fully *lulled* him into submission, then I will pounce on him, as his sister and his mother used to—he was often knocked about and whacked in childhood—females are imperious, he said, it is the "macho woman" time and again. After a while I was able to interpret the pouncing he was afraid of as being that I would say: "We are not going on any more." He replied very strongly—I suppose he was trying to loosen the grip of his fantasy of me as the "macho woman"—"Yes! I think you're going to say, '*That's it*, bugger off now.'" If I did, he added, he would be violent. I do not think he had read much, or indeed any Jung, so I was fascinated to hear him say he could remember reading Rider Haggard's *She* when he was a boy, and that was what he meant about imperious, macho women. You will remember that Jung thought *She* was a very good example of an anima figure. After I had written this I came across the particular foot- note about *She* in The Psychology of the Transference" (Jung 1954, p.220) in which Jung refers to "She" as "this 'royal' figure." That was like Leo's word "imperious." And I was doubly fascinated to see that my choice of the name Leo for this patient (to disguise his real name) might have come by cryptamnesia from that passage in Jung, as he says that the hero of the book is called Leo Vincey, and described him as "handsome . . . a veritable Apollo."

As a result of that session I knew that the sleepiness I had experienced was my part in his fantasy of me lulling him into submission, that I must have introjected; and that my feeling of being underused may have been defensive against his certainty that femaleness was always dangerous to him. It was a one-sided version of femaleness, and the session made me realize yet once more how self-analysis of the therapist has to go on for- ever.

In the following session effective analytic work was done on his need to fend off the woman, as he put it; he wants to be tough and male, but he cannot find out how. His mother hated his father's violence, and tried to bring up her son clean and obedient so that he should not be an- other aggressive man, but she did it in much too tough a way, which he feared would destroy his maleness. But he could not get on with his vio- lent father, he hated him, so he found it very difficult to make use of me taking care of him, which he said is what therapy should be. I thought he explained his dilemma very well. And it became equally clear that my being comfortable with good-enough maleness or the father in myself— namely, a healthy relationship with the animus—combined with a good- enough femaleness for him to sense that the anima is not going to de- stroy him, that was the internal *coniunctio* he needed in his analyst.

Following Jung's study of the *Rosarium Philosophorum* (Jung 1954) and his later book, *Mysterium Coniunctionis* (Jung 1963), it is now seen that the *coniunctio* is not so much a concept as a dynamic interaction. I think of it as a descriptive word which refers to the interplay within each of us of anima and animus images, and similar interplay between therapist and patient. In the same paper as I quoted before, I wrote: "Play and interplay between the mother and the infant set the tone of his later interplay and interaction with other people" (1974, p.8). We see transference and countertransference as "creative illusions" and it is worth remembering that the word "illusion" comes from the Latin, *ludo*, meaning "I play," so that the image offered or presented and represented by each person *plays in* creatively with the other. But the creative factor very often remains a mystery—and what Jung called "the demon of sickness" (1954, p.72) is an inevitable concomitant of the therapist's career choice. We have to get to know our demons, become conscious of them, and reduce their power over us.

References

Carotenuto, A. 1982. *A Secret Symmetry: Sabina Spielrein Between Jung and Freud*. New York: W.W. Norton.

Erikson, E. 1964. *Insight and Responsibility*. New York: W.W. Norton.

Goodheart, W. 1984. Successful and Unsuccessful Interventions in Jungian Analysis. *Chiron: A Review of Jungian Analysis* 1984: 89–117.

Hubback, J. 1969. The Symbolic Attitude in Psychotherapy. *Journal of Analytical Psychology* 14:1 (Chapter 1 in this book).

Jung, C.G. 1954. *The Practice of Psychotherapy*. In *Collected Works*, 16.

———. 1965. *Mysterium Coniunctionis*. In *Collected Works*, 14.

Milner, M. 1955. The Role of Illusion in Symbol Formation. In *New Directions in Psychoanalysis*. London: Tavistock.

Chapter 4

Manipulation, Activity and Handling

Descriptions abound of interactions between analysts and their patients, and much light has been thrown from many angles on what went on in particular sessions, in particular analyses, and in analysis in general. Despite the vast literature, additions can still be made to it because the nature of analysis itself is protean and not merely repetitive. General features, specific features, and changing features all need research. In "Principles of Practical Psychotherapy," Jung wrote: "*The individual signifies nothing in comparison with the universal, and the universal signifies nothing in comparison with the individual.* There are, as we all know, no universal elephants, only individual elephants. But if a generality, a constant plurality, of elephants did not exist, a single individual elephant would be exceedingly improbable" (1935, p.5).

My aim here is to join the discussion, on methods of work in analysis, which has been going on (though not always publicly), ever since Freud and Jung started to diverge. It is a discussion which carries on *pari passu* with the examination of content and process. At intervals it becomes possible for progress in the study of those two factors to be linked with attention given to method. And at the moment it is worth bringing out that recent work on countertransference (e.g., Racker 1968, Fordham 1969, 1972, Franz 1969, Kadinsky 1970, Plaut 1970, 1971, Lambert 1972) can be related to the direct examination both of method and the psychology of method. Method is being considered here in the light of patient-analyst interaction, in the light of transference and countertransference, and on the basis of the view that the most effective tool we have is our all-around understanding of those interactions.

I intend to draw attention to the activities of analysts for which the word handling is suitable, and is in fact often chosen by patients themselves, and to the activities of patients easily called manipulation. Ma-

Originally published in *The Journal of Analytical Psychology* 19:2 (1974), pp. 182–91.

nipulation is a term which has a pejorative flavor: we try not to be manipulated, even if we also like to see ourselves as capable of being adaptive and flexible. In studying our methods, our procedures, the term handling has been chosen here in preference to that of technique in order to focus on the more human or personal factors as compared to the more exactly technical ones. There is a tendency to associate, on the one hand, such qualifications as *correct*, or (as the case may be) *incorrect*, to technique, and, on the other hand, evaluative adjectives like *good* or *bad* to handling; but these scales of judgment and of evaluation need not be "either-or" ones and there is room for both of them, when analytic work is being examined.

Both terms, handling and manipulation, are metaphors. I am indebted to Kenneth Lambert for pointing out to me that, historically, a maniple was a subdivision of a Roman cohort, which itself was the tenth part of a legion. Such a group, or, as it were, handful of soldiers can be pictured as holding a critical position until further help arrived. Patients in analysis try to manipulate the analyst for various reasons such as anxiety, or simple fear, or out of fantasied omnipotence. Impatient of frustrations, they are trying, maneuvering to get what they want and get it quickly, forcibly, instead of more slowly and verbally. The patient's attempted manipulations often stem from as-yet-unanalyzed ego-defenses against minor or major anxieties, and they decline if analysis proceeds.

I should make it clear at the outset that in discussing manipulations and handling I am not writing about the occasional physical contact which does take place, whether it is fortuitous or intentional on the part of the analyst or maneuvered by the patient, in the course of therapeutic work which takes place mainly in words (Bosanquet 1970; see also Jacoby 1986 and Greene 1984). In using those analogic terms, it is *as though* physical hands were involved. These notes are on the subject of verbal actions and interactions though they take place in the material setting decided on and supplied by the analyst and within the principally psychological process of analysis; the patient's aim may be less predetermined.

Manipulation

Contact between therapist and patient may extend over many years, or last only a few weeks or less, but however short the therapy, there will have been activity on the part of both. Winnicott's therapeutic consultations are clear examples of how one individual analyst could sometimes do short work of (Winnicott 1971). Occasionally a therapist can do something, in a single isolated interview, and thereby enable the patient to do something after the interview, by mainly listening and not overtly affecting the course of the patient's talk. The full nature of "doing" includes its opposite, refraining from doing. Jung describes that as a "specifically Chinese concept, *wu-wei* . . . 'not-doing' (which is not to be confused with 'doing nothing')" (1921, p.217).

Refraining can be based on a positive decision to do, that is to say, nothing, with the conviction that that is the best action in the circumstances, as compared with keeping silent out of impotent confusion or lack of understanding. Uncomfortable experiences of that kind are probably well known to all analysts. They can also no doubt think of occasions, during perhaps various analyses, on which they carefully opted for silence and knew themselves to be actively partaking in the analysis. This is not to claim that such active silence is necessarily successful in the sense of immediately or steadily forwarding the analysis, even if the analyst feels convinced of having good reasons for remaining silent: I have on occasion positively chosen to say nothing and soon regretted my choice. All I could do then was to wait for a suitable opportunity later.

To illustrate this, I would like to instance some details from the analysis of a young homosexual woman, Miss A., who had great difficulty in speaking to me. She was often very seriously blocked. Her spontaneity was grossly repressed. The following incident occurred after she had been in analysis about three years. She mentioned someone only once, and I refrained from asking openly more about the person and, later, from even indirectly reminding her of the woman, although the matter sounded as though it were important. I refrained because it seemed to me at the time that it would be more valuable to her gradually to become more spontaneous and flexible in relation to me than to have the direct help of analyzing either her resistance or the problem at which she had hinted.

About a year later, she could no longer conceal how much the problem had grown and how painful it had become. In the course of now actively analyzing her passivity in relation to the other person, and recognizing how much she herself was suffering as a result, I was led to think that an earlier active grasping of it all on my part, and particularly the resistance, might have served her better than my refraining had done.

This long, drawn-out incident had points in common with something which had happened within a few weeks of the beginning of her analysis; namely, a resistance to the mother transference through falling in love with an older woman she had met in the course of her work. She only told me about her very gradually and had numerous devices for keeping out of the analysis all talk of this woman she now loved, while covertly behaving in the transference as though I were a direct replica of her father. Interpretations based on that projection were apparently ignored rather than demolished or rejected.

With hindsight it might be argued that I had been responding at a deep level to this patient's need not to be hurried, to her need to set the pace in the transference, within which she could get the necessary gratification of her unconscious infantile omnipotence, and it may have resulted in the analysis beginning to counteract the unfortunate effects of her developmental difficulties and fixations. I hope this was so. The analysis of Oedipal material was left until later. On reflection it seemed to me that she might have benefited more from a different method than the only one with which I found myself able to work.

While the problems described above are partly related to aiming for the optimum timing of interpretations, my principal object is to illustrate how an apparently passive patient actively deflected me from taking action. The interactions briefly outlined can be seen both as unconscious manipulations on her part, and of possibly too-cautious handling on my part, for fear of doing damage.

In the paper, "What He Is or What He Does," the psychoanalyst Springman studied the contrast of those two aspects of the working analyst as determinants of cure in "analytic therapeutic activity." He discussed the subject of the duality of the analyst and adduced two clinical examples to show that "noninterpretative interventions" (that is his phrase for the factor of "what he is") are necessary when the patient is initially very negativistic and can make no use of interpretations, whereas a cooperative patient needs to draw on "what he does," that is to say the analyst's interpretations. In the case of an uncooperative young woman patient, he suggested discontinuing the treatment for the time being: yet she came for the next session and was free from the resistance of her previously negative attitude. The suggestion had stemmed from his being able to rely on himself, rather than from established psychoanalytic rules (1970).

The contrast and the distinctions highlighted in Springman's paper are lucid, convincing and valuable, particularly if analysis is being seen in terms of cure, rather than of development. Yet it is possible to query whether the difference between "what he is" and "what he does" is as clear-cut in daily clinical work as Springman made it for the purposes of exposition. The analyst acts from the root and stem of what he is. So does the patient. Yet "what he is" is not a single or a constant state for either of them, though the analyst's being includes such previously split-

off elements which his own analysis enabled him to integrate, and his being is, mostly, reliable enough. Also, he is advisedly active in his attempts to discover and uncover what the patient is and how he acts and
why, as compared with the patient's usually lesser capacity; yet their respective activity, passivity and receptivity are in states of interplay all
through the analysis.

In considering Springman's formulations when I was trying to understand the way I was analyzing Miss A., it seemed to me that further
thoughts were necessary. The complement to, or the opposite of, activity
is usually taken to be passivity. The clinical events given above might be
analyzed at the time and examined later in terms of those two modes, as
well as in terms of whether she was being cooperative or negativistic.
There would result a relatively narrow analysis of the patient solely in
terms of her passive homosexual orientation and her penis envy. Such
narrowness would have the advantage of a certain sharpness of definition
and could be theoretically accurate. But Miss A. was passive in a manip-
ulative manner and I found myself working with her in a way which was
probably necessary to me, aimed at fostering in her a gradual discovery of
how to become receptive. The gradualness, which seemed right, points
to the presence of a factor in me with which I was feeling for the right
time for alerting her and for interpreting her defenses. I was fairly sure
she needed those defenses, as the anxieties behind the manipulations
were those associated with her infantile sexuality: she was very antagonistic to taking in anything from me in sessions when the father transference was in operation. She defended herself very strongly against both
the earlier envy of the breast and the later envy of the penis, and used
the one to try to conceal the other.

It seemed to me that with Miss A. the contrast active/receptive was a
more helpful formulation than that of active/passive. A woman analyst's
animus problem (or a man analyst's anima problem), if sufficiently
worked through and related to earlier personal experiences and fantasies,
will not interfere dangerously with the analysis of a patient's similar difficulties, provided the pathological defenses can be converted into healthy
and necessary ones. This is an aspect of self-analysis which calls for constant attention.

There is a further large area of analytic work where the themes of activity, passivity, and receptivity are relevant in both their benign and
their malign versions, and that is the analysis of a patient's passive-
aggressive reproaches, together with the analyst's style of analyzing
shadow problems.

I had a patient recently, Miss B., who could skillfully needle me with reproaches, having wiped out earlier interpretations of similar material and not daring to attack openly. She complained about circumstances and about people other than myself who were described as exerting control over her and as compared with whom she presented herself as innocent and powerless. On some such occasions there seemed to me to be just enough actuality in me, and also enough reality in the outer conditions of her life, for me to experience a certain compunction and uneasiness. My empathic response to her was not, I thought, good enough; guilt and persecutory anxiety beset me, at first fairly mildly and then in force, although I hoped that those kinds of reaction had been well enough understood and integrated as manifestations of the shadow. I was not fully satisfied with formulating to myself that the persecutory and projected anxieties emanated from Miss B., as I was not well enough defended against them to be sure which of us was attacking. I was the butt of destructive reproaches which I found more difficult to analyze than overt attacks. The patient did not trust me enough. She was attacking other people openly, and only needling me with reproaches.

With another patient, however, the same kind of difficulty can be seen, with a rather better resolution. Mr C. had come to England from a distant country for his analysis. He was unhappy, like a miserable whining child. He had been told that he had had feeding difficulties in the first few weeks of life, and from early childhood he had painful memories of being plagued, when constipated, by his mother's fierce use of soapstick suppositories.

In his analysis he could not receive anything useful from me unless he had done his own emotional excreting in his own way first; it was his way of trying to turn me into a tolerable mother. He complained in a reproachful way about all the conditions of living and working here; his colleagues were bone-headed, he had no energy for anything but to work in order to pay for his analysis, no time for his hobbies, his physical health was in jeopardy and such friends as he had, each being made to sound more insensitive than the last, were largely objects of envy.

It was obvious that in the analysis, whatever the realistic validity of these griefs and grievances, the complaints were envious reproaches which he was directing at me week after week, but they only came within reach when he was able to voice the bitter denigration of: "This horrible analysis wasn't worth coming for. I'd have stayed back home if I'd known what it would be like!" I answered that he was, now, hitting me and trying to demolish me; thereafter, with many ups and downs, a better (more workable) analytic relationship developed. With him, as compared with Miss B., my analytic persona had held reasonably healthily.

Handling and Certain Practical Matters

The extract I have just given leads me to the subject of handling, and to a consideration of the necessarily defensive aspects of certain practical matters.

There are many things I would include under the term handling that are recognizable from one analyst's practice to another, that is to say, professionally common and conventional persona manifestations, inevitable ones; but those matters take a particular form and, when considered together, demonstrate how in the combination of the material and the psychological, each analyst must have his own persona. On the one hand the needs of those seeking psychotherapy are being considered, and on the other hand there are matters in which the analyst considers himself. From the patient's point of view such material factors, procedures and aspects of the analyst's personality come to be data, like other reality features of life, to which he has to adapt.

The room and its contents either reveal or conceal the analyst to the patient (Jackson 1961, 1963). Its location also affects him in various ways. A friend of mine, speaking of her completed analysis, said: "I used to wish, in vain, that my analyst worked in Harley Street. I thought I did not want to know anything about his personal life: mine was too overwhelming at the time, and his home was an imposition on me!"

Ulanov, writing about birth and rebirth, examined closely the effect of her pregnancy on three women patients during their analyses, a pregnancy which had to be spoken about to them before it was physically evident (1969). A woman psychoanalyst, Ruth Lax, also wrote on the subject and pointed out that "a personal event in the life of the analyst, which cannot be hidden from the patient, intrudes into the analytic situation. The so-called anonymity and neutrality of the analyst is interfered with" (1969). She states further that "a situation occurs during the pregnancy of the analyst which offers the opportunity for making special observations about transference and countertransference." It is a matter where the analyst's sex had direct and specific effects which rarely have the corresponding ones in analyses conducted by a man, whose wife's pregnancy is less likely to be discovered.

Time

The analyst's style is revealed in the various procedures which become necessary during regressions to a preverbal stage of development. That is the time in an infant's life when the good-enough mother responds in action and does not expect her child to be able to wait long for her at-

tention. In a corresponding way a patient in whom "infantile reactions of
a total order are being reactivated . . . will identify in a very primitive
way with his analyst," in Michael Fordham's words. In that situation
there arises "that fusion which renders the patient unable to do without
the analyst and makes any separation, even for twenty-three hours, traumatic. Frequent interviews or keeping contact over the telephone during
the weekend can do much to help." The crux of the matter is to be able
to distinguish the stage of development which is being reactivated,
which defenses are operating, or have broken down, and whether there
is depression which is suicidal in degree.

With such a patient, or one who is regressed and also withdrawn in a
schizoid manner, the obvious useful action is to arrange a time for a telephone conversation before the next session. But it is possible for an analyst to play in with a patient's unexpressed persecutory belief that the
conventions of analysis do not include telephone calls. By thus protecting himself he may be in danger of closing the door to a really effective analysis of the patient's defenses and the resolution of his earliest
anxieties and demands.

Hospital Visits

Opinions differ on whether to visit a patient who has to be hospitalized
for physical treatment. There are cogent arguments on the side of those
who believe this is invariably a serious analytic mistake, that it is step-
ping beyond the limits of permissible activity, that it verges on social
contact. The patient might understand a visit (or several) in a way the
analyst did not mean; it could well be that such visits are evidence of
successful manipulation by the patient, that they will contribute to a
proliferation of infantile omnipotent fantasies which may become very
difficult to analyze. There is not, as far as I know, a common code about
such visits, so that each analyst presumably develops his own attitude
and practice on the subject. Any physical illness, or an operation under
an anesthetic, causes regression, and knowing the patient well enough to
sense in advance how he is likely to experience being hospitalized will be
an indication of whether to offer a visit. I have had one patient with
whom it happened that a visit could take place at the time of one of the
lost sessions, a material fact which was the first step towards later discussion and analysis of her reactions. It was clearly unsuitable to do so at
the time of the visit. I also said that the best time to telephone from the
hospital would be during one of her usual session times, and she took up
the suggestion. The visit and the telephone conversations were linked

soon after with discussion of the particular operation she had had, and its meaning within her psychopathology. It seemed to me sometime later that her analysis was not furthered, rather its progress had been hindered, by complicated affects which she had not been able to integrate, such as a feeling of being very special and also a rather cool complacency stemming from unconscious envy of my "kindness," and it was possible to say that I thought it had probably been a mistake.

On the occasion when I have thought it right to say that I considered I had made a mistake, I have tried to take account of the patient's current ego strength; if that is good enough, I believe maturation is forwarded, on the analogy of the child who is mature enough to be able to discover a parent's limitations without that being a traumatic disillusioning experience. There is disagreement among analytical psychologists and others as to whether an analyst can make mistakes. In commenting on what Fordham had called "the failure in interchange between a patient and myself" in his paper, "Technique and Countertransference" (1969), Kadinsky wrote: "An analyst does not make 'mistakes'—just as he does not allow his patient to claim to have made a mistake: whatever he does . . . is always an expression of his personality and valuable as a clue to self-understanding" (1970). Plaut, on the contrary, seems to think mistakes are possible, since he looked for one: "When I read through the notes much could be recalled. I found no *single* [italics mine] point in the analysis where I could put my finger and say, I made a mistake here" (1971). The search for "a clue to self understanding" may lead to discovering a strong affective factor. Following Winnicott writing about "objective and justified hatred" of the patient (1949), Little (1951) said, "The subjectivity of the feelings needs to be shown to the patient, though their actual origin need not be gone into (there should be no "confessions")."

The term countertransference becomes increasingly valuable as its manifestations and variations are studied. What Plaut was looking for, in the instance quoted above, what Fordham called "a failure in interchange," and what I think can on occasions be termed mistakes, are forms of unsatisfactory handling. There may be some hurt to the patient, at times when such a failure or mistake occurs, and it is ordinarily human to suffer at any rate the minor prickings of a conscience which is not excessively protected by the persona, while taking advantage of the occasion to study where and how the countertransference projection was at work. When I examined my motives for visiting my patient who had had an operation, I found it was not principally a "kind" response to the fact that she was lonely, but rather that I wanted to see what it felt like to me to break a "rule" that I normally accept. So that I believe the mistake lay in my using the patient for my own purposes, instead of considering her first. But I did not communicate that to her.

Conclusion

Neither a patient's attempted manipulations nor an analyst's idiosyncrasies are necessarily to be deplored—it is the *excess* of them which hampers good work. They are analyzable interactions relating to defensiveness or to experimental assertiveness in the transference and in the countertransference. Meticulousness, however, as the expression of an anxious obsessionality in myself as analyst, is a trait which it is worth working on: gifts of flowers on the eve of a break, or in the last session of all, are accepted, not analyzed. And the same held for a patient's genuine concern on an occasion when I was wearing a large bandage on my leg; other patients had made no comment: I could not be certain whether or not they had noticed. Shaking hands at the end of an analysis is probably usual, but I have detected the presence in myself of a reaction-formation in doing so, as this is a country where there is less hand shaking than in others (Jacoby 1986). It would be difficult to feel comfortable with oneself, when working to enable someone else to grow more natural and feel more at ease with himself, when working towards individuation, if natural and even idiosyncratic expressions were always or artificially held back. The patient makes the best use he can of his particular analyst's personality, handling and style, as well as of the general features of analysis. Many of the personal characteristics of his analyst will enter the transference, in an analysis which is even moderately thorough.

Jung wrote: "His [the patient's] system is geared to mine and acts upon it; my reaction is the only thing with which I as an individual can legitimately confront my patient" (1935). These notes have been recorded in order to draw attention to some particular aspects of patients' manipulations and one analyst's attempts to understand the connections between content and method.

References

Bosanquet, C. 1970. Getting in Touch. *Journal of Analytical Psychology*, 15:1.

Fordham, M. 1969. Technique and Countertransference. *Journal of Analytical Psychology*, 14:2.

————. 1972. The Interrelation Between Patient and Therapist. *Journal of Analytical Psychologist* 17:2.

Franz, K.E. 1969. The Analyst's Own Involvement with the Process and the Patient. *Journal of Analytical Psychology* 14:2.

Greene, A. 1984. Giving the Body its Due. *Quadrant* 17:2, 9–24.

Jackson, M. 1961 Chair, Couch, and Countertransference. *Journal of Analytical Psychology* 6:1.

————. 1963. Technique and Procedure in Analytic Practice with Special Reference to Schizoid States. *Journal of Analytical Psychology* 6:1.

Jacoby, M. 1986. Getting in Touch and Touching in Analysis. In *The Body in Analysis*. N. Schwartz-Salent & M. Stein, eds. Wilmette, Ill.: Chiron Publications.

Jung, C.G. 1921. *Psychological Types*. In *Collected Works*, 6.

————. 1935. Principles of Practical Psychotherapy. In *Collected Works*, 16.

Kadinsky, D. 1970. The Meaning of Technique. *Journal of Analytical Psychology*, 15:2.

Lambert, K. 1972. Transference/countertransference: Talion Law and Gratitude. *Journal of Analytical Psychology*, 16:2.

Lax, R. 1969. Some Considerations about Transference and Countertransference—Transference Manifestations Evoked by the Analyst's Pregnancy. In *International Journal of Psycho-Analysis*, 50:3.

Little, M.I. 1951. Countertransference and the patient's response to it. In *International Journal of Psycho-Analysis* 32:1.

Plaut, A. 1970. "What do You Actually do?" Problems in Communication. *Journal of Analytical Psychology*, 15:1.

————. 1971. "What do We Actually do?" Learning from Experience. *Journal of Analytical Psychology*, 16:2.

Springman, R.R. 1970. What he is or What he does. In *International Journal of Psycho-Analysis*, 51:4.

Ulanov, A.B. 1969. Birth and Rebirth. *Journal of Analytical Psychology*, 18:2.

Winnicott, D.W. 1949. Hate in the Counter-transference. In *Collected Papers*. London: Tavistock Publications.

————. 1971. *Therapeutic Consultations in Child Psychiatry*. London: Tavistock Publications.

Chapter 5

Acting Out

The old saying, "Fools rush in where angels fear to tread," is well known. I suggest it may be a precursor, on the folk level of the technical term and concept of acting out. Fools act, and act too quickly, whereas angels (and analysts usually) consider the matter carefully and may postpone comment or interpretation (which are forms of action) until the next day or session, or even the next week or month. Whether or not my speculation is apt, I forgot both the saying and the moral behind it when I was invited to be one of the speakers at a Day Conference on Acting Out in September, 1983. I fell for the flattery of the invitation. But the purposive and adaptive aspects of acting out (of which I will say more later) are that I probably needed to put a lot of thought into what acting out means, and means to me as a Jungian. The term does not feature in the *Index* to the *Collected Works* of Jung, but it is used by modern Jungians. I did not realize that only very little written attention has been given to it by us. In twenty-eight years of the *Journal of Analytical Psychology* not a single paper has been wholly devoted to the phenomenon itself, to clinical descriptions of its manifestations, to dynamic or structural considerations, or to the theory of it—let alone a discussion of the now several conceptualizations. But a review of only a few recent annual indexes of the *International Journal of Psycho-Analysis* revealed the existence of almost innumerable papers which either fully attend to several of the many aspects of the subject, or in which the concept is used and its meaning is assumed to be understood. Perhaps it appears as a seminar topic of psychoanalysts in training. Analytical psychologists learn about it in supervision, that is, in clinical experience rather than from the theoretical angle. Some discover it during their own analysis. It has been

Based on a paper given at a Day Conference of the British Association of Psychotherapists on 24 September 1983 and originally published in *The Journal of Analytical Psychology* 29 (1984), pp. 215-29.

pointed out to me by Dr J. Redfearn that the concept signifies a clinical judgment or a practical problem in handling, rather than an analytical attitude which takes account of the subjectivity of the analyst's feelings as well as of the patient's actions (personal communication).

For many Jungians, and especially in centers other than here in London, anything smacking of technique is suspect. It is sometimes even attacked on the grounds that it is "scientific," more particularly by those who call themselves archetypal psychologists, who favor working mainly with images, symbols and mythological amplifications. That suspicious attitude has resulted in it being all too easy to be a little casual about the use to which such a technical term is put. The term, "acting out" is the one which, before anything else, denotes something presumably identifiable, and in the past has been considered usually as done by a patient. As well as a denoting term, it is a descriptive one. The range of occurrences that it describes is, however, a wide one. Equally wide is the range of possible ways for the analyst to proceed, respond, or react, or techniques to use, when he considers that the patient is acting out. It is also possible for the term to be applied to the analyst, thanks to the development over the years of sophisticated thinking about countertransference, and in consideration of the view Jung expressed that the analyst is in the analysis as well as the patient.

This paper consists of some reflections on the concept and its manifestations, linked to the major lines of thought in contemporary analytical psychology. It is neither exhaustive nor definitive. For example, as I have no delinquent in my practice, I am leaving out the whole question of acting out and delinquency.

Short Selection of the Literature

The Jungian use of the term "acting out" is evidently based on Freud's (1914) formulation in "Remembering, Repeating and Working Through" in which he went into more detail than he had when it first appeared in the 1905 *Standard Edition* of his publication. Freud was explaining why the patient known as Dora broke off her treatment. In "Remembering, Repeating and Working Through" Freud wrote

the patient does not remember anything of what he has forgotten and repressed, but acts it out. He reproduces it not as a memory but as an action: he repeats it, without, of course, knowing that he is repeating it (1914, p.150).

That is a compact statement, and even more compact is the definition offered by Phyllis Greenacre, in a symposium held at the Thom Clinic for children in Boston in 1962: "We might define acting out, then, as memory expressed in active behaviors without the usual sort of recall in verbal or visual imagery" (1978, p.216). But Laplanche and Pontalis showed how those definitions fail "to distinguish the element of *actualization* in the transference from the resort to motor action—which the transference does not necessarily entail" (1973, p.4). When they composed the *Language of Psychoanalysis* they had the benefit of the work of the many contributors to the Copenhagen International Psycho-Analytical Congress held in 1967, and the commentators on the papers there, who added a wealth of sophistication to the subject. And since Laplanche and Pontalis, Dale Boesky (1982) has reconsidered the concept very thoroughly. Any Jungian wishing to study the subject has to take notice of contemporary Freudian work on it.

Among analytical psychologists, Michael Fordham has up to now most conspicuously thought and written about acting out. In the chapter entitled Notes on the Transference (significantly published in the book entitled *Technique in Jungian Analysis*) there appears this statement: "Acting out is a special form of defensive behavior whenever it occurs, and is based . . . upon a projection to which neither analyst nor patient has been able to gain access" (1974, p.126). He stated the same thing in longer form (in the same chapter):

> The gradual development of an analysis can lead to the analyst's becoming the center of it, so that the whole patient may become involved in the process of transformation. If, as sometimes happens, this concentration of libido is made into an aim, almost anything, whether adapted or not, that happens outside the transference in the life of the patient is considered undesirable. These supposedly undesirable activities have come to be termed "acting out," and this term seems to have received greater prominence than its more vivid equivalent of "living the shadow" (pp.124–25).

My next quotation from the same chapter, leads on from those statements:

> In using a psychoanalytic term, *acting out,* it is necessary to realize that it is being altered in the process [by analytical psychologists] and at the same time extended, to cover and emphasize the *purposive* [my italics] aspect of the act in question.

Then he refers to Stein (1955) who described certain women patients who "walked round the analyst's chair in a menacing manner . . . [in] increasingly narrow circles, reminiscent of the 'hag track' . . . *in order to try to stir him up.*"

I would interpose at this point that the hag was a witchlike creature, a female, probably elderly, believed to have supernatural powers which she used and worked up by means of circumambulating. The hag track, according to the Oxford Engish Dictionary, is another name for the fairy circle. The man was encircled with the bad archetypal power, the hag or the witch being the obvious opposites of the good mother and the good woman. The hag and the witch are the archetypal shadow figures of the woman.

In *Ancient Art and Ritual*, Jane Ellen Harrison wrote:

> The savage [primitive man] is a man of action. Instead of asking a god to do what he wants done, he does it or tries to do it himself; instead of prayers he utters spells. In a word, he practices magic, and above all he is strenuously and frequently engaged in dancing magical dances (1931).

Jung wrote about the shadow at the collective level as being evident in the present in such "counter-tendencies in the unconscious" of modern people as those which appear in "spiritualistic séances," in what he calls "puerile and inferior" character traits, in carnival customs and in other "traces in folklore" (1946, par. 469). He adds that "the main part of [the shadow] gets personalized."

The personal shadow, as is well known, consists for each of us of what we do not like about ourselves, what we repress from consciousness, what we postpone discovering, but it is also a factor that we need to find and accept for full personality development. The man partly wants to be stirred up by the woman (I refer to the quotation from Stein's paper), —perhaps even wants that to take a sexual form, but at the same time he does not want her to be more powerful than he is. He has a shadow problem about the powerful woman and the internal woman-image. Fordham writes that the patients who walked round the analyst's chair were "enacting a primitive drama . . . which was not realized at first by Stein or the patients. They were *living their shadow* which contains an archetypal image" (1974, p.126). That phrase *living the shadow*, conveys that the events referred to are potentially usable for purposes of bringing personal or archetypal shadow elements to consciousness, preliminary to their being integrated with the ego. But Fordham, in the chapter from which I am quoting, went on to say: "*Living the shadow* is likewise considered undesirable in analytical psychology, but for the added reason that it is acting in a primitive manner and is undesirable because it is consequently unadapted" (p. 126). And he explains that in Stein's paper called, incidentally, "Loathsome Women," the patients wanted to stir their analyst up, to get him to "man-handle" them, but also did not really want that, since they had come to the analyst "because of the failure of their primitive and guilt-ridden activities to produce adequate satisfaction" (p. 126).

Some Varieties of Acting Out

As the analytic attitude eschews, as far as is humanly possible, criticism, moralizing, and didacticism, I think we might notice, as well as what Fordham calls the undesirable fact of the primitivity of the patient's action, that this "undesirability" of acting out stems also from the analyst's feeling of defeat when acting out takes place (he may ask himself "What did I say, or fail to notice, that led to the acting out?"), and also where matters of technique are concerned that it is often difficult to get the patient to accept interpretations of it. Those may have been directed only at the particular form of action that has occurred, which probably will not have been mutative, rather than to the underlying transference fantasy, which is what is going on behind the reliving of earlier interpersonal experiences. Interpretation, I find, succeeds only after quite a lot of work has been done on the patient's unconscious transference projections, and at the same time privately examining the countertransference, so that the analyst and the patient both see what each is *doing*, as well as *being*, or claiming that the other is *doing* and *being*.

I would, however, add a caveat at this point: what I have just said might be taken to imply that I advocate blurring the distinction, which has always been at the center of the concept of acting out, between, on the one hand, remembering, thinking, and speaking, and, on the other, acting, or enacting, or reenacting. I only wish to point out that we have all—Freudians and Jungians alike—come to the stage of analytic sophistication when we know that thinking, fantasizing, and dreaming are psychological forms of action, so that the idea of a spectrum of actions is what we are dealing with, rather than a simple set of opposites. For example, a certain patient spoke several times one summer about her wish, and indeed her strong urge, to bring me a rose from her garden, but she refrained from putting the urge into action. Two years later, she did bring two roses—very carefully selected ones which were going to develop into perfect blooms. On each occasion analysis revealed the previously unconscious transference projections which were currently at work, their origins in the ways of interactions that there had been in the oedipal triangle in childhood, and, more significant of course, her feelings about her mother and her father, and what she took to be their respective feelings about her. I did not find that the act of bringing the roses impeded analysis, nor was it more "primitive" than telling me that she wanted to bring a rose. In fact there was positiveness in her having dared to take action.

I am somewhat cowardly about interpreting Christmas presents at the time they are given. They often signify a defensive maneuver against separation anxiety. One particular patient, whose father had left the family when she was still very young and who never gave her any presents or sent her birthday cards, used always to give me two presents, and a card at the same time; and she sent a second card through the post. I used simply to thank her. Later I came to see that I was meant to be good father as well as good mother. I hope it would nowadays be possible for me to interpret along those lines, which would not have been an attacking way to do it. I should have pointed out, perhaps, that bad father-me was giving her neither card nor present, and that there was a hidden attack by her, laced with irony, in her giving me two of each.

Acting Out and Archetypal Theory

At a different point in the spectrum of talk and action lie car accidents, which obviously don't happen *in* the consulting room as did those two examples I have just given, and which are clearer instances of what is generally meant by acting out. They can be suicide threats, and on one occasion some years ago, when the accident involved no other car, I felt I needed to find that out by asking whether or not the patient had been wearing his seat belt. He was in a hyper-manic state: acting out can precede a psychotic episode. I usually investigate the circumstances of a collision or a near miss in order to discover whether the patient considered himself or herself attacked by the other driver (who may be standing in for me in the transference) or whether he or she was the attacker. One woman patient knocked down an elderly woman on a pedestrian crossing after a session when her ambivalence towards both her analyst and a certain member of her family had not yet become adequately conscious. There was still a great deal of analytic work to be done on a number of major difficulties in her life; they could be conceptualized in terms of the archetypal conflicts highlighted in the transference projections at various times. When she had the accident, the feature most prominent in the analysis was the mother and child interaction, both in the day-to-day work and at a deeper level. The fact that she hit a woman much older than herself is an illustration of that. But she also had an animus problem with me, as she was far from sure that I was—in her terms—as intelligent and powerful as her previous analyst or as herself. That was the representation in the transference of the animus and anima problem that she and her husband had: the mutually unsatisfying marriage relationship had contributed to the tension between the couple and their nearly grown children. She was putting into action revengeful retaliations, impulses of which the meaning had not yet emerged. It is precisely in that primitive area of the psyche where lies the trouble which leads to acting out: the forces at the instinctual pole of the archetype are activated by powerful emotions, and the other pole, that of meaning, has not yet been reached.

On the one hand—or at the one pole—"the archetypes are the unconscious images of the instincts themselves, in other words . . . they are patterns of instinctual behavior" (Jung 1936, par. 91). But, at the other pole, "instinct brings in its train archetypal contents of a spiritual nature," it *"stimulates thought"* and thought activates the search for meaning (my italics). In acting out there is too little thinking, let alone hard thinking, as well as too little appreciation of meaning.

The example of the driving accident illustrates potentially many features of the Jungian view of the dynamics of acting out. There is, first, that bipolar quality of the archetype which is a valuable aspect of Jungian theory when we are working with developmental issues and the need for strengthening the ego. It was shown in that instance not classically, as it were through an image or a symbol in a dream or in a fantasy, but in what the patient *did*: first she used the maternal object, the car, as a weapon with which to attack the older woman; and, second, she misused what should be a container or a valid protective outer shell, because she was defending herself against what would have been very painful affects if she had discovered her anger against me in the transference. Her adolescent son was being very difficult at the time, acting out instead of having verbal rows; she felt angry with her husband, who she considered had been inconsistent in his attitude to the young man; she was also angry with her mother (long dead) who she believed had given in too easily in any marital disagreement and who had never been able to criticize her husband, my patient's father—and that had become one of my patient's own problems. The impulsive or instinctual pole of the archetype was responded to, in other words, the more primitive factor, or the more infantile one, the presymbolic forces were let loose and the meaning pole of so many archetypal affects could only emerge during the following weeks when the unfortunate accident was analyzed.

The second feature of theoretical interest to the dynamics of acting out was that shadow factors were at work. Fordham, in one of the passages quoted earlier, drew attention to a possibility whereby analytical psychology could make a substantial contribution to demonstrating and understanding the subtleties of the concept. The term "living the shadow" is a valuable one and it certainly applied to the patient about whom I have been speaking. She was obsessional in her attempts to get her behavior to reach an impossibly high ego-ideal, and that exerted a heavy-handed influence on her. She wished to see herself both as being more emancipated than her mother from a "little woman" pattern of life, and as being her father's favorite daughter. She was envious of her husband. She feared criticism both from him (she described him as being a passive-aggressive man), and from internalized parents, with whom she had identified more than she yet realized. A "forbidden" impulse was trying to emerge in the transference: she had been experiencing me in consciousness as likable and very different from either her mother, her father, or her husband, but from the unconscious area she was in fact striving to find a way to criticize and attack me. In the countertransference (I realized after she had knocked down the woman), I had been slow to appreciate the urgent need for her negative criticisms to emerge: they might have taken the form of her saying, for example, "you are not seeing what is going on," which might have led to: "you are like my mother who over protected my father." I had unconsciously colluded with her not-yet-analyzed transference fantasies. For her the important shadow problem was her fear of being, and being seen to be, what both her childhood family and her present one disapproved of, namely critical of authority and power figures. Her perfectionism got in the way of noticing and criticizing my imperfections. Instead of understanding the meaning of the shadow, she was dominated by it. In the immediate events it was the personal shadow which gripped her and which prevented valid ego development. There was also the archetypal shadow and an animus problem, the unconscious masculine element: the patterns of unintegrated potential were operating dangerously from generation to generation. The analyst's endeavor is to see to it that they are interpreted and enabled to contribute developmentally by becoming conscious through emotional experiences in the transference. The ego is strengthened by acceptance of the shadow. But that involves pain, which she naturally wished to avoid—she was already suffering much unhappiness.

"Living the shadow" may need to be worked through many times in a thorough analysis. The shadow in the form of antidevelopmental and regressive forces is a deep one. It is of course linked with trickster, *puer* and *puella* problems. Representations of both the *puer* and the trickster figures need analyzing and bringing to consciousness during episodes of acting out, since both of them are connected with attempts on the part of the patient to remain powerfully young in relation to the analyst or to other figures in his or her life. The appeal of the perpetual-small-boy kind of man, who is charming, delightful, perhaps even has a cherubic quality about him, disguised under a form which leads people to say such things as, "he's still a boy, even at seventy"—that appeal is certainly very strong, and particularly to sentimental women. The naïve woman who plays the kitten, who wins through by charm, or who pleads innocence, when unfortunately all she is innocent of is experience, and what she has refused is responsibility—she also gets what she wants, perhaps for a long time, and she enjoys tricking people into credulity. The boy, the *puer* archetype, the girl, the *puella*, and the trickster who of course is always a child at heart, are all three acting out, and they try to get the people in their lives to accept the implicit idea that they do not have to grow up, with all the loss of fun that that would involve.

The figure of the trickster is usually referred to as "he": I have been struck by the relative paucity of examples in Jungian papers of trickster possession in women; but I find in practice that women patients whose difficulties or pathology lie in the hysteric area rather than the obsessional, and who defensively develop somatic symptoms, can be enabled gradually to accept interpretation of those symptoms (which are a form of acting out) if I bear in mind that the trickster is at work. The trickster possession acts in an attacking way against my analytic efforts, and in a self-attacking way against the patient. The attempt to seduce the analyst-father and the alternative attempt to get him to change into being a kindly mother-analyst, who the patient hopes will be sympathetic towards her physical troubles, are ones which the analyst must sense, understand, and interpret. In the background of the somatizing and hysteric maneuver is the oedipal confusion between the desire for the mother's continued early mothering and the other desire for a love-affair with the father. The trickster and the incest archetypes both affect the patient severely, and acting out in the form of perhaps very obstinate psychosomatic illnesses may hold up the analysis until the transference fantasies of regression and incest have come to light and been worked through.

The trickster is always unwilling to be exposed—there is a lot of resistance against being shown up. It likes working out of reach of the adult, plotting, if it is a child-trickster, anywhere out of sight—in the bushes, or at the far end of the beach—where small boys and girls investigate each other's genitals. It does this to retaliate against the parents who do mysterious things behind closed doors and who do not wish to be interrupted or peeped at through the keyhole. Neither tricksters nor conjurors nor spies can bear the light of day, that is to say, interpretation. The trickster-patient who acts out wants it both ways: he or she in the short run wants magically to confuse the analyst-parent, owing to the very powerful loving and attacking impulses which are operating, and which are both feared. The acting out defensively protects the patient from insight. But in the long run, or at a deeper level, the patient wants the analyst not to be tricked. The therapeutic alliance does not consist simply of positive feelings on both sides; rather it is an alliance between the patient's developmental needs and the analyst's artistic skill in fostering them. Behind the patient's childlike desire to be special, or perhaps the favorite, to be charismatic and marvellous, lies a large inflation of the self. Physical actions seem to the immature mind to be more powerful than mental or psychic ones—and, of course, they very often are, in the short term. The immediate is at the instinctive pole of the archetype, the psychic and meaningful take longer to reach.

Acting Out and the Self

A strong case can be made for analyzing acting out in terms of ego possession by the self, whether "the self" is taken in the sense of the primal undifferentiated self of very early infancy prior to the development of the ego, or in the classic Jungian sense of the central archetype, to which Jung gave particular attention when working on individuation in the second half of life. Psychological development has been found by analysts of all schools, I think, to involve cyclical phases—or ones to which the image of the spiral applies perhaps even better. Acting out in one form or another occurs in most analyses, and recurs in many. At times ego, ego potential or ego features are difficult to discern: they are concealed within the postulate we name the self. The self may feel to be, or be expressed as a very small dot, a nucleus, or it may be felt to be all-inclusive, everything. In analysis we sometimes feel that the patient "is" a powerless baby or that the patient "is" omnipotent. As analysts we may oscillate between those two extremes. Both are presymbolic, and they precede ambivalence. Dominance by the undifferentiated self temporarily deprives the ego of all competence. People, whether they are patients or not, whose psychic development has been excessively harassed or sorely beset with difficulties, or who have suffered repeated losses, will

tend to regress to states where ego functions very largely disappear. And
this happens as many times as it needs working through. When there is
acting out and particularly the physically dangerous kinds, the *puer,
puella* or magical child has been reabsorbed by the primal self, the earlier
de integration has been negated.

The theory of deintegration in contemporary analytical psychology refers to the concept first put forward by Michael Fordham to the effect
that the earliest integrated psychosomatic state of wholeness at, and soon
after, birth, which he called the primal self, spontaneously divides into
parts (1974). The primal self is seen as containing in a state of potentiality all the necessary archetypal stages of development, including relationship to part objects and whole objects. Instinctual activity, or deintegration, takes place, which is the beginning of ego development. It
must, of course, not be confused with disintegration, going to pieces.
Deintegration is conceived as being essential for the infant to emerge
from its earliest self-enclosed state.

Using the other theory, that of the self as the central archetype, it can
be seen that a return to possession by an inappropriate psychic unity
and by the overpowerful archetypal contents of the self is dangerous to
healthy functioning. Each of us falls into possession by the self and in-
dulges in a form of acting out when we assume, as I suppose infants implicitly do, that we will be safe in acutely dangerous situations. It is a
kind of identification with immortality (Edinger 1960). It is closely allied to the loss of ego functioning which is evident at times when omnipotence is in the ascendant, which is so frequent in episodes of acting
out. And that, in turn, is allied to the omniscience which almost invariably tries to postpone acceptance of interpretation of acting out. It is not
just cussedness or resistance on the part of the patient: the analyst needs
to understand that there is a perhaps inevitable regression of the ego
in the direction of an undifferentiated self, so that renewed painful
experiences of deintegration are going to be necessary before insight is
admitted.

Many analysts have noticed that instances of acting out tend to be ignored (by the patient) as soon as they are felt to be over. They are sometimes called "attacks of acting out" and that is indeed an apt expression.
Moreover, ego development has been under attack. So has the analyst as
the representative of the ego. If ego functioning is then rapidly and defensively reestablished, the patient does not want to know about the attacks and tends to be surprised or even offended if the analyst refers to
them. The patient fairly naturally wants to be brought back, as it were,
like a child onto the lap after he or she has had a tantrum, and for the

misdeed to be forgiven. There is a diminution of the wish for insight, for elucidation, and for thinking, which are all aspects of ego. It is an effort to try to examine and think through what happened. In "Psychic Conflicts in a Child," Jung wrote

> I lay stress on the significance of *thinking* and the importance of concept-building for the solution of psychic conflicts. . . . the initial sexual interest strives only figuratively towards an immediate sexual goal, but far more towards the development of thinking (1946, p.4).

Two of my patients used to tell me at intervals of fearsome fights and rows, shouting and screaming, which erupted at home, usually at weekends, but neither of them ever screamed at me. The exciting orgiastic sexual character of the incidents was clear. Each would regress, at those times, to what was in fact a reproduction or representation of early infancy situations in which screaming was their only weapon of attack and defense. One of them toned down in the transference the manifestation of frustrations and used to nag, fuss, and niggle in a manner that I experienced as merciless. Invariably she would leave with a little girl smile and a quiet "thank you." The other one for many months on end regularly used the last session in the week to go at me nonstop, trying to wear me down. While the real tantrums took place with their men and against their men, the mitigated attacks were all they could allow themselves with me, presumably because ego possession by the self could be allowed to be more extreme at home than in the transference where protection of the mother-me was essential to their survival and their development.

The two patients who attacked their men much more overtly than they went at their analyst were both prone to have phases of envying me inordinately. The acting out at home was a defense against understanding how enviable they considered my analytic work to be. In trying to reduce me to reactiveness, to irritation, to defeatism, and self-reproach they were concealing from themselves the sharpness of their envious attacks. When it became possible to point that out, and to link their envy of me with childhood rivalries and with infancy attacks on the breast, the acting out diminished in intensity. It occurred less frequently when the patients had, after much working through, fully accepted the origins of their attacks. Acting out, which had had a high component of aggression, came to be seen as stemming also from hunger for development and understanding. That was an acceptable instinctual urge (Hubback 1969).

Finally, where ego possession by the self is concerned, I would draw attention to the connection between the victim-victimizer syndrome and acting out. The kind of patient who acts out in the transference and feels himself to be the victim of the analyst is likely to retaliate against others in his environment: they in turn are then victimized by his not-yet-analyzed persecutory anxieties, which he projects. Deep affects have been activated in the transference, stemming from presymbolic levels of ego development. The aggressive and destructive components of acting out have been delineated here, which situates them very early in life. The body, body affects, pleasures, and frustrations get expressed in activity and in reenactment.

I mentioned the purposive potential that there is in acting out at the beginning of this paper when I said that probably I had, when undertaking to write it, a need to study the whole question. Rather than merely fall into the trap, to be tricked, and to forget that one feature of appearing in public (and of publishing papers) is that it can represent a version of regressive childhood exhibitionism, I found when I began to reflect, to study the matter, and to put careful thought into it with a view to drawing attention to what analytical psychology has to offer on the subject, that that was ego functioning as compared with the earlier more primitive reaction. There is a symbolic intercourse between those who ask for a professional paper and those who give one, and it is to be hoped that the concepts which emerge are legitimate offspring.

Interactions

On the whole, as was said earlier, analytical psychologists have not tackled acting out as a separate topic, and on reflection I think this may stem from the view they have that analytical psychotherapy is in its essence a matter of interaction. Jung himself felt strongly that the analyst was in the analysis as much as the patient, and even on occasion told a patient a dream he had had, thereby resolving a countertransference/transference block in which both were stuck (1963, pp.133,138). I have heard recently that in Jungian circles in the USA increasing attention is being given to acting out by analysts. Even if trainee-therapists are made very anxious by open discussion of the danger of sexual acting out with patients, their anxiety has to be risked so that they can discover the dynamics of it. The trend among analytical psychologists who closely study "the infant in the adult" has resulted in a potentially good understanding of how easily psychic interactions with the patient can be distorted into acting out. For many years I have felt and found in practice that "in this work [psychotherapy] actions and interactions are of even greater interest than are concepts" (Hubback 1969), and that "the important happening in therapy is the interplay between therapist and patient, on the basis of the fact that play and interplay between the mother and the infant set the tone of his later interplay and interaction with other people" (*ibid.*). Those are only sketchy, outline remarks. They could be fleshed out with, on the one hand, examples of how the analyst's unconsciousness of what is happening (the puristic meaning of countertransference) delays effective therapy, and, on the other, examples of how self-analysis during interactions which might be physical helps them to move on to becoming properly psychic: the transcendent image may be brought to life by the analyst's dream, fantasy, reverie, and reflection. Then, if all goes well, there is not acting out on the part of the analyst: psychological activation and interaction develop instead. I do not think that description is unduly idealistic.

An important manifestation of the overall theme is the series of complicated interactions between Jung, his patient Sabina Spielrein, and Freud, which came to light as a result of Aldo Carotenuto's book in which he published her journals, her letters to Jung and those to Freud, together with Freud's answers (1982). The book was widely reviewed and continues to be discussed. It can be said that Jung acted out, as did also his patient, when he allowed her fantasies to dominate the later stages of her treatment, when presumably separation anxiety and the fear of loss were both at work in both of them, though neither he nor Freud, whom he consulted, seems to have named it acting out at the time. She did not physically conceive with him the fantasied son, Siegfried, but she became a very creative psychoanalyst. The concept of the anima came to Jung, I think, more easily during his major crisis a few years later (1914 to 1917), after those experiences with her, than it might have otherwise. He made open reference to several of her papers, written from 1911 onwards. But then Freud also acted out, in his relations with Jung, his not fully integrated father-son conflict. Transference and countertransference projections became very confused between the two of them. Moreover Spielrein's concept of the death instinct was taken up by Freud, and then by Klein.

Those events are now a lifetime ago. There have been innumerable observations and experiences of disappointments, disillusionments and losses contributing to depressive attacks and to phases of acting out. Less dramatic instances than the Spielrein one could probably be given by many analysts of occasions when the instinctual pole of the archetype was activated and a certain amount of acting out took place or nearly did. Though the risk of a male analyst acting out with a female patient is, I think, more often referred to than the other way around, most women analysts can probably recall times of being deeply affected by the erotic atmosphere of some sessions, and just like male analysts can retreat from the risk with a reminder of all they know of the force of the incest archetype. The early analysts would have had to be even more impressive giants than they were, to see what they were doing.

Summary

This chapter outlines a Jungian view of the originally Freudian term, "acting out." After showing what the author owes to some of the writers who have published on the subject, and giving an example of what can be called positive or valuable acting out, she shows how archetypal theory illuminates many aspects of a patient's dangerous acting out and the analyst's part in the interaction. The two contemporary theories of the self in analytical psychology (the archetypal and classical, and the theory of the primal self) are used to show how a better understanding of acting out may be reached. It is stressed how unanalyzed countertransference can become a kind of acting out by the analyst, and an attempt is made to show how the interaction between patients and analysts are dynamic and symbolic.

References

Boesky, D. 1982. Acting Out: A Reconsideration of the Concept. *International Journal of Psycho-Analysis* 63:1.

Carotenuto, A. 1982. *A Secret Symmetry: Sabina Spielrein between Jung and Freud.* New York: Pantheon.

Edinger, E. F. 1960. The Ego-Self Paradox. *Journal of Analytical Psychology* 5:1.

Fordham, M. 1974. Notes on the Transference. In *Technique in Jungian Analysis.* Library of Analytical Psychology.

———. 1978. *Jungian Psychotherapy.* Chichester: Wiley.

Freud, S. 1914. Remembering, Repeating and Working Through. *The Standard Edition of the Complete Psychological Works,* 12.

Greenacre, P. 1978. Problems of Acting Out in the Transference Relationship. In E. N. Rexford, ed. *A Developmental Approach to Problems of Acting Out.* Rev. ed. New York: International Universities Press.

Harrison, J. E. 1931. *Ancient Art and Ritual.* London: Oxford University Press.

Hubback, J. 1969. The Symbolic Attitude in Psychotherapy. *Journal of Analytical Psychology* 14:1 (Chapter 1 of this book).

———. 1972. Envy and the Shadow. *Journal of Analytical Psychology* 17:2.

Jung, C. G. 1936. The Concept of the Collective Unconscious. In *Collected Works*, 9/i.

———. 1946. Psychic Conflicts in a Child. In *Collected Works*, 17.

———. 1963. *Memories, Dreams, Reflections.* London: Collins and Routledge & Kegan Paul.

Laplanche, J., and Pontalis, J-B. 1973. *The Language of Psychoanalysis.* London: Hogarth.

Stein, L. 1955. Loathsome Women. *Journal of Analytical Psychology* 1:1.

Chapter 6

Uses and Abuses of Analogy

When I wrote this paper I stated that the theme of it had been in my mind for many years, in a diffuse form. Then a paper by Mary Gammon entitled, "Window into Eternity: Archetype and Relativity," was published (1973). It enabled me to develop the aspect of the theme which was of most interest to me. The introduction and the summary of her paper are reproduced here as they give the reader some of the necessary background.

Introduction: In *Monadology* Leibnitz perceived that "the connection or adaptation of all created things with each, and of each with all the rest, means that each simple substance has relations which express all the others, and consequently it is a perpetual living mirror of the universe."

Just as Einstein's special and general theories of relativity are a formulation based on the effects of the physical world, so Jung's concept of archetypes is a description based on the effects of the psyche. Jung observed: "Psyche cannot be totally different from matter, for how otherwise could it move matter? And matter cannot be alien to psyche, for how else could matter produce psyche? Psyche and matter exist in . . . the same world and each partakes of the other, otherwise any reciprocal action would be impossible" (*Aion*, p. 261).

Is there an analogous archetypal structure which connects psyche and physics and adapts them to each other? This paper suggests that there is such a structure common to both.

Summary: The event, conscious and unconscious, is defined as the quantum of the psyche's existence. It is examined in both its sub-

Originally published in *The Journal of Analytical Psychology* 18 (1973), pp. 91–104.

jective and objective aspects in Einstein's theory of relativity, Heisenberg's "principle of uncertainty," Jung's experiments in the process of association and in examples from classical mythology. Thereafter, meaning is defined in relation to the event's intrinsic qualities and extrinsic significance.

Einstein's description of the structure of space is then used to cast new light on the archetypal structure of the psyche, in particular Jung's "multiple consciousness." The physicist's concept of a hole connection in the structure of space is shown by examples of individual and collective symbols to be itself an archetype. The event, especially the category of synchronistic events, is also considered in relation to the hole in space. These subjects are then discussed in terms of potential meaning for the psychology of the individual.

The position of consciousness in Jung and Pauli's *quaternio* is examined in relation to the archetype. An analysis of chance and causality through their connection with the archetype follows and, in conclusion, an addition to Jung and Pauli's *quaternio*, or "whole judgment," is suggested. This addition incorporates an archetypal "window into eternity" within the psyche analogous to the hole in space developed by Einstein's theory of relativity.

Since the time when her paper and mine appeared, other writers have published books which analytical psychologists have found to be deeply interesting as throwing analogical light on some centrally important Jungian theories. Prominent among them are the following: the physicist Fritjof Capra's *The Tao of Physics* (1975), which led directly to Jean Shinoda Bolen's *The Tao of Psychology* (1979); the plant physiologist Rupert Sheldrake's hypothesis of morphic resonance and formative causation offered in his book *A New Science of Life* (1981); the physicist David Bohm's development of what he calls "a new model of reality," expounded in *Wholeness and the Implicate Order* (1980): and the chemists Ilya Prigogine and Isabelle Stengers' *Order out of Chaos* (1984) in which they step outward from theories of physics or chemistry into the philosophy of science and the study of change. Louis Zinkin is also interested in the analogies between systems theory and the deintegration of the self in infancy, and the way in which research in a variety of specialties can be of use to analysts' studies of change in individuals, and the large theme of "change in itself" (1986).

Each of those works throws further light on the aspect of Mary Gammon's paper that originally interested me, the way in which she used the theories of physics to "cast new light on the archetypal structure of the psyche." When I was reading her paper, there were times when I feared that if archetypes, structures and the psyche were as difficult as I find modern physics I had better follow Voltaire's advice in *Candide*; that is, retire and cultivate my garden. Then I remembered that my interpretation of his remark is, "You must *cultivate* your garden." And that led me to see that it would be a misuse of Mary Gammon's use of analogies to take the two sides of them as parallel in every way.

An analogy is a likeness in certain respects between two things which are otherwise different. So the object of using Einstein's and Heisenberg's theories on the structure of space as an analogy for the archetypal structure of the psyche is, I suppose, to enable us to understand how our psyches are constructed better than we would by studying this structure (or the model for it) directly. Because modern physics is difficult unless it has been studied properly, it does not follow that the attribute of difficulty need be carried over into psychology. In other words, any user of an analogy has to be careful that the element abstracted from one science for use in another casts light rather than causing further darkness. This thought disposed of my fear that the likely misuse of analogy rendered the whole device useless, or turned it into intellectual gymnastics or exhibitionistic juggling.

An analogy is a device. Or it can be called a tool. It is a way or a method towards understanding something, in this case the unconscious psyche, which cannot be studied directly. Because of that difficulty we must search for an effective indirect way. But its indirectness must be constantly remembered, or we will be in danger of believing we are doing more than we really are. The indirect way of studying the psyche that is taken most often is that of analogies. The use of analogy has penetrated into almost every branch of mental activity. I believe it to be the basis or substructure from which image-making develops, and to be a most powerful help in the constant effort to make sense of life. It is the central element in the kind of work we do when we try to repair the split in our psyches or in those of others. And the centuries-long controversy between dualistic thinkers on the one hand and the upholders of the one world thesis on the other is permeated with the biological analogy of one body, one truth, one God.

Images are a particular form of analogy. In a recent publication Rosemary Gordon defined an image as "a perception in the absence of an external stimulus, irrespective of the sensory mode in which this perception occurs" (1972, p.63). The actual external stimulus presumably happened in earlier experience—I think that the image occurs as a mental linking of the experience of that earlier stimulus with a later and different experience and that the nature of the linking process is analogic. To move from that perhaps rather abstruse proposition to our daily work as analysts, the thesis of this paper is that, when we are listening to a patient, our previous experience of ourselves, our experiences with more or less similar patients (analogous ones), combined with our knowledge of various models and theories, all act together as a conglomerate substantive image and that is how our way of being with that patient comes about. Emulating Bion, we may hope to live up to the ideal of beginning each hour of analysis with really cleared minds (1970); this is a counsel of perfection, for as we listen to patients, analogies (but not necessarily personal ones) are inevitably activated in us, and it is important to become conscious of them so that they do not dangerously intrude, but so that their possible validity for the particular patient on that particular day can be properly tested. The analogy may be to previous material the patient had brought, but had now split off. I currently think that making ourselves available as analysts to patients involves the fact that we analogize and the way we do it, as well as our attempts to allow them full freedom.

The other part of the paper to which I wish to refer in this introduction is that analogic thinking is characteristic of the unconscious intellectual approach. In *Symbols of Transformation*, Jung described the differences between "directed thinking or, as we might also call it, *thinking in words*" (1912, p.16) and fantasy thinking, much of which "belongs to the conscious sphere, but at least as much goes on in the half-shadow, or entirely in the unconscious, and can therefore be inferred only indirectly" (p.29).

But both the drawing of analogies and the use of intelligence are linking activities. The total process of analysis can plausibly be viewed in terms of healing or integrating split-off complexes and other portions of the psyche, and recurrent individuation experiences are stages in the development or advance towards some goal or end, this goal being the self and the whole man. Included in those tremendous undertakings is the relating of the individual to other people in his life, and beyond those linkings and relatings is the metaphysical adventure, the seductive excitement, of the unitary world, the *unus mundus* of the philosophical alchemists. Jung's remarks about this occur in several of his works, though he wrote about it in greatest detail in *Mysterium Coniunctionis*. The following quotation about it comes from "A Psychological View of Conscience" which was published in 1958:

> The psychoid nature of the archetype contains very much more than can be included in a psychological explanation. It points to the sphere of the *unus mundus*, the unitary world, towards which

the psychologist and the atomic physicist are converging along separate paths, producing independently of one another certain analogous auxiliary concepts (1955, p.452).

Alluring Analogies

Having, as I hope, established that the use of analogies is not only widespread but in fact intrinsic and essential to our mental operations, I
would like to go on to discuss the usefulness of them. There is a very
powerful feeling-value when the discovery is made that a truth established convincingly in one branch of human knowledge can be applied
in another branch and turns out to be valid there, too. This seems to me
to be nothing to do with thinking, it is a matter of pleasure. The fact
that it gives intellectual satisfaction is distinct from, and additional to,
the feeling-tone. It is a bonus. In getting pleasure from such analogies we
are responding to a deeper layer of ourselves than the intelligent one, the
layer where we want to find similarities and where we are afraid of differences. I shall return to this point later.

In Jung and Pauli's book, *The Interpretation of Nature and the Psyche*,
the effect of the joint publication of their two papers was to show how
Jung the psychologist could apply the principles of scientific investigation to the large or macrophysical and statistical truth of causality, in relation to conflicting small or microphysical events, and develop the
theory of synchronicity, and Pauli the physicist could investigate the archetypal basis of the formation of scientific concepts (1955). Pauli made
the valuable connection (p. 155) that Kepler worked in an age (the sixteenth century) when "the view of the universe was not yet split into a
religious one and a scientific one," that his discoveries of the laws of
planetary motion (on ellipses, on radii and on times of revolution) were
not what he was originally seeking, and that the mental background was
that "he was fascinated by the old Pythagorean idea of the music of the
spheres . . . and was trying to find in the movement of the planets the
same proportions that appear in the harmonious sound of tones and in
the regular polyhedra." "Geometry," wrote Kepler, "is the archetype of
the beauty of the world" (p. 156).

In the late seventeenth century and the early eighteenth century,
Newton's synthesis of mathematical rationalism, fashionable on the con-
tinent of Europe, with a perhaps more English experimental approach,
opened the way for modern physics which was at that time still called
"natural philosophy." But Newton who is usually thought of as so essentially a thinking scientist, a mathematician, and a physicist, also used his

powerful intellect in a series of papers and letters arguing for the existence of God, using arguments from all levels, from this lofty one: "This
most beautiful system of the sun, planets and comets could only proceed
from the counsel and dominion of an intelligent and powerful Being"
(1953, p.42) to this lowly one: "Can it be by accident that all birds,
beasts, and men have their right side and left side alike shaped (except
in their bowels); and just two eyes and no more, on either side of the
face; and just two ears on either side of the head; and a nose with two
holes . . . ?" (p. 65).

Those four men, Kepler, Newton, Jung, and Pauli, all seem to me to
be working from the ground thought and the inner wish for a unitary
world which psychologically works on the basis of the mind's need for
analogy. Speaking of what I believe was their wish carries no criticism. I
am not referring to wishful thinking, with the connotations and the disadvantages that it has in daily life.

The biologist, Medawar, wrote in 1968 on the themes of "What goes
on in the head when scientific discoveries are made?" and "What is the
scientific method?" in a book called *Induction and Intuition in Scientific
Thought* (p.8). He argued strongly against inductive thinking and in favor of intuition. Induction is "arguing from the particular to the general," which I suppose is the popular view of what a scientist does and of
how theories are constructed. But Medawar champions intuition; he is
interested in what he calls "the generative act in scientific inquiry" (p.
55), and thinks that "scientists are usually too proud or too shy to speak
about creativity and 'creative imagination'" (p.55).

In describing various aspects of intuition as it occurs in scientific work,
he details this one: "the instant apprehension of analogy, i.e., a real or
apparent structural similarity between two or more schemes and ideas,
regardless of what the ideas are about" (p. 57). He also wrote: "the scientific method . . . like other exploratory processes . . . can be resolved
into a dialogue between fact and fancy, the actual and the possible; between what could be true and what is in fact the case" (p. 59).

The contribution of a biologist to the nature of intuition is valuable as
he has drawn attention to the fact that some intuitions are generative or
creative acts; they bring together two previously unassociated things or
ideas which in the unconscious have been perceived as analogous— similar in some respects. Kekulé's famous vision of the benzine ring has been
paralleled recently by an engineer of Pakistani origin, who, while working on the chemistry of plastics, developed an important invention as a
result of working on a problem long, doggedly, and miserably: then one
evening, when he was very tired, he happened to remember Charles

Lamb's story of the mythical Chinese discovery of roast pork, and during the night he had a dream which linked the problem and the roast. He awoke from the dream able to add the third necessary contribution, which solved his problem (I cannot trace my source for this story).

Specialists in their own field, who yet have minds of an all-around kind, use the work of parallel disciplines to convince themselves that they are on to something valuable in their own field. It helps them to heal the split between their pride and their shyness (to take up one of Medawar's remarks), or, one could say, between their confidence and their diffidence. They need this reassurance.

Before moving on to the application to clinical analytic work of the theme so far developed, I would like to introduce two other disciplines in which, in our own time, there is a wish to benefit by analogies with other spheres of work: namely, social anthropology and linguistics.

Without making claim to more than an interest in anthropology, I think that the tone of some contemporary anthropologists' writing and the background of their ways of thought are analogous to ours. Professor Levi-Strauss is not *persona grata* to those anthropologists here and in America who study tribes and societies empirically and in depth, in the field, and who concentrate on how those groups function. He has done relatively little fieldwork. But he does try to link observed facts in such a way as to forward, on his terms, the study of psychological structures. In his inaugural lecture as the first holder of the chair of social anthropology at the Collège de France, in 1960, he said: "Social facts do not restrict themselves to scattered fragments. They are lived by men, and subjective consciousness is as much a form of their reality as their objective characteristics" (1967). And again: the "empirical and subjective synthesis offers the only possible guarantee that the preliminary analysis, carried as far as the unconscious categories, has allowed nothing to escape" (p. 14). Writing of the work of anthropologists, he might almost be writing of analysts: "By comparison with the natural sciences, we benefit from an advantage and suffer an inconvenience; we find our experiments already prepared but they are uncontrollable. It is therefore understandable that we attempt to replace them with models . . . the boldness of such an approach is, however, compensated for by the humility—one might almost say the servility—of observation" (pp. 25–26). He also wrote of "this alternation between two methods (each involving its rhythm)—the deductive and the empirical—and the strictness with which we practise each in its extreme and most refined form" and of how anthropology makes "the most intimate subjectivity into a means of objective demonstration" (p. 26).

My last excursion into a discipline which has clear analogies with psychology is into linguistics, the science of language. Modern linguists have developed their science in clear-cut opposition to traditional grammar, which originated in Greece in the fifth century B.C., and which was current until very recently. They do not, as I think old grammarians did, believe that there is a fundamental difference between "civilized" and "primitive" languages. They analyze the structure of language where the old grammar was merely descriptive. Just as psychology has moved beyond the descriptive stage, so linguistics now claims to be structural and generative. Linguistic scientists lay stress on the open-endedness of language—some of them call that its creativity—by which they mean "the capacity that all native speakers of a language have to produce and understand an indefinitely large number of sentences that they have never heard before and which may indeed never have been uttered before by anyone" (Lyons 1970).

The principal exponent of modern linguistics, who is now known outside his own field, is Noam Chomsky. This appears to be not only because of his intellectual and creative eminence as a linguist, but also because he is extending his range and interest into critiques of behaviorism and into practical political philosophy. He has opponents, both where details and where general lines of thought are concerned. He is not the only important contemporary linguist, but the way he thinks and works has much in common with the way we do. It is interesting to discover what is happening in linguistics, seeing that so much analytic work takes place through the medium of words, and that Chomsky is investigating the relationship between language and mental processes. His view is that the most interesting thing about a language is not what can be observed, but what the native speaker knows intuitively about the structure of his language.

His concern is for the underlying, the nonobservable, the abstract structure of the sentence. And beyond his concern for structure is a more important one for meaning. One of his exponents in England, James Thorne, has written: "My own experience has been that one feels on the right track with something when one begins to find that one's explanation of one particular phenomenon will also help to explain what had previously appeared to be a disparate phenomenon" (1971).

In *Aspects of the Theory of Syntax*, Chomsky was studying "deep structure relations" and declaring that the understanding of them was essential for correct interpretation of language. He claims that the principles underlying the structure of language are biologically determined, part of "human nature" and genetically transmitted from parents to their children (1965).

In *Language and Mind* he asserts the importance of his kind of linguis-

tics (generative grammar) for the investigation of the structure and predispositions of the human mind (1968). His views have a strong link
with the theory of archetypes. His idea that children are predisposed to
be able to learn language and to speak creatively—that is, to understand
and to produce sentences which have never been made before—seems
to me to be analogous to how archetypes are thought to operate. He
holds that the principles of language and grammar are genetically transmitted, as are complex instinctual patterns, but not on a behavioristic
stimulus-and-response model. His way of viewing the child's creative
predisposition to learn to speak the language he hears spoken is fundamentally similar to that of analytical psychology about archetypal
predispositions.

The "common structural denominator" (Plaut 1972) between Chomsky's linguistics and our theory and practice is that the probably archetypal predisposition and ability to understand and speak a language still
has to be activated and worked up in personal relationship between the
child and others; language is not just handed down, mechanically or
impersonally; analysis does not simply happen, and it also is between
people.

I titled this section of the paper "alluring analogies." I find it alluring
and encouraging that human sciences other than psychology are working
on parallel and analogous lines of thought. But I think I should acknowledge that this feeling of encouragement almost certainly stems from some
deep-seated anxiety; it seems to me unlikely that it is a merely personal
anxiety, which no one else shares; I believe it is closely associated with
the wish for the unitary world and I suspect that the centuries-old idea of
unus mundus is an intellectualization of the regressive wish for a symbiotic reunion with the archetypal great mother.

The Unitary World (*Unus Mundus*)

Mary Gammon's investigation of the analogies between Jung's theory of
archetypes and developments of Einstein's theory of relativity incorporates many substantive references to the idea of the unitary world and
she draws on models and images of this from widely scattered sources, including a reference to the alchemist Dorn who was the originator of the
image "window into eternity," which is the first part of her title. I am
not certain whether thinking about ideas, such as that of the unitary
world, does not take us into the pitfall-riddled world of metaphysics: it is
rather like Molière's M. Jourdain who discovered he had been talking
prose all his life, and was unduly impressed; or again, it is that "fools

rush in where angels fear to tread." My justification for taking a look at the unitary world idea is to throw light on the psychology of it and to connect it with the theory of transference and with an inherent and general tendency towards analogizing. The idea of the unitary world acts in the mind as an analogy towards which thinkers try to get whatever they are thinking about to approximate. It is not that they are necessarily "arguing by analogy" or idealizing about the unitary world as an analogy from which they would deduce other ideas which do not truly concur; it is rather that if they do not use the idea (of the unitary world) as an ultimate test those who reflect on life miss the deep emotional satisfaction that they get if they do appeal to it. There is a really very widespread wish and hope to find unity in spite of the blatant diversities of the material world. To take up what I said earlier, we are frightened by differences, we seek similarities. We are afraid of going to pieces, in rage; we long to come together, to integrate. We want to repair dangerous splits. The idea of the unitary world is a projection. We can only get the true measure of it by studying it in that light. Its intimate connection with Jung's formulation of the nature of the self is simple and evident.

Transference is a form of analogy, memory, and imagery. Two people who are in actuality distinct and different from each other, that is analyst and one or the other parent at different times during an analysis, have their common characteristics selected by the patient and acted on psychologically. This plays in with some of the undifferentiated contents of the unconscious regions of the patient's psyche, in that it meets there the regressive wish to reestablish an intimate closeness with the mother only, the first experienced parent, for experiences with her were, in physical terms, approximations to a unitary world; but the reality of development is towards duality, their two parents, their oedipal problems, leading to the acceptance of multiplicity, paradox, and the opposite poles of archetypal experience.

Jung was in the Indian province of Orissa in 1938, taking part in the celebration of the twenty-fifty anniversary of the University of Calcutta. In *Memories, Dreams, Reflections*, remembering that time, he wrote: "I grasped the life of the Buddha as the reality of the self which had broken through and laid claim to a personal life. For Buddha, the self stands above all gods, a *unus mundus* which represents the essence of human existence and of the world as a whole. The self embodies both the aspect of intrinsic being and the aspect of its being known, without which no world exists' (1963, p.261). That is a valuable reference to the idea of the unitary world as it informs most intimately one of the eastern religions. Much earlier in his life, Jung had become interested in extending

his reading: in the 1900s he was, according to the editorial preface to
Psychiatric Studies, conducting "researches . . . [which] . . . brought
about the transformation of psychiatry, as the study of the psychoses,
from a static system of classification into a dynamic interpretative science" (1957). In the years leading up to writing *Symbols of Transformation* (first published in 1912 as *Wandlungen und Symbole der Libido*) he
had read a great deal in and around the subjects of gnosticism and of the
unitary world, or monism, versus the alternative philosophical idea of
dualism (Hubback 1966). The anxiety about the break from Freud and
the terrifying experiences in 1916 which led to him writing the *Seven
Sermons to the Dead* and, I think, "The transcendent function," were part
of his long work on monism and dualism. He was thinking about it
again, as I have said, in India in 1938. He brought it in in "Flying Saucers: a Modern Myth of Things Seen in the Skies" which was first published in 1958, where he made use of the analogy of the action of number as being the bridge which spans "the splitting of the world picture,"
since "number . . . belongs to both worlds, the real and the imaginary"
(pp. 409–10). He was also in that essay concerned with linking modern
physics with his theory of synchronicity.

It was in *Mysterium Coniunctionis*—which was written between 1941
(when he was 66) and 1954 (when he was 79)—that he investigated the
relations between the unitary world idea and the use various alchemists
made of it, particularly Gerard Dorn (whose writings were published in
1702). It is, in my experience, impossible to read that book and particularly the final and culminating chapter without getting carried away and
without linking Jung's commentary on Dorn with subjective material and
personal thoughts. The idea of the unitary world comes alive across the
centuries and across very different intellectual premises, as a result of
Jung's analysis of the psychological validity of the philosophical alchemist's search for inner truth. The languages are different, but translation
is possible.

I am not among those perfectionists who maintain that poetry is
untranslatable, but translators of poetry have to have the feel of the original poem in its own language, and the feel of the language into which it
is going to be rendered; and I think the analogy holds, that the form the
alchemists used in their search for psychic totality need not deter us from
translating their experiences into a form which we find suits us, namely
the psychological.

In the foreword to *Mysterium Coniunctionis*, Jung wrote:

However abstruse and strange the language and imagery of the alchemists may seem to the uninitiated, they become vivid and alive

as soon as comparative research reveals the relationship of the symbols to processes in the unconscious. . . . The heterogeneous material adduced for comparison may seem in the highest degree baffling to . . . [someone] who does not know their psychological affinities with analogous formations (1955, p. xvii).

Towards the end of the book, in the last section, Jung wrote extensively about the unitary world idea and it is not easy to select in such a way as to give a really comprehensive account. In what follows I am merely choosing a few passages which connect with my themes of the use of analogies and the examination of how they are the substrate of our clinical work, work on the ego's splitting defense against anxiety, work on the earliest discernible splits, and work towards individuation.

Jung specifically links his thinking about *unus mundus* with patients' shadow problems. For example, "Confrontation with the shadow produces at first a dead balance, a standstill that hampers moral decisions. . . . Everything becomes doubtful, which is why the alchemists called this stage *nigredo, tenebrositas*, chaos, melancholia" (p. 497). He also stated, "If the patient's recognition of the shadow is as complete as he can make it, then conflict and disorientation ensue . . . here the logic of the intellect usually fails, for in a logical antithesis there is no third. The 'solvent' can only be of an irrational nature" (p.495). The idea of the *unus mundus* is a rational one: Jung (pp. 464–5) suggests "that there *an interconnection or unity* (my italics) of causally unrelated events, and . . . a unitary aspect of being which can very well be described as the *unus mundus*" (pp. 464–5). In other words, he is saying that when we make, or experience, an interconnection (a link) it is tantamount to getting in touch with or uniting with, the unitary world. This happens first in the unconscious and nonlogical areas of our minds, but we can become conscious of it.

As well as writing about "coming to terms with the other" in ourselves, about active imagination for which, to start you off, "you can . . . use a bad mood" (p.495) (in everyday unglamorous analysis, that is working with the negative transference), Jung goes on to demonstrate that "it is . . . a question . . . of a view which can be translated from medieval language into modern concepts. Undoubtedly the idea of *unus mundus* is founded on the assumption that the multiplicity of the empirical world rests on an underlying unity" (p. 537). That assumption can be scrutinized and subjected to analysis through the activation of associations. In the attempt to construct a bridge across the wide gap that exists between such an abstract statement and the body-basis from which it may have been derived, different individuals respond each in his own way, each with his own imagery, and unsubstantiated speculation would be out of place. The observation of infants can tempt towards hypotheses for which the evidence is effectively introjective on the part of the adult observer, so that all that can be surmised is that "the assumption" of "an underlying unity" has an experiential basis, though the question of precisely what it is has to be left unanswered.

In another passage a little earlier, Jung had written:

> While the concept of *unus mundus* is a metaphysical speculation, the unconscious can be indirectly experienced via its manifestations . . . The contents of the unconscious, unlike conscious contents, are mutually contaminated to such a degree that they cannot be distinguished from one another, and can therefore easily take one another's place, as can be seen most clearly in dreams (pp. 462–3).

That can also be seen in the transference, at stages when the patient cannot distinguish emotionally between analyst and parent. With ego growth the capacity to distinguish grows.

To return to Jung, he went on to say:

> The indistinguishableness of [the contents of the unconscious] gives one the impression that everything is connected with everything else and that . . . they are at bottom a unity. . . . The mandala symbolizes, by its central point, the ultimate unity of all archetypes as well as the multiplicity of the phenomenal world, and is therefore the empirical equivalent of the metaphysical concept of *unus mundus* (p. 463).

The center point of the mandala can be thought of as an abstracted representation of the infant's early perceptions of the parts of the mother on which he discovered how to focus, namely the nipple and the eye, and as carrying from that body-origin the potentiality of the symbol of the self to which Jung refers, in that last passage. His studies of *unus mundus* and of the self can be linked to Fordham's work on mandala symbolism in childhood (1957), the self in childhood (1969) and the primary self (1971).

My last quotations (from *Mysterium Coniunctionis*) are the following: "the alchemical *mysterium coniunctionis* . . . is the western equivalent of the fundamental principle of classical Chinese philosophy, namely the union of *yang* and *yin* in *tao*" (pp. 463–4). And: "We should at all events be able to understand that the visualisation of the self is a 'window' into eternity, which gave the medieval man, like the Oriental, an opportunity to escape from the stifling grip of a one-sided view of the world, or to hold out against it" (p. 535).

There is a close analogy between working through in analysis and the way the alchemical "adept had to experience again and again how unfavorable circumstances or a technical blunder or . . . some devilish accident . . . forced [him] to start all over again from the beginning." A sense of inner security has to be tested out time and again before it is stable enough to withstand the disturbing influences of ordinary life.

The "again and again" motif is demonstrated by the way in which sympathetic magic, which is magic by analogy, and the repeated rites in all more sophisticated religions are performed over and over again. Jung, in the "Structure of the psyche" refers both to the Catholic mass and to various Christianizations of preChristian rites (1927, p. 149). A modern example comes from as recently as 1969: an anthropologist, John C. Messenger, working in the Aran Islands, off Western Ireland, reported that on St. John's Day, in midsummer, boys light a huge bonfire just after sunset, "and a few islanders carry brands from it to their homes and fields for protection and to guarantee the fertility of their wives and female livestock" (1969). Anxiety about procreation, about their livelihood, about cyclical events and, I would surmise, about getting in touch with a power beyond themselves, lies behind such a survival. It is anxiety about going to pieces which informs all efforts to get life from the original fire and the unitary world. It is behind the sophisticated theories of intellectual writers and the hopes of rural islanders.

The Abuse of Analogies

The thesis up to now needs qualifying and elaborating in connection with Jung's views on integration and individuation, and with respect to the difference between *unus mundus* and the self. In our analyses we frequently strive to make conscious the ego's previously unconscious splitting defenses and the contents against which it defends itself. In trying to reactivate the damaged "natural process of maturation inherent in the nature of man" (Fordham, 1969), we are working towards the integration of the personality. But a difficulty arises in connection with different uses of the same word, not only as between analytical psychology and other disciplines discussed in the foregoing pages, but within the corpus of analytical psychology itself. The current use of "splitting" as meaning a defensive maneuver against anxiety is different from the use to which

Jung put the word "split" in 1928 in the following passage from "On psychic energy"

> Thus every child is born with an immense split in his make-up: on
> one side he is more or less like an animal, and on the other side he
> is the final embodiment of an age-old and endlessly complicated
> sum of hereditary factors. The split accounts for the tension of the
> germinal state and does much to explain the many puzzles of child
> psychology, which certainly has no lack of them (pp. 51–2).

Jung uses the word differently in "Psychological factors in human
behavior":

> Let us turn first to the question of the psyche's tendency to split.
> Although this peculiarity is most clearly observable in psychopa-
> thology, fundamentally it is a normal phenomenon, which can be
> recognized with the greatest ease in the projections made by the
> primitive psyche. The tendency to split means that parts of the
> psyche detach themselves from consciousness to such an extent
> that they not only appear foreign but lead an autonomous life of
> their own (1937, p. 121).

An abuse of analogies can occur if one is unclear about the other person's exact frame of reference and his use of terms; it is essential to aim
at seeing where the analogy breaks down, it must not be overworked. It
is also an abuse of analogy to use the wish for the unitary world idea as a
factor with which to work in analysis on early splitting defenses as that
could lead to confusing *unus mundus* with the self; it is another abuse if
we use if unconsciously for facile reassurance. But it is not an abuse if we
use analogies consciously in the region of ego activity. We are free to
look back somewhat nostalgically to the time when men such as Kepler
put into one volume "religious meditations, an almost mathematical
symbol of the Trinity, modern optical theorems, essential discoveries in
the theory of vision and the physiology of the eye" (Jung & Pauli 1955,
p. 155), but that combination is no longer our world. In the language of
mythology, we have been turned out of paradise where humans and God
lived in the same walled garden. The unitary field of knowledge of Kepler's day has now been divided into many areas. That division is not
helpfully described in the word "split," if "split" is used analogically—the
early stages of the infant's psychic development are unconscious; splitting
as an ego defense is also at first unconscious. It needs interpreting to

bring it into consciousness. Dividing, distinguishing, and discriminating are essential ego activities. It is on those grounds that I think we have to be careful not to be totally seduced by the *unus mundus* idea.

There is, in conclusion, a real distinction between, on the one hand, the experimental way of apprehending the world and its contents, and on the other hand the contrasted ways: the immediate, the intuitive and (for some) the religious. It is important to know and to distinguish when we are operating in each or either of those ways, even if it is impossible to move as easily between the two as the particularly gifted people, whom I have discussed, have shown themselves to be.

To bring all this down to daily practice with patients: the application of it is that we are working for development from the earliest stages of psychosomatic unity towards the more complex psychological structures. The early stages and states of unity, of narcissism and the psychotic-type defenses of infancy are represented in adult patients in idealization of sameness, in analogy, in homosexuality, in the unitary world idea, and at those stages there is projective and introjective identification. In the more developed stages and states realistic dualism, multiplicity, and heterosexuality can be accepted. The patient experiences painful oscillations between these and the intermediary states; he or she moves forwards and backwards between simplicity and complexity; between aloneness, fusion, and relatedness; between experiences of the self and of individuation. The analyst uses at times his or her working acquaintance with the nature and functioning of the psyche (an acquaintance which grows only slowly, with experience, into generalizable knowledge) and, at other times, perhaps in quick succession, the very different kind of immediately apprehended confidence which stems from trustworthy intuitions about the particular patient, in the transference and in the countertransference.

Summary

There are four primary themes of this paper.

The use of analogy underlies both image-making and the unconscious stages which precede conscious thinking; it helpfully gratifies the wishes of many workers in different disciplines and it is associated with the desire to reunite with the archetypal good mother.

Sciences other than psychology, where analogous processes are currently evident, are briefly discussed in that connection: specifically in physics, biology (Medawar); anthropology (Levi-Strauss); and linguistics (Chomsky).

The unitary world idea (*unus mundus*) is discussed with reference to the theory of transference and to Jung's use of it in the analogy of alchemy and developmental psychology, in *Mysterium Coniunctionis.*

An attempt is made, in conclusion, to point up the difference between splits and distinctions.

References

Bion, W.R. 1970. *Attention and Interpretation.* London: Tavistock.

Bolen, J.S. 1979. *The Tao of Psychology.* London: Harper & Row.

Bohm, D. 1980. *Wholeness and the Implicate Order.* London: Routledge & Kegan Paul.

Capra, F. 1979. *The Tao of Physics.* London: Fontana.

Chomsky, N. 1965. *Aspects of the Theory of Syntax.* Cambridge, Mass.: M.I.T. Press.

———. 1968. *Language and Mind.* New York: Harcourt Brace.

Fordham, F. 1969. Some Views on Individuation. *Journal of Analytical Psychology,* 14:1.

Fordham, M. 1957. *New Developments in Analytical Psychology.* London: Routledge & Kegan Paul.

———. 1969. *Children as Individuals.* London: Hodder & Stoughton.

———. 1971. Primary Self, Primary Narcissism and Related Concepts. *Journal of Analytical Psychology,* 16:2.

Gammon, M.R. 1973. Window Into Eternity: Archetype and Relativity. *Journal of Analytical Psychology,* 18:1.

Gordon, R. 1972. A Very Private World. In *The Function and Nature of Imagery,* Sheehan, P.W. ed. New York: Academic Press.

Hubback, J. 1966. *VII Sermones ad mortuos. Journal of Analytical Psychology,* 11:2.

Jung, C.G. 1912. Symbols of Transformation. *Collected Works,* 6.

———. 1927. The Structure of the Psyche. In *Collected Works,* 8.

———. 1928. On Psychic Energy. In *Collected Works,* 8.

———. 1937. Psychological Factors Determining Human Behavior. In *Collected Works,* 8.

———. 1957. Editorial preface to *Psychiatric Studies.* In *Collected Works,* 1.

———. 1958. Flying Saucers: a Modern Myth of Things Seen in the Skies. In *Collected Works,* 10.

———. 1958. A Psychological View of Conscience. In *Collected Works,* 10.

————. 1963. *Memories, Dreams, Reflections.* London: Collins and Routledge & Kegan Paul.

————. 1965. *Mysterium Coniunctionis. Collected Works,* 14.

———— & Pauli, W. 1955. *The Interpretation of Nature and the Psyche.* London: Routledge & Kegan Paul.

Levi-Strauss, C. 1967. *The Scope of Anthropology.* London: Cape.

Lyons, J. 1970. *Chomsky.* London: Fontana/Collins.

Medawar, P.B. 1969. *Induction and Intuition in Scientific Thought.* London: Methuen.

Messenger, J.C. 1969. *Inis Beag, Isle of Ireland.* New York: Holt, Rinehart & Winston.

Newton, I. 1953. *Newton's Philosophy of Nature: Selections from his Writings,* Thayer, H.S., Randall J.H. jr. eds. New York & London: Hafner.

Plaut, A. 1972. Myself as an Instrument (unpublished).

Prigogine, I, Stengers, I. 1984. *Order out of Chaos.* London: Heinemann.

Sheldrake, R. 1981. *A New Science of Life.* London & Boulder: Shambala.

Thorne, J. 1971. Nature and Human Nature. In *The Listener,* 29 July 1971.

Zinkin, L. 1986. The Hologram as a Model for Analytical Psychology. *Journal of Analytical Psychology,* 32:1.

VII Sermones ad Mortuos

In Jung's *Memories, Dreams, Reflections* the chapter entitled "Confrontation with the unconscious" contains a detailed description of the experiences leading to the writing of the *Seven Sermons to the Dead*, but there is next to no information about the contents of the text. This work of Jung's forms the appendix to the German edition of *Memories*; here I am quoting from the English translation by H.G. Baynes (1916b). Stephan A. Hoeller has also translated the *VII Sermons* and his text is in *The Gnostic Jung and the Seven Sermons to the Dead* (1982).

I shall examine the text in some detail, first, in relation to the stage in Jung's development at which he wrote it; second, as containing some of the image material from which he drew his views on the ego, the self, and the unconscious; and third, as most likely to be the expression of the personal experience which formed the basis of the paper entitled "The transcendent function," written in the same year, 1916, but not published until 1957.

The Background

While reproducing here as little as possible of the chapter "Confrontation with the unconscious," it will be valuable to point out some of those aspects of it which are particularly interesting in this connection. The first is the way in which Jung reacted to the period of disorientation and inner uncertainty that followed his break with Freud in 1912. Then there is the way of making use of what he allowed and encouraged to occur during the next four years. In his own words he was "dealing with his own neurosis" by allowing free play to dreams and fantasies, and by reflecting on them in the light both of "Freud's view that vestiges of old experiences exist in the unconscious" (1963, p. 167) and of the knowl-

---

Originally published in *The Journal of Analytical Psychology*, 11:2 (1966), pp. 95–112.

edge he already had at this stage of gnostic writings. He did not know where this conscious submission to unconscious impulses would lead him; what he did know was that it was a painfully humiliating experience in some of its aspects, and really frightening to a psychiatrist who had observed what psychosis means to those who do not recover from it.

A surging stream of multitudinous fantasies began to flow in him, and one in particular "kept on returning: there was something dead present, but it was also still alive." Out of this paradoxical and intense personal experience grew, later, the totality theory of the archetype of the self; it was confirmed by clinical material, but of this we have, regrettably, far too little.

In those years (1912–16) Jung was frequently in a very wrought-up state, almost lost in the swirl of tempestuous emotions. By a tremendous feat, on his own, he translated these emotions into images; he found the images which were concealed in the emotions. Postponing for a moment the examination of Jung's experience, I should like to put forward a view of the way in which emotions and images are, in some people, functionally connected. In the grip of an intensely frightening emotion, in the midst of an almost overpowering sense of personal danger, the only certainty of which a person may be sure is the wish to survive. In this situation, which is experienced as crudely extreme, the pressure to live through fear engenders and sets in motion the image-making capacity in the person. There is a life-saving quality, at this point, in the capacity to make one thing out of another, to transform, which is the only kind of creation available to human—limited—beings. The hypothesis may be advanced that the mental sequence occurs along the following lines: "I am frightened, I behave in a frightened way, something must have caused me to behave in this way. Someone outside me embodied fright, or else it was that fright took form in me." *Fright* is an abstraction. In the midst of a purely emotional experience, such abstraction is intolerable, even impossible. So the abstraction has to be made into an image to represent it; it is then actually present in the mind of the frightened person. Then it can be met. Only in this way can there be any positive and effective outcome from the emotional crisis. The form the image takes selects itself, internally, for personal reasons. The image-selecting process, with its individual appropriateness, baffles description.

When Jung wrote down his fantasies—*Seven Sermons to the Dead* was the culminating one—he was able to do this only in "high-flown language" which "corresponds to the style of the archetypes . . . high rhetoric . . . even bombast. It is a style I find embarrassing; it grates on my nerves, as when someone draws his nails down a plaster wall, or scrapes

his knife against a plate" (1963, p.161). The *Seven Sermons* is indeed a
peculiar document. It is not more interesting for that reason than it
would be if it were written in his more usual style; it is, rather, that this
quality must be acknowledged and allowed for, seeing that Jung considered it intrinsic to the production; it is, perhaps, like some poets' man-
nered and unindividual styles of writing, which the reader may happen
to find at first most uncongenial, but which he almost ceases to notice
if he is drawn on enough to want to elucidate the contents and their
meaning. It should also be remembered that as well as Jung's personal
need to resolve his own inner uncertainties there is the fact that he was
responding in advance and alone to what those now practicing deep
therapy learn in the structured experience of the training analysis: "a cogent motive for my making the attempt was the conviction that I could
not expect of my patients something I did not dare to do myself . . . the
so-called helper could not help them unless he knew their fantasy material from his own direct experience" (1963, p. 172). And in another passage he writes: "At almost every step of my experiment I ran into some
psychological material which is the stuff of psychosis . . . This is the
fund of unconscious images which fatally confuse the mental patient"
(1963, p. 181).

  During the time when Jung was beginning to allow these fantasies to
take shape in him, a number of figures formed themselves. One of the
first was the "Elijah figure," who soon developed and changed into someone he named Philemon. Although as the dreams and images succeeded
each other Philemon acquired a character of his own, at the beginning
his significance was vitally linked with Jung's knowledge of the second-
century gnostic deviations from what was then already becoming a dominant form of Roman Christianity. He states that Philemon had "a gnostic coloration."

  The original of Jung's Philemon was probably the one to whom St
Paul wrote a very short Epistle, enjoining him to take back a runaway
slave, who was also a Christian convert. Philemon was a prosperous and
influential member of the Christian community in Asia Minor, living either at Ephesus or at Colossae. The Epistle contains almost no doctrinal
matter, so that it did not have a great interest to the dogma-creating fathers of the early church; but there is in it a rather obscure sentence
which may have had a particular appeal to Jung. This sentence expresses
Paul's hope "that the fellowship of thy faith may become *effectual*, in the
knowledge of every good thing which is in you" (my italics). Effectiveness
will be shown later in this paper to be a vital concept in the *Seven Sermons*, and gnostic knowledge was based on inner experience. It is possi-

ble, but it cannot be said with certainty, that what Jung calls Philemon's "gnostic coloration" can be accounted for in this way, since there seems to have been no identifiable individual member of a gnostic sect with that name. Marcion, the founder of an important sect in many ways closely akin to gnosticism, included the Epistle to Philemon in his collection of canonical works, but that would not make the name Philemon any more "gnostic" than, say, the name Paul.

Jung's Philemon has other reasons for his "gnostic coloration." In his role of the initiator and guide who made possible Jung's psychic exploration, he has affinities with other figures beloved of gnostics: for example, the Greek-Egyptian god Hermes, John the Baptist, Poimandres of the *Corpus Hermeticum*, to name only the best known. Virgil played a comparable part for Dante. Jung's Philemon became the most important of the fantasy figures, from the dynamic point of view, because he was the origin—an image form—of the later conceptualization of the objective psyche. He came to represent, Jung wrote, "a force which was not myself," *the other* within. It was from the presence of Philemon which he experienced in himself that Jung abstracted the idea of "psychic objectivity, the reality of the psyche." So he decided that there were things in his own psyche which he himself did not produce.

Another short digression is necessary at this point to examine what is likely to be the significance of Jung's selecting a gnostic figure in these early stages of the growth of his own particular contribution to the knowledge of various forms of unconscious events. The historical gnostics were mostly syncretist Christians collecting beliefs from many different sources, living mainly in various settlements in Egypt, some both learned and influential such as Valentinus, who had a chance at one time of being chosen Bishop of Rome, or Basilides of Alexandria, who was particularly fascinated by what he took to be the religious significance of the Persian dualist philosophy which was based on the two principles of Light and Darkness, independently created and not derivable from each other. It is Basilidian gnosticism that seems to have left most traces of itself in Jung's *Seven Sermons*. There were also other groups such as the Naassenes ("worshippers of the serpent"); there were most likely extra-Christian gnostics; and there had been pre-Christian ones, such as a group living in Samaria. The sect of the Essenes, whose writings have been found near the Dead Sea, were possibly heterodox Jews, with their own views on the nature of the deity, on the creation of the world, and on the origins of good and evil. The gnostics held, essentially, that Gnosis (Greek *knowledge*, hence salvation) was to be reached through inner experience rather than as a result of imposed authority; illumination

would lead to regeneration and divinization; self-knowledge and renewal
were seen in terms of union between the man who *knew* these things and
God. Immediacy was all-important and central to the experience of true
gnostics.

Gnostics of whatever kind were deviants in religion at the time when
Christianity was establishing itself, in the teeth of much opposition. The
Church in the second and third centuries found it impossible to include
them under the Catholic (but not catholic) umbrella; their views were
too far from the main stream at a time when the strength that unity
gives a struggling body is essential for its survival.

It will be clear at once that to Jung the appeal of the gnostic way of
seeing inner, or psychological, events was bound to be very strong at a
time of his life when he was moving away from unquestioning acceptance of Freud's view of the unconscious and its workings. His reading
in gnosticism and allied fields can be surmised from examining the bibliographies at the end of *Psychiatric studies*—papers all written before
1907—and at the end of *Symbols of Transformation*, but the results of
such an examination must be checked against internal evidence in the
Seven Sermons, because the bibliographies were not composed by Jung
himself, but by the editors of the *Collected Works*. In the first of these
bibliographies there appears, among the otherwise mainly medical and
psychiatric references, the autobiography of Cellini. Cellini was an Ital-
ian Renaissance goldsmith, who took part in magical devil-raising rites
in the Colosseum, who wrote poetry, who had a vision of the sun and of
Christ, in which he also saw "all those who have ever been born and
then suffered death." The experience which culminated in the writing of
the *Seven Sermons*, when the dead crowded into Jung's house, could perhaps be a personal echo of Cellini's vision. The most likely original
sources for Jung's knowledge of gnosticism are the *Acts of Thomas* (otherwise known as the Hymn, or the Song, of the Pearl), the *Museum Hermeticum*, the Mystical Hymns of Orpheus, the *Pistis Sophia*, the "Septem
Tractatus seu capitula Hermetis Trismegisti," and the works of several of
the early church fathers who described gnostic thought in order to expose the thinkers' errors.

To return now to the conversation with the gnostic-like Philemon and
with an assertive, insinuating, plausible feminine figure (whom he left
nameless at this stage): it may be remembered that Jung felt that in this
situation his ego was painfully devalued. He conceptualized the female
figure as the soul within him, an abstraction transformed into an image-
person, who kept him in touch with the unconscious part of himself. But

in 1916 he experienced in fantasy this soul having flown away from him and having gone to the "land of the dead, the land of the ancestors"—the area beyond the personal past—and he was convinced that there she activated and animated those extrapersonal or collective "dead," who were past but not finished.

Then a parapsychological phenomenon occurred, on a bright summer day, towards the end of the afternoon. All the members of the household are reported by Jung to have taken part to some extent in the hallucination—they heard the ring at the front door bell which he was convinced was the action of the returning dead, who then crowded into the house. For the next three evenings he wrote down the conversations which took place between himself and the dead. After their initial statement that they had not found what they sought in Jerusalem, the dead mainly restricted themselves to questions, and he himself functions as the mouthpiece of an internal figure whom he called Basilides in Alexandria. The result is a document of about five or six thousand words in which it is possible to find, in imaginative form, a great deal about the ego, the self, and the unconscious.

The Text

First a note about the title. The word "sermon," as well as the meaning it normally carries, denotes "any serious address, any serious counsel, admonition, or reproof" (Chambers's *English Dictionary*). One of the sources of Jung's knowledge of gnosticism was the work of the early third-century schismatic bishop of Rome, Hippolytus, whose *Philosophumena, or Elenchos* (at one time thought to have been written by Origen) is now considered to be a collection of lectures, or sermons, exposing the facts about a large number of heresies and refuting their falsities. Jung preferred to call this work by the alternate title *Elenchos*, under which title it appears in the bibliography. This is possible because this technical term used by Plato, and more especially by Aristotle, meant an argument of disproof or refutation, and this aspect of Hippolytus' work perhaps appealed most particularly to Jung precisely because he was using the book as a source of information, and he delighted in paradoxes. The root of the word "sermon" is the Latin *serere*, to join or bind together, to compose. So it is clear that the intrinsic aspects of the work—the conscious area, their joining, and the results—are implicit in the title, in addition to the fact that seven has its "gnostic coloration."

Among the intricacies of gnostic thought and texts the importance of the number seven is prominent. It need not be taken as particularly mys-

tic, mystifying, or magic. Its significance lies in the fact that the real object of the gnostics' efforts was to tease out of the available evidence
some further understanding of the origins of good and evil. In an attempt
to fathom this problem of the presence and the workings of evil in a
world supposedly created by a good God, the idea was evolved that from
this supreme God there emanated a rather lesser world, from that world
a second, and so on, until divinity and goodness were so far attenuated
that evil came into being. The school of the Egyptian Basilides apparently worked on this theory more than any other gnostic group or sect,
and a link was made between the emanations theory of the origin of evil
and the belief that the lowest or last set of emanations comprised seven
powers which created the material world, that these were in some occult
way really the five Babylonian planet-gods together with the sun and the
moon. Basilides seems also to have confused the issue by trying neatly
to attach seven mental qualities to those seven astrological quasi gods:
mind, reason, thought, wisdom, might, righteousness, and peace. These
elaborations are an example of the very different approach to the problem of evil that he had, as compared with various approaches then current. From this confused collection of notions stemmed, later, various
medieval heresies which were passionately followed by both intellectuals
and nonintellectuals who were, in their own different settings, struggling
also with the problem of the origin of evil. And it is still a live issue, although in the second half of the twentieth century it is more usual to see
it in straightforward psychological and developmental terms.

In the *Seven Sermons* there are three main concepts which Jung en-
dows with attributes and characteristics, and with ways of functioning.
They become psychic entities. They are: the *pleroma*, the name he gives
to the thing that is nearest to what he later called the self; *creatura*,
which can be taken to be the ego; and *Abraxas*, the unconscious.

The pleroma is introduced as early as the second paragraph of the first
sermon: "I begin with nothingness. Nothingness is the same as fullness.
In infinity full is no better than empty . . . A thing that is infinite and
eternal hath no qualities, since it hath all qualities. This nothingness or
fullness we name the PLEROMA . . . In the pleroma there is nothing
and everything. It is quite fruitless to think about the pleroma, for this
would mean self-dissolution" (1916b, p. 7). The statement of the fruit-
lessness of *thinking* about the self is particularly interesting.

Jung's own use of the gnostic word pleroma will emerge later in this
paper, and the way it became a useful tool in his hands will be best demonstrated if the description of it written by Irenaeus in his refutation of
Valentinianism (perhaps about 160 A.D.) is read in advance:

There is a perfect pre-existence Aeon, dwelling in the invisible and unnameable elevations; this is the Pre-Beginning and Forefather and Depth. He is uncontainable and invisible, eternal and ungenerated, in quiet and in deep solitude for infinite aeons. With him is Thought, which is also called Grace and Silence. Once upon a time, Depth thought of emitting from himself a Beginning of all, like a seed, and he deposited this projected emission, as in a womb, in that Silence who is with him. Silence received this seed and became pregnant and bore Mind, which resembled and was equal to him who emitted him. Mind alone comprehends the magnitude of his Father; he is called Only-Begotten and Father and Beginning of all. Along with him, Truth was emitted; this makes the first Form, the root of all: Depth and Silence, then Mind and Truth.

When Only-Begotten perceived why he had been emitted, he too emitted Logos and Life, since he was the Father of all who were to come after him and was the beginning and form of the whole Pleroma (Irenaeus, quoted in Grant, 1971, p. 163).

The second concept that is treated as a psychic entity is creatura, which (this is the first reference to it in the text) "is not in the pleroma, but in itself . . . we are distinguished from the pleroma in our essence as creatura, which is confined within time and space" (Jung, 1916b, p. 8). Creatura is the imaginative prototype of the Jungian ego. In all gnostic thought and teaching occurs the basic idea that the phenomenal world in any form—that which has been created—is inferior to the earlier and spiritual pleroma. Dualism in both time and space pervades gnosticism: earlier and higher are good, later and lower are bad. Similar feelings, or value judgments, are very common in all ages and places.

The third concept with which the *Seven Sermons* is concerned, Abraxas, is introduced near the end of the second sermon: "This is a god whom ye knew not, for mankind forgot. We name it by its name Abraxas . . . it is improbable probability, unreal reality" (p. 17). Such is evidently one way of describing the unconscious, which Jung on many later occasions referred to as having been acknowledged to exist by those living in early historical times (and among primitive peoples today), but dangerously ignored throughout more recent centuries.

Historically, Abraxas occurs frequently in Basilidian gnosticism. The sources of information about it are the writings of those who set out to refute heresies, Irenaeus, and Hippolytus. They describe it variously as "the unbegotten Father," "the power above all," "the cause and first archetype of all things."

The Basilidians believed that there were 365 parts to the human body, as well as 365 days in the year, that the sum of the numbers denoted by the Greek letters in Abraxas is 365, that "the unbegotten Father" generated a series of powers, who in turn originated a second series, who created a second heaven, and so on until 365 heavens were in existence; and the angels of the last visible heaven were the authors of our world. There is also thought to be an ancient Semitic origin for the word Abraxas—and therefore, possibly, another root of Jung's conceptualization of the unconscious in 1916—which would connect it with "the breaking forth of light" and with a solar god (Smith and Wace, 1877).

Each of the sermons begins with the returned dead either requesting unspecific help: they "besought my word" (p. 7), "Speak to us further . . ." (p. 19), or asking a particular question: "Where is God? Is God dead?" (p. 15), "Teach us, fool, of the church" (p. 27), "There is yet one matter we forgot to mention. Teach us about man" (p. 33). The anima figure had certainly activated them effectively. The dead were not passive and easily satisfied questioners: in some ways, indeed, they were very much alive. For instance, they "now raised a great tumult, for they were Christians" (p. 18); or again (and this is an experience we have all shared), "Now the dead howled and raged, for they were unperfected" (p. 22); or, "with disdainful glance the dead spake: cease this talk of gods, and daemons and souls. At bottom this hath long been known to us" (p. 32) (but they had apparently not been able to make full use of their knowledge, or they wanted more help in learning to digest it).

At the very end of the three days they were, apparently, convinced and satisfied: "Whereupon the dead were silent and ascended like the smoke above the herdsman's fire, who through the night kept watch over his flock" (p. 34). The genuine poetic note in the last sentence can frequently be heard in the *Sermons* in contrast to a certain amount of rather painful archaism. The poetry is reminiscent of the Naassene Hymns quoted by Hippolytus and of the "Hymn of the Pearl," contained in the *Acts of Thomas*, to which Jung may have had access in a Greek version of *Acta Apostolorum Apocrypha* published at Leipzig in 1903. Many of the poetic passages in the *Seven Sermons* are concise, lyrical, vigorous, and effective.

Effectiveness, in fact, is the quality which, nor surprisingly perhaps, emerges clearly from the many paradoxes, contradictions, and confusions. There is the actual effectiveness which the writing of the *Seven Sermons* had for Jung himself—the development of his thought and work consequent on an experience of symbolic character which he was able to understand—and the inherent concern with effectiveness in that the sermons are a representation of unconscious forces *at work*. Even taking the matter at the most superficial verbal level, the word itself appears very frequently throughout. In the list of pairs of opposite qualities which he says are in the pleroma (the self) and "which are not, because each balanceth each," the effective and the ineffective are the first set he gives. Though in the self the pairs of opposite qualities cancel out, in the ego they are "distinct and separate . . . not balanced and void, but are effective." The idea of pairs is common among gnostics but particularly in Basilides for whom the idea of transcendence involved the denial of existence so that God was the nonexistent God (M.F. Wiles, personal communication).

The list of opposites in the *Seven Sermons* is: "The Effective and the Ineffective. Fullness and Emptiness. Living and Dead. Difference and Sameness. Light and Darkness. The Hot and the Cold. Force and Matter. Time and Space. Good and Evil. Beauty and Ugliness. The One and the Many, etc." (p. 11). And this list is preceded and followed by passages in which Jung is grappling with the problem of the genesis of the ego: "Our very nature is distinctiveness . . . indistinctiveness is the quality of the pleroma . . . The natural striving of the creatura . . . fighteth against primeval, perilous sameness." (pp. 10–11). Half a century later it may be more fruitful, in trying to understand patients, to reword this in terms of infantile psychic development. The healthy infant's growth depends on his being able to distinguish himself from the mother, the first carrier of the archetypal image of the self.

God and the devil (in the second sermon) both contain opposite qualities also; they have been "distinguished out of the pleroma" by the action of creatura. "Common to both . . . joining them . . . above them" is effectiveness, which thereby becomes a sort of super god. Jung names it Abraxas. No wonder the dead howled and raged: "Abraxas is effect" (pp. 16–17). It was the unconscious. The dead did not relish being lost in it, unreclaimed. They insisted on coming back. The personal repressed past and the general, collective, unconscious elements pestered Jung most effectively to be brought into relation with creatura, the ego.

In the last sermon, which has an inspired but obscure quality to it, the nature of Abraxas emerges again, but less clearly than in earlier passages. Speaking to the dead, who at this final stage ask him to teach them about man, Jung writes of the small and transitory man who is needed by the unintegrated unconscious elements as a kind of gateway, a man who looks to a single star as to a god—his world, his pleroma, his divinity. In this world is man Abraxas, the creator and destroyer of his own world (p. 33). There is perhaps discernible here a reference to omnipotence, though no warning is given of its dangerous workings. Also, perhaps, there is a hint of what can be seen as unconscious persecutory fantasies which wreck more in anyone's life than external enemies do.

Alternatively, the seventh sermon can be read as an intriguing if obscure statement of the self-evident truth that only with a body, housing an ego, and in our lifetime, can expressible contact be made with both the personal and the collective unconscious. Smallness and transitoriness can be taken as attributes of man and considered in a religious or in a philosophical sense. Other associations may lead readers to what they know of the Homunculus idea, to the young men (the Kouroi) of the Dionysian spring rites, to Tom Thumb, to the phallic Green Man, and back, spiralwise, to needing to devote the maximum available libido to the exploration of the unconscious and its workings. But these are occupations for living people, with functioning egos, not for disembodied souls.

With effectiveness, the other quality which is given a great deal of attention is distinctiveness, particularly in the first sermon, where creatura's power of discriminating is fully elaborated, and in the second, which follows up the ideas closely. The focus is on the points of distinction between pleroma and creatura, self and ego. The nature of each is sketched in lightly at first, then contrasts and paradoxes are piled up gradually. Jung's constant concern with opposite qualities pervades the whole work and colors the picture he paints of the two concepts. He was at this stage giving more attention to the differences between ego and unconscious, and their complementary qualities in relation to each other, than he was to the way in which the ego grows out of the unconscious.

In two important passages, "man discriminateth because his nature is distinctiveness. Wherefore he also distinguisheth qualities of the pleroma which are not" (pp. 9–10) and "when we distinguish qualities of the pleroma, we are speaking from the ground of our own distinctiveness and concerning our own distinctiveness" (p. 10), it is possible to recognize the link between the break with Freud, which led to the four years of self-analysis, and the evolution of the type theory owing to the tensions between two men of such contrasted personalities. Certainly no thinking takes place within this self-area; but a sorting out, an ordering, a capacity to separate distinct entities each from the other is the ego quality with which he is most concerned here. "The pleroma hath no qualities. We create them through thinking;" yet, "thoughts flow to you out of the pleroma" (p. 13). This suggests that thoughts are created, made real, only as a result of action on the part of the ego. And this is indeed a way of considering creativeness which can be used to throw light on both fresh ideas and newly-made objects. If the pleroma is understood here in the sense of the original self and if it is postulated that the mother embodies it for the infant and that the infant's major activity is to emerge gradually as a new and distinct individual both physically and psychologically, the infant can do this only on the basis of making something out of what he or she gets from the mother. The infant creates himself or herself as he or she is at each stage on the basis of what flows to him or her out of the pleroma (both milk and suitable psychic releasers of responses which lead to development), but no stage may be missed, and activity on the part of the infant is essential.

The possible usefulness of these prototype versions of the concepts of the ego and the self is suggested in the rather obscure sequence: "Not your thinking, but your being, is distinctiveness. Therefore not after difference, as ye think it, must ye strive; but after YOUR OWN BEING . . . if ye had this striving, ye would not need to know anything about the pleroma and its qualities, and yet would ye come to your own right goal by virtue of your own being" (pp. 13–14). In spite of what looks like an idealization of the primitive man whose nature has not been distorted by the development of rational powers, there is in those words an outline suggestion of the impetus towards the effective increase of ego functioning, which experiencing the self but not being overwhelmed by it leads to, when understood as much as each individual can.

The loss of the ego in the self, as a later theoretical formulation, is expressed in concrete terms: if we do not distinguish "we get beyond our own nature . . . we fall into the pleroma itself and cease to be creatures . . . this is the death of the creature . . . The natural striving of the creature fighteth against primeval, perilous sameness" (pp. 9–10). That ability not to lose ego nature is an essential part of the positive principle of being an individual. And Jung writes that in creatura opposite qualities are not cancelled out—they are lived, we are their victims, "the pleroma is rent in us" (p. 12). There is an obvious hint here of the mythical seamless garment of Christ and of Jung's much later elaboration of Christ as an image of the self (cf. *Aion*).

There is another ancient source on which Jung was most likely drawing when he wrote the *Seven Sermons*, namely the *Hermetica*. This is a collection of Greek and Latin writings dating from the third century A.D., ascribed to a certain Hermes Trismegistus, who pseudonymously fills the role of teacher or guide and who discourses with pupils singly or

in small groups. In some of the talks he takes on the name of Poimandres, and he is certainly reminiscent of Jung's Philemon. The topics discussed were religious and philosophical. The sources of the ideas in the
Hermetica were Platonic, Pythagorean, and Egyptian; they date from the
time of the diffusion of Greek culture which the Roman Empire made
possible; they are almost entirely free from any Jewish or Christian influence. Jung would have been able to read Reitzenstein's edition of these
writings, the first scholarly study of them, which appeared in 1904. Wal-
ter Scott's edition (Scott, 1924) makes it clear to English readers how
close a connection there is between these third-century explorations and
those Jung was undertaking in 1916.

The text of the Seven Sermons is almost overwhelmingly rich, and it is
impossible to enter here into the many allusions to the archetypal image
of wholeness which it in fact contains. The reason for drawing attention
to at least some of the variety if offers within an apparent repetitiveness
is that many years after writing it and having been able to consider the
clinical material of many patients who were seeking his help to activate
development in themselves, Jung came back, in Aion, to the gnostic
symbol of the self in order to show that he found value in studying the
historical forerunners of current imagery. And the specific value to him
lay in the attempt to counteract what he calls the mass-psychoses of our
time which he saw as resulting from suggestibility—ego-weakness—and
ignorance of the fact that "psyche is really par excellence" (Jung 1951).

Another passage has more mundane associations to at least this one
reader of the Sermons: "When we strive after the good and the beautiful
we thereby forget our own nature . . . we labor to attain the good and
the beautiful yet at the same time we also lay hold of the evil and the
ugly, since in the pleroma these are one with the good and the beautiful"
(Jung, 1916b, p.12). Is that not an excellent comment on the inflations,
both positive and negative, in which otherwise admirable people can get
lost at times, unaware of their smugness and scorn for others? There is
also perhaps a foretaste of the good and the bad breast which have to be
discovered both to belong to the same mother, either in actuality or in
the transference projection, so that we are not stuck forever in persecutory anxieties, and can pass on through ambivalence, concern, and depression to a more effective development of ego functioning.

In the sixth sermon, where there is a disquisition on sexuality seen "as
a serpent" and spirituality "as a white bird," the serpent quality is associated with woman and with exclusively evil things, and "the bird hath a
nature like unto man, and is effective thought" (p. 31). That sermon is
sketchy, consisting of not fully-worked-out passages. It is possible that

Jung was wilting under the intensity of the effort needed to record the conversations. In the fifth sermon there are some rather more valuable remarks on spirituality and sexuality, distinguished the one from the other instead of being crudely contrasted.

An exhaustive scrutiny of the text of the *Seven Sermons* would certainly yield many more early aspects, in image form, of later ideas and formulations. A few are worth mentioning, almost at random. There is the Medusa quality of the unconscious: "Before its countenance man becometh like stone" (p. 22). There is incest, and there is the great mother (who appeared as a principal figure in many gnostic thought-systems): "It is the son's horror of the mother. It is the mother's love for the son" (p. 21). There is the number four: "Four is the number of the principal gods, as four is the number of the world's measurements" (p. 24). There is the dangerous but necessary Pandora-behaviour of the devil who "openeth all that is closed" (*ibid.*). There are the contrasexual elements in men and women. There is deep concern for human suffering: "Men are weak and cannot endure their manifold nature. Therefore they dwell together and need communion, that they may bear their separateness. For redemption's sake I teach you the rejected truth, for the sake of which I was rejected" (p. 25)—and the danger of being possessed by the saviour-archetype is there also. There are, finally, numerous apparently simple statements which yet contain a wealth of possibilities for the individual reader prepared to develop them, for example: "Communion giveth us warmth, singleness giveth us light" (p. 30).

The *Seven Sermons* and *The Transcendent Function*

Jung wrote both these works in 1916. The theoretical essay can, I think, safely be presumed to have been written after the personal experience, but it was not published until 1957, and it is interesting that although the processes described in it (ways of coming to terms in practice with the unconscious) were among those which occupied Jung very closely for all the intervening years, he left *The Transcendent Function* in manuscript form. It is possible to wonder whether the abstract thinking and writing which followed the *Seven Sermons* held such a strong personal flavor for him that he did not publish it for that reason. In a prefatory note to it written in 1959 he stresses the dangers he sees in the liberation of intensified unconscious contents: "The method of active imagination . . . is not a plaything for children." It is essential to find "the meaning and value of these fantasies . . . through their integration into the personality as a whole."

The last few pages of the chapter of his memoirs, "Confrontation with the unconscious," suggest that after writing the *Seven Sermons*, and then painting his first mandala, which he did not at the time understand, "the prelude" was over and he felt confident of being able to communicate "the pattern of order and interpretation" which he discerned in the confused contents of the unconscious. It seems that the stages of the experience had been: the hallucination itself, the imaginative activity which followed his accepting it, the symbolic and integrative value he was able to discern in it and to make out of it, followed by the increase in ego functioning which was demonstrated by abstracting and formulating the essential features of the transcendent function, a phrase with mathematical connotations which he adopted for his own psychological use at that time.

A close study of *The Transcendent Function* yields many links between it and its basis in experience, the *Seven Sermons to the Dead*. Those that it is possible to establish within the limits of this paper are not exhaustive; they are offered here as indications which others may care to follow up for themselves.

In describing the complementary character of the unconscious tendencies in relation to conscious attitudes, he writes of "the definiteness and directedness of the conscious mind," a phrase that has close affinity with the discrimination and distinctiveness which he attributes (in the *Seven Sermons*) to creatura. In the passage on evaluating the symbol—"the word *symbol* being taken to mean the best possible expression for a complex fact not yet clearly apprehended by consciousness" (Jung, 1916, p. 75)—there is a strong hint of a description of what he had himself endured and benefited from earlier in the year.

"Why is it so absolutely necessary to bring up the unconscious contents?" he asked in *The Transcendent Function*. He gives the answer two paragraphs later: "We are searching for . . . a way to make conscious those contents which are about to influence our actions, so that the secret interference of the unconscious and its unpleasant consequences can be avoided" (Jung, 1916, p. 79). He himself had found the experience "absolutely necessary." He met the challenge of that secret influence and interference with the determination to cooperate, and to do this in consciousness, which is the area of the mind where action can be taken. The individual's range of responsibility for his actions is thereby greatly enlarged. I think this is what he means when he refers to the "moral demands" of fantasies which are integrated into the personality as a whole.

Having shown the necessity of raising unconscious contents to consciousness if they are causing acute anxiety, such as Jung had been suffering over the widening rift between Freud and himself, he asks another basic question concerned with the long-term value of this confrontation and the way of ensuring the continuance of benefit. He describes "the mental and moral attitude [which it is] necessary to have towards the disturbing influences of the unconscious" as being that of recognizing the compensatory significance and the tendencies of both the conscious and the unconscious. And the insistence in *The Transcendent Function* that conscious and unconscious must alternate in taking the lead in the process of bringing together opposite tendencies in the interest of reducing excessive anxiety was based on his own experience of first allowing unconscious material to emerge, even though in a frightening form, and then decidedly swinging over to a conscious working on the material, its meaning and its results. He was quite clear that "the position of the ego must be maintained as being of equal value to the counterposition of the unconscious, and vice versa."

That reads like a reflection of the powerful personal experience which had, I surmise, earlier in the same year been expressed in this way: "If we do not distinguish, we get beyond our own nature, away from creatura. We fall into indistinctiveness . . . We fall into the pleroma itself . . . We are given over to dissolution in the nothingness . . . Hence the natural striving of the creature goeth towards distinctiveness . . . This is called PRINCIPIUM INDIVIDUATIONIS. This principle is the essence of the creature" (p. 11). And although he makes it clear in the *Seven Sermons* that creatura cannot *think* about the pleroma, it can do something which is perhaps better expressed as considering it, giving it due weight, due consideration. Turning to *The Transcendent Function* at that point yields the following: "Thanks to the fundamental insight of Freud, we know that emotional factors must be given full consideration in the treatment of the neuroses . . . Taking the other side seriously does not mean taking it literally, but it does mean giving the unconscious credit, so that it has a chance to cooperate with consciousness instead of automatically disturbing it" (p. 88). Jung's view of the unconscious, distinct from the then Freudian view of it as the dangerous repository for unacceptable, and therefore repressed, personal contents, was beginning clearly to emerge as a result of Jung himself discovering some of the historical and philosophical antecedents of his inner experiences, the gnostics' deliberations on the problem of evil.

During the years of growing anxiety on the subject of whether he could continue to follow and to collaborate with Freud, Jung evidently tried to disentangle the intellectual from the most personal aspects of disagreement. It became increasingly clear to him that if he followed his

own bent he would lose the friendship of Freud. Both men were interested in archaeology, but Jung's reading in that subject (and in other allied ones) led him to a different kind of exploration of mythology from
Freud's. And at the time when he was plunging into a frenzied reading of
mythology he was also diving into the not very limpid waters of gnostic
writing. Analytical psychology cannot dispense with one result of Freud's
excavations, the archetypal Oedipus complex, but the extension and ex-
pansion of personal psychological experience which Jung found to be essential through the activity which resulted in writing the *Seven Sermons*
had no close parallel for Freud. Jung's dissatisfaction with the view Freud
then had on the nature and functioning of the unconscious was no doubt
grounded in their individual personalities and in the age-relationship between them—Freud was nineteen years older than Jung. The question of
"how the ego and the unconscious are to come to terms . . . the bringing
together of opposites for the production of a third: the transcendent
function" had a burning personal activation behind it.

The connection between gnosticism and the totality definition of the
self remains an exclusively intellectual one unless confirmed by the symbolic experience which the writing of the *Seven Sermons* was for Jung.
That is why there is such a vivid quality to be sensed in several passages
in *The Transcendent Function*, for instance: "The confrontation of the
two positions generates a tension charged with energy and creates a living, third thing . . . a living birth that leads to a new level of being, a
new situation" (p. 90).

In the 1916 version of "The Structure of the Unconscious," later expanded and renamed "The Relations Between the Ego and the Unconscious," Jung brought together, in a startling and illuminating manner,
the schizophrenic locksmith's apprentice and the philosopher Schopenhauer. The patient tried to communicate in "the primitive language" of
an intuitively-produced image which was an impersonal one springing up
spontaneously from an archetypal source. Schopenhauer's conception of
"the world as will and idea" seemed to Jung to be the philosophic equivalent. The philosopher, he wrote, can be credited with "proprietary
rights" only if he turns an intuitive and impersonal image into an abstract idea. His mind becomes a channel for conveying it to others.
So the situation is reached in which Jung calls an individual's image-
statement impersonal (he later dignified it with the description "archetypal"), yet at the same time an abstraction, which sounds so entirely
nonpersonal, can belong to an individual: he has performed a personal
mental action to produce it. Philosophers, and presumably also ordinary
people, may be credited with possessing their ideas if by means of ego ac-

tivity they have worked on the images which spring from the unconscious. They have earned possession of the abstraction through work;
they are not possessed by dangerous and deceptively impressive, unconscious, raw material. In the words selected on the bright summer afternoon in 1916, the locksmith's apprentice was lost in Abraxas where the
pleroma dominated the situation, and the philosopher—or the man who
understood his experiences—was creatura, about to enjoy his distinctive
and effective, but limited and human, individuality.

Summary

Jung's work Seven Sermons to the Dead is examined in the context of the
time of life at which he wrote it, a time both of internal crisis and of difficulties connected with the widening rift in his relations with Freud.
The contents of the document are examined in order to try to establish
their meaning and value. They seem best understood as image material
from which evolved and were abstracted his later theoretical views on
the ego, the self, and the unconscious. They are postulated to be the experiential basis of later reflection and thought. Further, the suggestion is
made that the writing of Seven Sermons to the Dead was the personal experience out of which the paper The Transcendent Function emerged later
in the same year, 1916.

   The document under consideration is incomprehensible without some
knowledge of the historical background; this includes Jung's wide and
deep reading in gnosticism, and in particular his attraction to two gnostic conceptions of entities, the pleroma and Abraxas. Some exploration
is attempted into the roots of those words and ideas. A brief excursion is
reported into some of the gnostic and hermetic writings which it can be
fairly safely assumed that Jung had already read at this stage in his life,
into the systems of early Christian non-Catholic thinking into which he
had delved, and into the origins of the gnostics' use of pairs of opposite
qualities. Some attention is given to the more obvious or striking concepts to which Jung is giving attention, such as consciousness and unconsciousness, effectiveness, persistence (by implication), discrimination, and distinctiveness. The use to which he evidently put this early
example of a kind of active imagination, under the safe conduct of a
gnostic-type internal figure, is shown to be the integration of dangerous
material from unconscious sources, and the consequent improvement in
ego strength. Allusion is made to some other important aspects of the
contents of Seven Sermons which it has not been possible to go into.

   The relationship between the contents of Seven Sermons and the paper

The Transcendent Function, which treats of active imagination and its attendant dangers, is deduced from internal evidence and worked out in accordance with the theme of the confrontation between the conscious functioning mind and material welling up from unconscious sources. The need to understand the forces at work in such an actively encouraged process is shown as having originally been Jung's own need to experience fully and to analyze his own psychotic anxiety. Finally, it is suggested that there is a link between the material outlined above and "The relations between the ego and the unconscious." The paper describes the connection between imagery and theoretical abstraction.

References

Cross, F. A. 1955. ed. *The Jung Codex: A Newly Recovered Gnostic Papyrus*. London: Mowbray.

Grant, R. M. 1961. *Gnosticism, an Anthology*. London: Collins.

Hippolytus. *Philosophumena: or The refutation of all Heresies*. Translated by Francis Legge. (Translations of Christian Literature.) London and New York: SPCK 1921 (two volumes).

Hoeller, S.A. 1982. *The Gnostic Jung and the Seven Sermons to the Dead*. London & Wheaton: Theosophical Publishing House.

Jung, C. G. 1916a. The Structure of the Unconscious. In *Collected Works*, 7.

———. 1916b. *VII Sermones ad mortuos*. Trans. 1925 H.G. Baynes, London: Watkins 1967. New York: Random House.

———. 1916c. The Transcendent Function. In *Collected Works*, 8.

———. 1936. The Concept of the Collective Unconscious. In *Collected Works*, 9/1.

———. 1951. *Aion: Researches into the Phenomenology of the Self*. In *Collected Works*, 9/2.

———. 1963. *Memories, Dreams, Reflections*. London: Collins and Routledge & Kegan Paul.

St Paul. *Epistle to Philemon*. New Testament.

Scott, W. 1924. *Hermetica*, vol.1. Oxford: Clarendon Press.

Smith, W. & Wace, H. 1877. *A Dictionary of Christian Biography, Literature, Sects, and Doctrines*. London: Murray.

Chapter 8

Envy and the Shadow

The theme of this paper is that the emotion of envy manifests itself in two major forms: the genetically earlier, hungry, wanting form and the later or shadow form. These manifestations are observed, not necessarily in that order, in a wide variety of individual patients. They are experienced in the transference, where they can come within reach of the analyst and of his possible therapeutic redirection of them into more positive and ego-developing channels. To substantiate and illustrate the theme I will draw on material from work in which the all-around actuality of various sessions is relevant but not necessarily easy to convey: the tones of voice, the body movements, the whole emotional atmosphere, the interplay between patient and analyst.

The intention is to see whether an acceptable link can be made between on the one hand the work which has already been done on the theory of envy and on the other the specific contribution to the nature of psychic functioning which the theory of the archetypes provides. While Klein's work on envy has been valuable in a direct way to many analysts, it can also serve as a stimulus for further research. There is always room and time for reassessment of accepted, or partially accepted, theories and for seeing whether they can be worked in with other and different approaches.

I have been finding increasingly that Klein's theory of envy does not always fit patients quite closely enough, and that it is only by being just as aware of the shadow as of the emotion of envy that we can satisfactorily extricate the nature and meaning of the anxieties which are at work in both envy and shadow experiences. I am attempting to study the nature and workings of unconscious envy from the specific point of view of analytical psychology, and particularly the characteristics of the shadow, both

Originally published in *The Journal of Analytical Psychology*, 17:2 (1972), pp. 152–65.

personal and collective, and to select from what I have been experiencing
of both, noticing and thinking about them, for some years.

Envy

Klein writes (1957, p. 6):

> Envy is the angry feeling that another person possesses and enjoys
> something desirable—the envious impulse being to take it away or
> to spoil it.

I do not find myself fully satisfied with that. Being envious does involve
being angry but it also involves hating: I believe the impulse to take something, and to have it for oneself, is the earlier and simpler form of the affect, and that the desire to spoil it, which is malicious, belongs only to the
later form. Intrinsically I am writing about envy as including three features, the first being the desire to get what another person has and enjoys,
the second being that the desire is colored with hate and the third that in
its later form it is toned with the impulse to spoil. This last aspect develops
as a result of repeated failures to get the wanted thing; the dog-in-the-
manger denigratory spoiling occurs in connection with the projection of
the subject's defeat and disappointment.

Insofar as the emotion of envy is the experience of wanting (as in the
French phrase *"avoir envie de,"* which means wanting, wishing for) it belongs in the infant's life to the stage before concern has been experienced.
To the extent that the emotion of envy involves hating his object for having the thing which he wants, it is experienced in association with most
powerful impulses directed towards attacking the object. This early envy is
ruthless, but not at that time of life anything to do with moral values as
they are regarded in and by more developed individuals.

With patients who are very envious (whether constantly and blatantly
in his outside life, or phasically in the transference), the problem is to
bring to light the stage of development to which the current envy belongs
or refers. When it is a question of an equivalent of the very early ravenous
demanding attack on the breast, an even minute amount of opprobrium by
the analyst (such as the use of the word "envy" can be for some people)
will mobilize in the patient an angry paranoid defense in the attempt to
protect himself or herself from the concern and compunction for which
they are not yet ready, and which occur more truly in association with
emotions of a later stage, after super-ego fragments have begun to co-
alesce. That is the stage at which envy becomes a true shadow problem,
when spoiling, denigration and malice set in. A patient who is envious

can regress in the safety of the transference and bring representations of the very early experiences of attacking the breast hungrily, angrily—apparently but not actually destroying it; that reexperiencing, with accurate interpretations which relieve his anxiety, can enable him or her to go forward securely towards acknowledging more developed envies as manifestations of the shadow.

While I have no alternative to offer, I do not find the terms "good breast" and "bad breast" fully satisfactory, though I realize that the words good and bad are necessary in trying to understand splitting as a defense against anxiety. It is difficult, if not indeed virtually impossible in our language, to use the words "good" and "bad" with no moral undertones at all. I could illustrate what I mean by pointing to the difference between the word "hunger" which is a genuinely neutral one, and the word "greed," which does not sound neutral.

Klein thinks that "no rigid dividing line can be drawn [between greed and envy] since they are so closely associated" but that an essential difference is "that greed is mainly bound up with introjection and envy with projection" (1957, p. 7). I suggest distinguishing in a slightly different way between envy as described earlier, and greed as being the impetuous, compulsive craving for more than the subject needs. An infant feeding with great energy, with great attack and taking in more milk than it needs, through ignorance and inexperience, depends to some extent on its mother's handling to help it to sick up the extra before being laid down to sleep. It may give the impression of feeding greedily, but I think true greed does not occur in earliest infancy. The word serves us best if reserved for a later activity, referring developmentally to a time in which the infant has begun to experience a variety of tastes, and finds some more pleasing than others. The infant can become greedy for them.

Those observations of more or less normal infants are borne out with patients. Patients are sometimes hungry, psychically speaking, and sometimes they are being greedy. Or, from internal adult moralizing, they see themselves as greedy when more truly they are hungry. It is important to be able to discern which they are at any particular time. It is also important to feel reasonably confident about whether to respond to a patient as the grown-up which he or she is, with the morals of the childhood family or those which are the patient's own individual version of contemporary collective ones, or as the infant which he or she was earlier. Morals do not apply to infants, and the absence of overt morals in analysis stems from the analyst's effort to reach, with the patient, earlier times, experiences and affects. Yet attention must also be given to the present where the shadow is at work, and to the possible future.

Note added to the earlier text:

Reviewing in 1987 these observations on envy (which were first published in 1972), I would like to add some further thoughts on hunger and greed. It now seems to me important to analyze the anxiety which is almost certainly contained within the compulsive quality that there is in greed. With the benefit of more years of observing and interacting with envious, hungry and greedy patients since making the above remarks about the moralizing feature in the use of the term *greed*, my present view is that the analyst should always try to find out precisely what the patient is anxious about, when greed is in evidence. During the interaction, and within the transference projections, it is usually possible to discover the nature of the anxiety which has led to normal hunger taking on a compulsive and greedy character. The adult patient may be self-critical when greed comes to light, and may need the analyst to point out that there had been some particular, unseen, anxiety at work, and that criticism does not apply while any affect is still unconscious.

The limits within which I hope to examine the nature and workings of unconscious envy in analytical work are set by my aim of trying to link my observations with the theory of the shadow. I shall not be concerned, except incidentally, with the theory of envy as a primary emotion. At present I hold the interim view, that all individuals are born with a capacity for emotions both conscious and unconscious, including the capacity for experiencing envy in situations likely to evoke it. But the stage and the circumstances in which this occurs probably vary considerably according to constitutional factors in the object, e.g., the mother as an individual.

The basis for this view is that, in the transference projections of patients, unconscious envy occurs in psychic events representing a very wide spread of earlier developmental stages. The theoretical point as to whether or not it is a primary emotion is at present of less interest to me than its nature and manifestations, and the question of whether, with each particular patient, the analyst can discover how best to use it, to work through its destructive aspects, reach its positiveness and thereby assist ego development. Shadow elements have to be worked through at many stages of an analysis, not only when the patient is in a stage of "confession" which can occur early on and then recur at intervals later, but envy also crops up either frequently or from time to time, in connection with many different people in the patient's life.

From the point of view of pure research (by which I mean in the interests of the development of an intellectually respectable theory, irrespec-

tive of the patient's health improving) it could be interesting to discover
with certainty whether envy was experienced so early in life that it could
be called primary or innate. Yet, on reflection, I think that both considerations go together, research and therapeutic endeavor: the test is effectiveness. Among those analyses with which I have not been satisfied, those
which were for any reason clearly incomplete although ended, are those
where the envy was not sufficiently analyzed and integrated, where a considerable shadow problem still persisted. It was examining them retrospectively which principally led me to try to find out more on the theoretical
side.

The Background and Collective
Considerations

Anyone who examines the indexes in the various volumes of the works of
Freud and Jung might be forgiven for jumping to the conclusion that, as
between the two, Freud had almost the monopoly of views on envy. But
Freud was more knowledgeable about women's penis-envy than about any
other manifestation of it. Another preliminary to this present study of
envy was to see how often there had been papers in the *The Journal of Analytical Psychology* specifically about envy: there was Michael Rosenthal's in
1963, and Mary Williams's contribution (1972). There was a critical notice of Klein's book, by Michael Fordham and Rosemary Gordon, in 1958.
In the *International Journal of Psycho-Analysis*, Joffe (1969) examined what
he called "the status of the envy concept."

   Others than analysts have experienced and thought about envy and envious people. There is a compendium called simply *Envy* by the sociologist
Helmut Schoeck (1969), which shows clearly what a very wide spectrum
of thinkers have given the topic their attention. He shows how many of
them dislike it, criticize it, regret its existence and testify to its widespread
incidence: Schoeck himself contributes a valuable sociological "Theory of
envy in human existence" (pp. 348-60), within which are included the
positive values of envy as promoting civilization, as domesticating power,
and as promoting creativity, provided envy is kept within bounds. He ar-
gues that

> envy is a drive and a mental attitude so inevitable and so deeply
> rooted in man's biological and existential situation, that no scien-
> tific consideration of this phenomenon ought to start from the pos-
> tulate that its consequences in the process of social change and the
> differentiation of social forms were exclusively negative (p. 350).

The deeper understanding of the troubles of envious patients, their connection with the collective unconscious and their archetypal nature, their special connection with shadow problems and the possibilities that these troubles open up if they can be worked through creatively, is forwarded by considering some of the astute descriptions of envious people, and observations on envy, made by poets and humanists who both come close to seeing the unconscious working of it which are the analyst's prime concern. Legends about the devil, Milton's Satan, Shakespeare's Iago, easily come to mind. With considerable psychological acumen St Augustine (A.D. 354–430) noted: "Myself have seen and known even a baby envious; it could not speak, yet it turned pale and looked bitterly at its fosterbrother" (397, and 1907, p. 7).

There was also Robert Burton, whose large treatise on depression, *The Anatomy of Melancholy*, was first published in 1621. The seventeenth century was not unlike our own time in terms of viciousness, turbulence and idealism. Some of his remarks are very relevant and based no doubt on accurate observation. Burton wrote:

> Envy so gnaws men's hearts that they become altogether melancholy, and therefore . . . Solomon calls it the rotting of the bones . . . it crucifies their souls, withers their bodies . . . As a moth gnaws a garment, so . . . doth envy consume a man, for so often as an envious wretch sees another man to prosper, to be enriched, to thrive and be fortunate in the world, to get honors, offices or the like, so he repines and grieves.

The passage about envy consuming a man sounds like a preanalytic formulation of the theory of envy of the breast, and of the impossibility of taking in an envied analyst's interpretations.

Burton also wrote:

> Cain was not angered because of a wrong—it was his brother's good fortune galled him . . . 'Tis a common disease, *and almost natural to us* [my italics] . . . to envy another man's prosperity.

That sounds like the theory of envy as primary affect.

> Every other sin hath some pleasure annexed to it, or will admit of an excuse; envy alone wants both. Other sins last but for a while; the gut may be satisfied, anger remits, hatred hath an end, envy never ceaseth.

That last quotation reminds me of the pessimism about effectively ana-lyzing, relieving and transforming women patients' penis-envy in the es-say "Analysis Terminable and Interminable," pessimism of Freud's to which I hope we as analytical psychologists do not have to succumb, provided we make the best possible use of the workings of archetypal conflicts, particularly shadow and negative animus ones.

It will have been noticed that Robert Burton calls envy at times a dis-ease, at times a sin. Experience of the shadow often comes very close to being a simple sense of sin.

The Shadow

Early Christian moralists held that the worst, the seven deadly sins (the sources of all others), were anger, envy, and pride (we still use these three words), avarice, lust, gluttony and sloth: there are modern words for those four, but the old ones sound more sinful. I noticed that in the works of Jung, whether I browsed here and there, looking for remarks about envy and the shadow, or read them in a concentrated way, the word *moral* appeared very often, and most particularly in connection with shadow problems. Here are a few:

> The shadow is a moral problem that challenges the whole ego-personality, for no one can become conscious of the shadow with-out considerable moral effort (1951b, p. 8).

In "The Relations Between the Ego and the Unconscious," he describes an undifferentiated person as being neither at one with himself nor able to accept responsibility for himself:

> he feels himself to be in a degrading, unfree, unethical condition (1928, p. 223).

In the same work, he writes:

> The universal problem of evil and sin is another aspect of our im-personal relations to the world . . . It is a notorious fact that the compulsion neuroses . . . not only have the surface appearance of a moral problem but are indeed brimful of inhuman beastliness and ruthless evil, against whose integration the otherwise very deli-cately organized personality puts up a desperate struggle (p. 179).

In discussing the case of "a highly intelligent young man" with a compulsion neurosis, Jung writes that the man's

> want of conscience was the cause of his neurosis . . . his fundamental error lay in his moral attitude. He found my way of looking at it shockingly unscientific, for morals have nothing to do with science. He thought that he could scientifically unthink the immorality which he himself, at bottom, could not stomach. He would not even admit that any conflict existed, because his mistress gave him the money [for holidays at St Mortiz or Nice] of her own free will (1934, pp. 355–56).

In drawing attention to moral points and in linking ethics and psychology Jung was not, as the young man had said he was, being moralistic. Rather the reverse: to understand ethics psychologically can result in detaching neurotic guilt from inappropriate areas of the personality and in enabling the freer ego to grow and to take greater responsibility in a more truly ethical direction. It is precisely work on the concept of the archetypal shadow and the application of this to particular interpersonal and developmental difficulties which can contribute most fruitfully to personality growth and a greater ethical articulation.

While experience of the shadow, both personal and collective, is so very much part of the everyday work of analysts that it tends to be regarded as somehow less prestigious than experience of what might be called the "greater" archetypes, it would be a pity if familiarity with it led us into believing we know all about it. Its very familiarity shows what a family thing is. And this results in it being difficult to distance ourselves enough from it to get a clear, nonmyopic view.

The principal characteristic of the shadow is that it contains the thing a person has no wish to be; a patient is getting into his shadow when he stumbles on attitudes in himself which he did not know he held and does not approve of, when he finds himself doing things which he feels do not suit him, things which do not fit with the idealized view of himself which he perhaps hardly realized was not how others saw him. In addition to the shadow as archetype, there is each one's personal shadow which Jung defines as "the uppermost layer of his unconscious" (1951a, p. 124) and he also makes it clear that the shadow belongs to the ego (1946, p. 260).

Someone who had had a psychoanalysis once told me she thought the greatest benefit she had derived from it was the series of home truths to which her analyst had treated her. As an only child she had had, she said, too little of the helpful side of ordinary family life. In a similar way, a patient of mine who was still relatively free from obvious paranoid fears (he was carefully defending against them) found that I had pointed out a characteristic which he then said his girlfriend had recently commented on. He had been annoyed at her noticing it: it had reminded him of his mother's perennial disappointment in him and her disapproval; he could never reach the standard she expected of him. He claimed that my comment had reminded him more of his father, who was his preferred parent, from whom he could accept criticism.

The personal shadow was most minutely and effectively pointed up in Freud's work, which was of course one of the reasons for his long-continued unpopularity, especially in scientific circles. The important years of his publications about repression coincided with a period of history when the optimistic belief in progress and reason, so widely held before the First World War, was being blown to bits. The economist Maynard Keynes, writing in 1938 about the beliefs of his circle of friends at Cambridge in the early 1900s, said:

> The attribution of rationality to human nature, instead of enriching it, now seems to me to have impoverished it. It ignored certain powerful and valuable springs of feeling . . . Even some of the feelings associated with wickedness can have value (1949, p. 101).

Jung thought that "Freud and his school" had presented "a biased portrayal of man from the shadow side alone. After all, the essential thing is not the shadow but the body which casts it" (1929, p. 63–4).

So the problem has shifted later in the twentieth century to trying to find how the shadow can be integrated with the ego and lived with, without it precipitating further and increasingly global murderous disasters. This is another way of conceptualizing the shadow as composed, in the first instance, of personal repressed contents, but as being also the archetype of evil, constituent of and contributory to, the collective unconscious. It is far from easy, and perhaps in any case unhelpful, in working toward a satisfactory theory of envy, to distinguish sharply between the personal repressed shadow and the shadow as archetype of evil. The two go together.

Whereas the personal shadow, so often featuring envy, is very largely but not exclusively made up of ingredients from the individual's upbringing which he has been taught to see as wrong, bad or evil, the shadow as archetype has an extremist as well as a generalized quality. It is more than a consensus of the collective ethical views of earlier generations, it also has a certainty to it which stems from its instinctual basis which is of course general and collective. It contains what Jung called "beastliness" and "ruthlessness" because it is rooted in instinctual, animal, experience and behavior. The condemnation given to envy, as well as the recognition of its ubiquitous occurrence, likewise testify to it stemming from an instinctive soil and growing in all stages of historical and personal development. Clearly, then, the analytic working on envious shadow-features with any particular individual, with a view to releasing libido for psychic growth, will bring analyst and patient into the region and the possibilty of individuation, through the integration of previously split-off elements. Neumann (1969), while not writing about envy, discusses this point very fully in the broad context of the twentieth century problems of evil and ethics.

In thus describing the field of enquiry, the principal feature has been to apply the main lines of knowledge of the shadow to the particular instance of the affect of envy. The question arises whether such an activity adds anything substantial to previous thinking about envy, as distinct from being merely a semantic exercise. If it is a real refinement of our tools it will carry its own justification in clinical practice.

Envy In Analytical Psychology

Analysts have often observed how unconscious envy operates and how rendering it conscious is followed, classically, by a greater flexibility in the patient's personality and an ability to acknowledge good in others. Klein calls this gratitude. It is in effect being able to give, to credit the other with something which the patient had previously been trying to deny him, notionally to take away from him; he had been trying to help himself to it, or to steal it. I would like here to take for granted such aspects of clinical work with envy (to help myself to them, while certainly expressing gratitude that this work has already been done) and to examine a few instances of envy occurring in the difficult frontier land between ethics and archetypes. The ethical atmosphere of our time in general (even if somewhat polluted) and the specific ethical characteristics in any particular patient's upbringing have to be taken into account.

Clinical Examples

Shadow, Reversal and Disorder

In psychotherpeutic work as well as in ordinary life many instances occur of men envying women, women envying men, the older envying the younger, the young ones envying their elders. Racker (1968, p. 110) writes that the male analyst may love the female patient genitally and he "hates her if she then loves another man, feels rivalry of this man and jealousy and envy (heterosexual and homosexual) of their sexual pleasures," and Racker says that this and other similar countertransference phenomena are due to the patient having become, in the countertransference, the representative for the analyst of his or her parent of the other sex.

With candor it is possible to echo his experience. While the genetic background and origin are clearly derived from unconscious infantile envy of the feeding and phallic mother, the essential ingredient is a wished-for and idealized reversal of the mother-infant relationship, which has occurred as a result of the infant's attempt to defend itself against the anxiety with which its hunger flooded it. A patient protested, in response to a comment of mine: "I can't bear it! That makes me sound just like my mother. And you reminded me of her, in the way you said that. I can't bear you!" Another patient, when I had made an observation which inevitably implied that my experience of life was more extensive than hers (she was about half my age), muttered half under her breath, "You win that round," as though there had been a contest going on. Her manner and physical bearing (which were always particularly important with this patient, who found it difficult to speak out) suggested that she felt squashed, as would-be protesters sometimes do in large families. She had had an anxious and overbearing father, and was the oldest of five children. She was trying to bite back, having felt bitten, and thus reverse the power situation as she felt it. All her demeanor conveyed sarcastic envy. She did not feel she was getting what she wanted, nor indeed did she want that day to feed off anything I had to offer her. She wanted to be the one who bit. Her attempt at reversal, if it had succeeded, would have been in the direction of development. She needed to find that she could protest, but the incident was colored with discomfort and displeasure for her. She felt I had hurt her and disliked me for that.

On a later occasion this patient was in the grip of a known fear and an unacknowledged wish to be seductive with me. She had almost realized this, in the previous session, in the course of the analysis of an incident in which she complained that I was being soft, by which she explained that she meant seductive, towards her. She was battling with a desire to disagree with me for saying that nothing which passed through her mind was irrelevant. Towards the end of the time she was silent for quite a while after telling me she had had an irrelevant thought. Finally she said it was a very embarrassing thought: she had been wondering whether I had ever noticed her facial hair, she disliked it very much.

The shadow quality and the envy in this passage of her analysis lay in her wish to avoid a physical aspect of herself which she believed to be derogatory to her attractiveness and one which represented an unconscious wish to be male in relation to me. This was combined with a subtle attempt to undermine me as an analyst-parent, to seduce me into giving way to inquisitiveness during the long silence, and to put forward her view of what would, and what would not, be productive in analysis. Later, her wish to solve her oedipal conflict by supplanting my husband came out into the open.

This patient demonstrated not only regressive wishes but also attempts at reversal. And such psychic activities were in fact intrinsic to the homosexual problem in her adult life, which her excessive early envy had led to, and her shame about her difficulties. The archetype of the self has an ordering aspect and power, and I think this patient's envy of my possible capacity in the transference was a manifestation of her unconscious attempt to disorganize her relationship with me, and thereby to resist the natural ordering power of the self. She feared that I would forcefully impose my point of view on her, as the circumstances of her childhood, and most particularly her father's personality and profession, had disrupted the natural development of her ego. There was envy of me as representing the all-giving mother, and there was an attempt omnipotently to deny me the use of the professional ability which she experienced as a father-quality and which, in other ways, she wanted to be put at her disposal.

In so far as she was trying to deny ability to me she could be said to be wanting it herself, emulating it or even stealing it, and at a later stage of development in the transference she felt very guilty in relation to me, that is to say after the shadow quality had set in openly. That was shown, for example, when she took almost the whole of a session battling with the block caused by her difficulty in telling me that the snowdrops in my room were good and large, whereas the ones she had planted were proving disappointingly small.

Hate and the Discovery of Love

In studying Jung's remarks made about the shadow at various times it is interesting to notice their increasing complexity and subtlety. In *Mysterium Coniunctionis* there are several passages which have a bearing on the conceptual connection between envy and the shadow. For example:

> The shadow, as we know, usually presents a fundamental contrast to the conscious personality. This contrast is the prerequisite for the difference of potential from which psychic energy arises. Without it, the necessary tension would be lacking. Where considerable psychic energy is at work, we must expect a corresponding tension and inner opposition. The opposites are necessarily of a characterological nature: the existence of a positive virtue implies victory over its opposite, the corresponding vice. Without its counterpart virtue would be pale, ineffective and unreal. The extreme opposition of the shadow to consciousness is mitigated by complementary and compensatory processes in the unconscious. Their impact on consciousness finally produces the uniting symbols (1955–6, p. 497).

The accuracy of the description in that passage struck me most particularly in connection with a patient whose fantasies for many years centered on his belief that his inner blackness was evident to people outside him, that he had blackheads on his face, was hideously repulsive, that I could not tolerate him and was terrified of him as being such an evil person. One fantasy was of snatching my books from the shelves, tearing them up and throwing the bits out of the window. He longed to return to the intellectual life which his illness denied him. He could normally not bear light, as that would make it possible, he feared, for me to see what a black person he was. He did not like me looking at him, and could not look at me. He was in far closer touch with the archetypal manifestation of the shadow than he was with his potentially positive characteristics.

The analysis gradually revealed how dangerously he had introjected the bitterly quarrelling parents: depression and vindictiveness had been thick in his childhood home. His early ego development had been much blocked by this totally bad atmosphere. His mother had seemed to him very depressed, bitter, and especially hostile to his father. While he invariably made out that he had received little but fear and confusion from them, he was desperately trying to cling to the good in himself which he had not yet consciously or convincingly experienced, while gradually allowing me to have some too. He was trying to get to this, to get at me, to go at me, and to get me, while the corresponding shadow pull was away from me.

He hated me intensely for long periods of time. The physical space between himself and me in the room was sometimes fantasied to contain
an actual barrier or fence—he drew a semicircle with his arm to show
where it was. He kept me at a distance to avoid quarrelling. At a somewhat later time the space was felt to be an unbridgeable emptiness, there
would never be a meeting. It was only by taking each of these phenomena in the transference as being representations of his mother's early difficulties with him and his difficulties with her, and interpreting them in
whatever physical way was appropriate at the time, that his infantile
hunger could be detached from his later shadow problem. His hating and
envy far more often felt to me, in the countertransference, like sup-
pressed energy, of which the positive pole had not yet been appreciated,
than like a really nasty attempt at vicious demolition of what I provided,
although of course his certainty of his blackness had to be taken into account and his projective assertions of my fear of him.

Improvement set in only when he found he could allow himself to believe in, and then to recreate for himself, the experiences of receiving
worthwhile things from me. The first present he gave me was an attractive variegated stone in two shades of grey, which he had picked up on a
beach. Some months later he brought a large pot of marmalade, which
he had made. Later, he played me tunes on his Jew's harp and then on
his penny-whistle. It seemed that only through giving actual presents or
making music could he come to believe that he contained goodness as
well as blackness.

His angry attacks became less destructively envious as their hungry nature emerged more clearly, through interpretation. His hunger for the
good was only gradually met by him finding that the attitude and the interpretations which I offered were of some use to him. By then he had
discovered so much of his intense envy, the hungry and the denigratory
variants of it, that he was able to say, one day, "You are telling me just
what I want to hear about myself, and what I am sure is true, and at the
very same time, *now*, I'm envying your knowledge."

During stages of the analysis when depression and ambivalence pre-
vailed, he would arrive looking gaunt, haggard, and half-dead; dreams at
those stages all included deaths or killings. The black was going to over-
come the light. The moral atmosphere of his upbringing in a remote and
harsh community had been calculated to produce a grossly exaggerated
sense of sin in a very sensitive boy. Rather like Van Gogh, who was
called after a dead brother, this patient had been called after two uncles,
from each side of the family, both of whom had been drowned. On attacking envious days his scowl could be ferociously forbidding. His smile,

when he discovered it, was correspondingly and compensatingly attractive.

Conclusion

The sense of sin is another way of talking about the shadow and has to be taken into account in considering psychic development. Or, to put it the other way round, the concept of the shadow is analytical psychology's contribution to, and extension of, theology's *sin*. Western religions speak openly of sin in various forms and with various attitudes. Philosophical schools usually pay attention to the study of notions or systems of ethics, the science of morals. Political theorists from Aristotle onwards have studied the problem of the limits of personal freedom in social living from the moral as well as from the cooler intellectual point of view.

All those disciplines tackle the problems inherent in the need for the individual actively to develop a capacity to consider other people and they offer a variety of solutions to this basically psychological problem. Depth psychologists, without setting out to do so, and in the course of doing much else, are inevitably caught up in their patients' need to improve their disturbed and unsatisfactory relations with the people in their current lives and with long-established imagoes. After an approximately beneficial analytic experience, most patients are capable of a more genuine altruism than before they start; they are more likely than not to have developed an ability to give at any rate as much emphasis to others' needs as to their own when this is appropriate, and even precedence to them on occasions when a developed moral sense requires them to do so.

The affect of envy is essential to adequate personal development out of the earliest stages of life when there is more self than ego. A person has to want to take in from outside himself in order to set going deintegration of the earliest self, and ego growth; this is the positive aspect of the hungry, wanting, and emulating ingredient in envy. Its negative aspect is the absolutely essential shadow-opposite of this very real wanting. Excessive envy becomes a block on development in those people for whom circumstances were such in the second stage of infancy that deprivations of instinctual needs were more frequent than gratifications of them. If their introjections of both food and consistent loving care were not adequate for normal ego growth, their angry, disappointed, and damaging affects became overpowering and had, therefore, to be projected. Consequently, they were experienced as coming from outside, and had to be destroyed if possible; hence the spoiling and denigratory forms of envy.

Instinctual and developmental needs are more complicated after teeth are cut and the stage of concern has replaced primary ruthlessness, than they are earlier. More subtle manifestations of envy occur in analysis when the stage of development to which they refer is post-teething than are the hungry envies of earlier stages. As those very early envious hungers, or hungry envies, occur at a time of life when the defenses of the incipient ego against terrifying anxiety are more often those of introjection, projection, splitting, and reversal than any others, and these defenses operate in very absolute ways, there is a theoretical as well as an empirical justification for distinguishing between the early wanting form, and the later shadow form, of envy.

Summary

The theme of this paper is the attempt to link collective and individual analytical knowledge of envy with the theory of the personal and the archetypal shadow.

In the early part of the paper, envy is described and discussed. It is broken down into its three constituent elements of wanting, hating, and trying to spoil. These elements are located in the stages of development of the normal infant. Greed is discussed. The theme is stated that the moral problem of the shadow (and envy as one frequent constituent of the shadow) does not apply at the earliest stages of life, but sets in at the stage when concern for the object becomes possible. The idea is advanced that research on theory and therapeutic endeavor go together, as a result of having examined analyses where too little attention was given to the patient's envy.

In the next section, some of the background is described with reference to the work of other analysts and other literary sources. The shadow is then described with reference to certain passages in Jung's works, particularly stressing his moral and ethical concerns, and the clinical application to compulsion neuroses and problems of integration. The necessity is stressed of taking into account both personal and collective aspects of the shadow, and connecting them to basic instinctual levels and problems.

Clinical examples follow, designed to illustrate in detail the way in which two particular shadow-features emerged in analytical and synthesizing work. The first set is about the shadow manifested in patients' unconscious attempts enviously to reverse and cause disorder. The second clinical illustration is about a patient who was "living the shadow" with the potentially creative impulses grossly repressed behind fantasies of inner and outer blackness, with hate dominant in the transference.

In conclusion the notion of the shadow as sin is linked with analytical formulations. Reference is made to the way in which hungry envy affects development, especially in the early stages of life when the incipient ego is defending itself against sometimes almost overwhelming anxieties, and how relative defeat at that stage leads on to the shadow form of envy.

References

Burton, R. 1621. ed. 1931. *The Anatomy of Melancholy*. London: Routledge & Kegan Paul.

Fordham, M., & Gordon, R. 1958. Critical Notice of Klein, M. *Envy and Gratitude. Journal of Analytical Psychology* 3:2.

Joffe, W.G. 1969. A Critical Review of the Status of the Envy Concept. *International Journal of Psycho-Analysis* 50:4.

Jung, C. G. 1928. *Two Essays on Analytical Psychology*. In *Collected Works*, 7.

———. 1929. Problems of Modern Psychotherapy. In *Collected Works*, 16.

———. 1934. Basic Postulates of Analytical Psychology. In *Collected Works*, 8.

———. 1946. The Psychology of the Transference. In *Collected Works*, 16.

———. 1951b. *Aion: Researches into the Phenomenology of the Self*. In *Collected Works*, 9/ii.

———. 1965. *Mysterium Coniunctionis*. In *Collected Works*, 14.

Keynes, J. M. 1949. *Two Memoirs*. London: Hart-Davis.

Klein, M. 1957. *Envy and Gratitude, a Study of Unconscious Sources*. London: Tavistock.

Neumann, E. 1969. *Depth Psychology and a New Ethic*. Trans. E. Rolfe. New York: Putnam (1949) *Tiefenpsychologie und neue ethik*. Zürich: Rascher.

Racker, H. 1968. *Transference and Countertransference*. London: Hogarth.

Rosenthal, M. 1963. Notes on Envy and the Contrasexual Archetype. *Journal of Analytical Psychology* 8:1.

St Augustine 397, ed. 1907. *Confessions*. London: Dent.

Schoeck, H. 1969. *Envy: A Theory of Social Behaviour*. London: Secker & Warburg.

Williams, M. 1972. Success and Failure in Analysis: Primary Envy and the Fate of the Good. *Journal of Analytical Psychology* 17:1.

Chapter 9

Depressed Patients and the Coniunctio

There are six particular people—my former patients—whose lives and therapies are at the empirical core of this paper. What they have in common is that each of their mothers were seriously depressed during these patients' infancy and childhood. The other thing they have in common is that they had their analytical therapy with the same analyst.

Over the years I have had a growing interest in trying to find out more about what it is that enables some patients effectively to emerge from long-term depressions. I would like to isolate one particular factor from those often explored and discussed, concerning the nature, the manifestations, and the treatment of depression. I am thinking of a factor whose absence could be a great disadvantage, but whose presence can enable a patient to become, in the course of therapy and time, less depressed, less frequently so, and less paralyzingly; such a factor might also help the person to be less aggressive towards others and facilitate the development of a truly viable sense of self.

Depression as a form of feeling ill, and as a clinical syndrome or illness, has been known for thousands of years and described from the earliest days onwards both by sufferers and by their doctors. A precise or short definition cannot be offered here, particularly as I am not a psychiatrist and because all authorities agree that there is a wide spectrum of symptoms and indications. At one end of that spectrum, depression is a natural reaction to painful emotional experiences, to bereavement and loneliness, to physical ill health or the approach of death—all features of the human condition. At the extreme melancholic or pathological end of the spectrum the mood change is extreme and persistent. If more of us had time to read (rather than occasionally dip into) Robert Bur-

An expanded version of a paper read at the Ninth International Congress of the International Association of Analytical Psychology held in Jerusalem, March 1983. Originally published in *The Journal of Analytical Psychology* 2 (1983), 313–27.

ton's *The Anatomy of Melancholy*, first published in 1621, as well as to study modern psychiatric textbooks, we would appreciate even more widely than we do from introspection and as Jungian psychotherapists, the many aspects of the whole depression picture. Its main attributes are (1) alteration in mood to sadness, apathy and loneliness, (2) a negative or otherwise self-attacking self-concept, with self-reproaches and self-blame, (3) regressive wishes, the desire to escape, to deny, to hide, to die, (4) crying, irritability, insomnia, loss of sexual appetite, (5) a low level of general activity, loss of decisiveness and of other ego capacities, sometimes a heightened level of inappropriate anxiety, fear, or agitation. In this paper there is no possibility of describing or accurately naming in psychiatric terms just which kind of depression afflicted the mothers of the patients about whom I am writing, e.g., whether they were basically endogenous depressions reactivated during their son's or daughter's infancy; the more important common feature was that the mothers had suffered a serious personal loss, a bereavement from which it appeared they had not recovered. None of them was hospitalized; the patients each had a far clearer impression of the depressed moods than of any intervening manic ones that there may have been; and the suicide of one of the mothers undoubtedly affected her daughter's life most deeply. The manifestations of depression in the patients themselves will emerge, I think, in the course of the paper.

The following thoughts have become the theme of this paper: too many and too strong negative archetypal images are absorbed by an infant or young child from a depressed mother, most particularly if she is a bereaved woman who is still caught up in her anger and sadness, so that she cannot direct herself towards the baby and genuinely smile into its eyes. Not enough validation of its lovableness is offered to such an infant at the stage in life when that experience is essential for a healthy self-belief to develop, which will be based on enough internal feeling that there is more growth than destructiveness both in itself and in its environment. To alter the attitudes stemming from those early inner and outer pathological experiences, an analytical therapist makes herself available for a relationship to grow within which a number of *coniunctiones* can occur: if, at the level of the objective psyche as manifested in the analyst, there is a well-established *coniunctio* of internal images, and if the patient is able to identify with that inner healer—whose outer scars may still be evident—then what is happening is that both archetypal structuralist concepts and the findings of developmental research are confirmed.

I am not speaking simply about the patient's need to (I quote Jung) kill the symbolic representative of the unconscious, i.e. his own *participation mystique* with animal nature . . . the Terrible Mother who devours and destroys, and thus symbolizes death itself (1912, par. 505).

The patient with a depressed mother does need to emerge from an unconscious identification with his or her mother because of the killing quality of her depression, and needs to cease participating in her anger and sadness. After the passage quoted above, Jung added in brackets:

I remember the case of a mother who kept her children tied to her with unnatural love and devotion. At the time of the climacteric she fell into a depressive psychosis and had delirious states in which she saw herself as an animal, especially as a wolf or pig. . . . In her psychosis she had herself become the symbol of an all-devouring mother.

And, following that clinical vignette he went on:

Interpretation in terms of the parents is, however, simply a *façon de parler*. In reality the whole drama takes place in the individual's own psyche, where the "parents" are not the parents at all but only their imagoes: they are representations which have arisen from the conjunction of parental peculiarities with the individual disposition of the child (*ibid.* par.505).

If for the term *participation mystique* we substitute the words and concepts *unconscious identification* then I can go along with the way Jung used the anthropologist Levy-Bruhl's term. Many writers since Jung have used the concept of *participation mystique* in a more simplistic manner than he in fact did, at least in the passage quoted. And it is regrettable that Levy-Bruhl should have had his phrase overused and distorted, when the perhaps rival psychological concepts of projection, introjection, identification, and the transcendent function really serve us better. Identifying with those structures in the analyst which have developed as a result of her working on instinctual "animal nature" in herself, can and does happen within the therapeutic relationship; projections and introjections can be discerned and described. I think they are marvellous, but not mystical.

The patient with a depressed mother is suffering from a serious narcissistic wound. I hold that such patients benefit greatly—perhaps essentially—from the analyst using to the full a combination of developmental observations and her own internal search for harmony, for *coniunctio*.

From the following brief descriptions of the patients (with fictitious names) it can be seen that the character and quality of their mother's depressive reactions to the loss of either their husbands or an earlier child ran the whole spectrum of possibilities: paranoid, manic, animus-ridden, schizoid, closed, sulky, aggressive, obsessional, and suicidal. Some of these patients made images, or allowed the images to make themselves, easily and early on in their analyses, others with difficulty and only much later. They also varied in their ability to fantasize in the transference, and to dream. Each of them suffered from internal impoverishment.

Anthony

A's father abandoned A's mother when he was very young; the precise age is unknown. This unsupported woman suffered all the rest of her life from a depressive and persecutory reaction to that loss. In addition to having to try to learn to live with such a mother, A (who became my patient in middle age) had certainly inherited some of his father's capacity to opt out of emotional commitments. He was evacuated at the age of six from a large city, with his school, for the duration of World War II, and billeted with several different families, who treated and ill-treated him in various ways. His parental imagoes were of course very confused. He related to other people in as distant a way as possible. Virtually the whole gamut of possibilities reappeared in the transference, from delusional idealization, via distancing coldness, to destructive hatred. Trust and self-confidence grew only slowly, through many discouraging phases.

Belinda

B's father disappeared even earlier in his child's life than did Anthony's; she thinks he was not told she had been born, and he may even not have known she had been conceived. All through her childhood her mother suffered from that, to her, crucial object-loss; it came after other similar losses. As a mother she seems to have been unable to emerge enough from her own narcissistic wounds to offer her daughter (my patient) a reliable self-feeling as a reflector of the child's potential belief in herself. The mother's long-drawn-out self-attacks, sulky depressions and obsessional cleanliness were partly introjected by her daughter and partly defended against; the defensive maneuver was fairly successful, perhaps

as a result of the daughter having inherited from the father what may
have been a self-protective ability to push "the woman" to one side. But
analysis, as it progressed, revealed how very powerful the damaged and
damaging mother still was.

Christine

C was the younger of two children and was in her fourth year when her
parents' marriage broke down in violence, and her mother never forgave
her father for the loss not only of economic support but, more dangerously, of personal happiness. While the mother saw herself as the injured
and wronged one, the father also had in fact been deeply hurt and de-
prived of his children. My patient C grew up with an aggressively depressed mother and an absent, rarely mentioned, unmourned father, for
whom all the same she hankered. C's depression had, for a time, a paranoid quality to it. In her the defenses of the self (Fordham 1974) were
obstinately structured, and early in her analysis she was blocked against
using her imaginative or symbolizing capacities.

Dominic

D's mother had lost her eldest son, when he was aged about eight
months, before D was born, and although there was no factual evidence
that he was a mere "replacement baby," his insistent conviction of hardly
having his own real identity was tenaciously held onto for many years.
His mother's depression was so thoroughly introjected that it acquired a
most powerful melancholic grip on him. He knew a great deal about the
losses of other significant males in his mother's and his maternal grandmother's lives, each of those males having either died suddenly or been
killed in various wars. In analysis the transference projections were intense, violent, cold, envious, and haunting; the countertransference affect was inescapable. But, as in the cases of A and B, he had internal
warmth, which, however strenuously he used his splitting defenses to
ward it off, always came back sooner or later.

Erica

E's mother had had to leave her country of birth and childhood when, as
a teenager, her parents became refugees. This woman apparently never
fully accepted the loss of her mother country: she gave all her children,
E and her brothers and sisters, names that were clearly foreign in the

country of *their* birth, which was in the Antipodes. E could not identify with a mother who was still mourning, everlastingly yearning for the impossible. She came to England. She developed moderate anorexia nervosa; in spite of that somatization of her mother complex she made a fair beginning in analytical therapy. But the shadow of her mother's depression came between her and all attempted relationships with men or women. And my offer of intensifying her analysis, which would have taken it a stage forward, into a deeper commitment, and would have involved the underlying, archetypal structures, led to her abrupt flight to the place where her parents still lived, as far away from me as possible: the other side of the world.

Freddie

F was the first of three children of his mother's second marriage: before that she had twin sons in a marriage which had broken down in a way or from a cause which F never heard mentioned. Her intensely erotic relationship with F when he was a baby and a child, her grousing attitude to life, her constant denigration both of the twins and of F's father and a number of physical ills, probably indicate a long-term depression. There was a mysterious or glamorous other man between the two marriages. She does not seem to have mourned the failure of the first relationship, nor the disappointment over the mystery man, but moaned about her marriage. F was very closely bound to her and decided one day early in puberty that he was a homosexual. He would not move from that decision: it meant to him that he was not an ordinary or banal man like his father, he was going to be extraordinary, his mother's lover. He himself was not a depressed man, but his psychic development was held up by the bond to a mother who had—as far as I could tell—not been able to mourn losses which occurred before F's birth.

In the interests of analytic theory it would be satisfying if it were possible to point to some factor in those people which seems to have made them especially liable to identify with their mothers, and to receive the projection of the mother's damaged self. For example, the stage of the patient's life at which the mothers were bereaved might be significant: but it was not the same for all, e.g., the first year of life, or one of the later developmental stages, such as the oedipal one, when the incest archetype dominates. Then, another possible factor would be personality type; they were all certainly more introverted than extraverted, but in terms of the classical Jungian typology of the four functions I can discern no categorical significance.

Another possibility, to which I incline, but it is a speculative one, is that the characterological feature of both the mother and the father by which each of them was both victim and victimizer had been inherited by the son or daughter, and the component of aggression-passivity led the child to identify with the available parent, namely the mother, in whom the victim-victimizer syndrome had led to depression. That factor would be a somewhat subtle version of the well-known defense of identifying with the aggressor. The theme of identification needs more examination than is possible here, and contributions from several angles, with clinical examples.

Self-Feeling, Narcissistic Deprivation and Depression

Many analytical psychologists have studied both the self in the sense that Jung used the term, and the patient's sense of himself, self-feeling, or self-experience. Moreover, the originally psychoanalytic (Freudian) term, narcissism, is currently used in studies relating to the Jungian self and the primal self, more frequently by analytical psychologists than Jung favored, for example, Ledermann (1982), Gordon (1980), Humbert (1980), Schwartz-Salant (1982), Kalsched (1980) and Jacoby (1981). The study of narcissistic personality disorder is proceeding apace, within a current Jungian frame of reference. Jungians are also making use of Kohut's and Kernberg's post-Freudian observations. My impression, derived from depressed patients in analysis, is that the relation between narcissistic unsatisfaction in infancy and depression in adulthood is extremely close. Further analytical studies of different groups of depressed adults may, if they are undertaken, lead to deeper understanding of exactly how the two kinds of suffering are related.

The depressed patient, whose mother was *not* subject to depression, brings to his analyst pathological material which is principally his own. The one whose mother is known to have been seriously depressed when he was very young will be listened to by an analyst with her ear ready to try to extricate the mother's bad internal self-view from the patient's fantasies about it. There are crosscurrents of identifications which can be navigated successfully, if slowly, through the patient's transference manifestations and the analyst's countertransference self-analysis. It is not just the familiar process of enabling the patient to separate out from his mother and to develop firm but not rigid boundaries between himself and every later representative of that first object, that first partner, but rather it is the task of analyzing his fantasies about his mother's inner life. They cannot be assumed to be totally fantastic, or "merely" subjective. The analyst's familiarity with her own inner life and willingness to use it indirectly in her work will be a major factor in analyzing the patient effectively. She has to be bold, and enough *in* her own residual depression, or depressive phases, and at the same time have good enough boundaries, to distance herself enough from her depressive tendencies so that the patient can use them in the transference—symbolically.

The symbolic attitude and approach (Hubback 1969) to the patient whose mother was depressed brings together the understanding of environmental influence, of developmental studies, and of archetypal disposition. Jung has written that the "appearance of the mother-image at any given time cannot be deduced from the mother archetype alone but depends on innumerable other factors" (1936, par.155). Jung also insisted that "the archetype in itself is empty and purely formal . . . a possibility of representation . . . the representations themselves are not inherited, only the forms, and in that respect they correspond in every way to the instincts, which are also determined in form only" (1936, par.155). The ethologists' theory of internal release mechanisms is in line with that formulation. In another passage Jung wrote: ". . . *the contents of the child's abnormal fantasies* can be referred to the personal mother only in part, since they often contain clear and unmistakable allusions which could not possibly have reference to human beings" (par. 159).

We can also observe normal infants when they are in the grip, early on, of desperate hungry anxiety, infants who gradually grow less anxious and angry when there have been repeated experiences of someone responding to their hungry, demanding, and envious attacks. Working for many months or even years may be necessary with patients who despair of ever becoming free from hatefulness. They feel overfull of hate against the apparently ungiving mother analyst, and overfull of terror that she will hate them for hating her.

The fantasies that such patients have are very extremist. On two separate occasions, with two different patients, I took marginally longer than usual to answer the door-bell when they arrived. One, a woman, said she had, in those instants, imagined me lying on the floor of my room, dead from a heart attack. The other, a man, fantasied that my husband had been killed in a motor accident and I had been called away. On another occasion, a man patient fantasied dying then and there while lying on the couch, of heart failure, which would give me, he hoped, the most difficult situation I had ever had to deal with. That was the day after he had voiced both a grossly idealized description of me, and his miserable envy, saying, "You have a really good, balanced, internal self-feeling, you believe in yourself. I don't." I told him I saw the imagined "heart attack" in the present session as a suicidal fantasy of self-punishment following the envious attack on me of the day before, but that he was also telling me that he was very much alive, to be able to go at me like that, with such attacking hunger. His response was, "Yes! I'll attack and attack, and attack again! I'm very hungry!" The following week, the atmosphere between us changed. The feeling arose in him that there was a "we," and he remembered some of the earlier positive phases of the analysis. He smiled on arrival, ruefully, he grew gentler. And he even managed a joke.

In therapies with such patients it was never any use to skimp on the long process of working through the experiences of unsatisfied narcissism or the images associated with them. Time and again the transference and countertransference projections, when elucidated, showed how the lack of outgoing and positive response of the personal mother had contributed in a major way to the patient having not only a consciously poor self view and an unconsciously grandiose and arrogant one, but an actively negative one. It was when that self-attacking view was in the ascendant that the structures informing the analysis were put to the greatest strain. The patients I am talking about were all either extremely sensitive to even the minutest alteration in externals, such as my appearance, or the contents of the room, or they defended themselves against their sensitivity being apparent. Each of them in his or her own particular way would make use of whatever came to hand to try to demonstrate how inadequately they considered I was treating them and how impossible was any change. Things were as bad as they could be, always had been, and always would be. There was no time any more, only timeless hell. Their very present despair could only be reached with the help of accumulated experiences in the analysis, from which they gradually discovered that change, time, and development do exist. They began to recognize the alternation of hell and heaven. Then, in time, those extremes were modified.

Both patient and analyst have their own personal and actual selves which stem from primal body-experiences of psychosomatic unity. The self is a concept which is the best possible way of referring to the sense of selfhood that each person needs if he is to use, rather than be misled by, what he gets from other people—identifications. He needs to have boundaries, and a sense of those boundaries, before he can identify healthily. If the actual mother fails to grant the infant boundaries, otherness, individuality, and aloneness, as she has not detached herself from the image of another person to whom she was ambivalently overattached, then she ties the infant in a false closeness based on her unconsciously identifying with her own abandoned self that she has projected into the infant. That infant is then grossly overburdened. His mother's angry depression is experienced by him in infancy and childhood as though it were his own capacity to attack, to defeat and to be defeated. Each of us in our original undifferentiated libido has the potential to direct it positively or negatively (experiencing the world as giving us nourishing food or destructive poison, love or hate, life or death, and so on), but the infant whose mother is depressed overdevelops his negative potential. The infant's need to discover the difference between despairing loneliness and positive separateness is not met by a mother who has not achieved it herself. Such a mother offers the infant a model of much more bad than good, as compared with a model (or image) of a person who discovers that the self contains both, and that the loving, constructive, forces can defeat the destructives ones.

Questions Connected with Technique And Countertransference

The problem of where the most powerful source of pathology lies for any particular patient may or may not affect the course of the analysis. How much does it matter whether the analyst gives great weight (in the reflections she does not communicate directly to the patient) to the presumed influence of the mother's unworked-through mourning, or adopts the other course of paying major attention to the patient's autonomous imagery? How much difference does it make to the healing process, to the development of reconciling and integrating forces, to the patient's potential for continued self-analysis and further improvement of personal relationships after he has separated from the analyst, if there has been concentration on one approach to the problem and neglect of the other? Or, is the wisest course to work with no framework of theory at all, no model associated with any group or school?

Only tentative answers can be offered here. Several of the patients produced images of quite exceptional force. But the transference projections were very powerful, whether there was much or little imagery. The mother's unworked-through mourning seemed to me to be still exerting a pathological influence, so that I consider attending to the images on their own is not enough. I observed that the introjected image of a depressed mother became more amenable to analysis at times when I myself either was, or was believed by the patient to be, depressed. The analysis became more stressful. It was important then that I should try to understand which losses or personal failings I had not yet faced, mourned, and accepted. It would be defensive idealization to see myself as fully individuated, or so free from ever being disturbed by personal emotions, that no affect leaked from me to a patient.

Integration of all kinds of shadow material proceeded when I was able to use a combination of intuition, memory and well-tried theoretical concepts to come to something I hoped could be dignified with the name understanding. That is where acquaintance with, and reflection on, other schools of analysis and other arts and sciences can be of great help.

Granting full acknowledgement to powerlessness is very necessary if the analyst is to avoid getting enmeshed in the patient's projective identification. The illusion of omnipotence must be dissolved. Being myself a parent, I find that unhappy or anxious affects in relation to one or other of my children can on occasion intrude and cause me to associate (privately) to a patient's perhaps similar experiences. Usefully, however, I find that they tend to see my professional persona as giving them a convenient experience of me being a sort of father to them. None of those I am speaking about had an effective father—he was either physically or psychologically not available to them. With most of these patients, the father transference has been frequent, necessarily negative at first, gradually or intermittently becoming positive, and useful in both ways. The evidence of dreams and fantasies has, however, accumulated and attacks on the-father-whom-the-mother-had-come-to-hate could be convincingly detected via attacks on me or self-attacks. A male patient's self-attacking actions make me feel angry with myself, as I believe a father does, when he worries about whether he is being a good-enough father to his son.

As a mother in the transference, I find that the countertransference affect, perhaps more frequently experienced than anger, is that of a nearly despairing kind, with predominance of a defensive splitting of affect. One patient in particular had received a great deal of despair projected from her mother, who seems to have been oblivious of her own pathological attitudes. In the mother and the daughter the negative animus was very powerful. In the countertransference, I had phases of losing self-confidence, and at times felt that I was not the right analyst for her.

An adequately functioning partnership within the analyst of libido both from the self and from the ego structures is necessary for treating a patient who is defending against ego development by blanking, which can represent total destruction. I remember the dream of one of my patients: she looked in a mirror and saw no one, nothing. Some time later, she was feeling upset and was talking about my approaching holiday: she described how I "vanish into thin air" when she knows I am away from home. If she cannot make an image of me being in a particular and familiar place, she is imageless. She cannot reconcile terror and hope. The parental imagoes are, in her, not so much negative (e.g., hated or feared or despised) but more dangerously they disappear completely at difficult junctures. I do not know whether they have an existence of their own, so that their disappearance happens *to* her, or whether she has an as yet not fully known anger aganst them so that unconsciously it is she who *makes* them disappear.

From the point of view of the day-to-day work with that patient, my experience is that if I interpret that she is actively blanking and destroying, that feeds her capacity to develop on the ego side and to begin emerging from the dangers attendant upon such imagoes. The central criterion I use is to try to speak within the transference in such a way as to foster her potential for experiencing herself as an individual, subject to certain forces but not entirely at their mercy.

When a patient begins to feel sure of being an individual he will credit the other person with individuality. When the healing process is at work and the old imago of *mater dolorosa* is less in power, and the introjection of her is less strangling, then a reconciling symbol appears in a dream or a fantasy. For example: The dreamer was mixing a drink at a party, for his sister, his wife and his daughters; the drink was made up of milk and semen. Also at the party, in a communicating room, were his professional colleagues.

Some months later I came across the following in "Transformation symbolism in the Mass," in which Jung is explaining a passage in an alchemical text of Simon Magus, who was quoting Hippolytus' *Elenchos*

> It [the divine pneuma] is the very ground of existence, the procreative urge, which is of fiery origin. Fire is related to blood, which is 'fashioned warm and ruddy like fire'. Blood turns into semen in men, and in woman into milk. . . . The operative principle in semen and milk turns into mother and father (1938, par.359).

The dreamer had not read the book.

His dream shows, first, a patient's use of body imagery; second, his desire to reconcile himself and get back into harmony with certain closely related females who usually received various anima projections from him; and third, the desire that there should be a better internal communication than previously in his feelings about himself as the son of his parents, as a family man, and as a worker. There were transference and countertransference features at the time which contributed significantly

to the dream and the combination of those with the symbols in it her-
alded a new phase of development.

The purposive nature of instincts releases healing and creative symbols
since, in the analytical treatment, the patient has been put in touch
with his capacity to connect the conscious mind with growth processes
from the unconscious. It is *his* own capacity: the analyst is the assistant,
similar to the alchemical *soror*.

Attacks of Envy and Envious Attacks

The flow of reconciling symbols is often held up by renewed envious attacks on the analyst. The stage of hungry envy (Hubback 1972), is followed by the second stage of denigratory envy. Sarcasm, scorn, and cyni-
cism are the consulting-room versions of the emotions belonging to the
stage at which "the infant in the patient" is trying to emerge from its
deep-seated fears of another abandonment.

So it happens that there is a new envious attack in a fantasy or a
dream just when it seemed possible that real progress had been achieved.
For example, the absence of my car from its usual place in the street
outside was said to "mean" that I had gone off to enjoy myself with
someone I found more atractive than the patient. Another patient
dreamed that he met me on the doorstep of my house as I departed, most
elegantly dressed, with a high and mighty Afghan hound which bared its
teeth fiercely while I took no notice of him.

The patient who has been enviously attacking the analyst as the present representative of the once-powerful mother gradually comes to recognize the character of the images in such dreams and fantasies, and discovers how to reconcile the warring emotions. Where work with such a
patient is concerned, there is an optimistic passage in Jung's paper entitled, "Concerning the Archetypes with Special Reference to the Anima
Concept": "The projection ceases the moment it becomes conscious,
that is to say when it is seen as belonging to the subject"—but a footnote to that runs as follows:

> There are, of course, cases where, in spite of the patient's seem-
> ingly sufficient insight, the reactive effect of the projection does
> not cease, and the expected liberation does not take place. I have
> often observed that in such cases meaningful but unconscious con-
> tents are still bound up with the projection carrier. It is these con-
> tents that keep up the effect of the projection, although it has ap-
> parently been seen through (1936, par. 121 and footnote).

Conclusion: Mysterium Coniunctionis

The dissociation between spirit and matter, of which Jung wrote a great deal in the last chapter of *Mysterium Coniunctionis*, is comparable—in the inner world of some of the patients described here—to the dissociation between the imagoes of each of the two parents. Other patients could not make contact with any image of loving parents, and less despondent images about life emerged only gradually during their analyses. Early in the paper I used the concept of *coniunctio* to refer to the kind of healed split which I think the therapist of depressed patients should—if possible—be able to offer. My thesis is that, via the transference/countertransference, there can be a carry-over of the psychological possibility of *coniunctio*, from the analyst to the patient. The theme can be worded in the fully Jungian form of granting *coniunctio* archetypal status, so that the constellation of that archetype can be postulated to activate in the patient the capacity to move from dissociation to internal harmony, or integration—the integration of the father and mother imagoes. The analogy of Jung's concern with spirit and matter in *Mysterium Coniunctionis* seems to me to be one which can validly be used, and other writings of his, e.g., "Transformation Symbolism in the Mass," and "The Transcendent Function" also give the background and basis for this theme.

Much work has to be done before the depth and extent of the dissociation is well enough appreciated, which lends weight to Jung's statement that "a *conscious* situation of distress is needed in order to activate the archetype of unity" (1956, par. 772). Then, in the "Epilogue," he enquires whether the psychologist can throw out the antagonistic forces, or whether he had not better "admit their existence . . . bring them into harmony and, out of the multitude of contradictions, produce a unity, which naturally will not come of itself, though it may—*Deo concedente*—with human effort" (par. 791).

I have often been struck by just that—the great and total "human effort" that the patient puts into the therapeutic work at this difficult stage. He or she is often in a renewed state of depression, angry and sore, or again in an ambivalent mood towards me. The affect in dreams and fantasies is either painful, or split off. One patient, for example, who was recovering from a serious schizoid depression, dreamed of the parental pair in a car, under which there was a smouldering fire, perhaps a bomb, and the dreamer/son saved them just before the fuel tank blew up. Presence of mind—ego capacity—was required of him, as well as a warmth of feeling toward his parents. The dreams of a woman patient over many months grew around images of the limitless sea and then other kind of water, with a gradual diminution of boundlessness, of isolation, of nameless terrors, and a steady growth of pictures in which some focus of safety was perceptible, places or situations where there were square enclosures or encircled areas, a potential coming-together, a possible *conciunctio*. Many months later, the images were again of a vast sea, greyness going on for ever. A renewed and strenuous effort had to be undertaken. Although the sea had no boundaries, there was fish pâté in a bowl on her kitchen table, ready to be made into sandwiches: bread from the earth, fish from the sea, a modern *coniunctio*.

The *coniunctio* and harmonization of internal imagoes is unlikely to take place if the analyst does not find the right combination within herself of responsiveness and self-boundaries. If she can keep her sense of self she will be able to become the internal representative of the union of the opposing pair. Unless she can respond from out of her own sense of healed self, the imagoes do not come together well enough for the patient's healing to be soundly enough based.

The last chapter of *Mysterium Coniunctionis* is a mine of wealth. For example, "The adept produces a system of fantasies that has a special meaning for him" (par.694). "The alchemists called their *nigredo* melancholia, 'a black blacker than black' night, an affliction of the soul, confusion, etc." (par. 791). "It was . . . of the utmost importance to him [the adept] to have a favourable familiar as a helper in his work." That "familiar" analyst knows in herself that *nigredo, mortificatio, separatio* and *divisio* precede *coniunctio*. The illustrations from the *Rosarium Philosophorum* and the use Jung made of them in "The psychology of the transference" (Jung 1946) are not always easy to connect in a living way with clinical material. Their initial impact can be one of major fascination, which is of little use in day-to-day work. When they, and Jung's other studies of the psychology of alchemy are returned to—perhaps again and again with personal development having taken place in the meantime—then the possibility grows of applying them in understanding clinical interactions with patients whose experience of parental imagoes has contributed substantially to splitting defenses.

Mysterium Coniunctionis uses much material from alchemists living, broadly, at the same period as those men studied by the historian Frances Yates, whose works are now essential companions for students of Jung's work on alchemy. Most of those men were written about by both authors: they include Ramon Lul, Marsilio Ficino, Pico della Mirandola, Cornelius Agrippa, Paracelsus, Giordano Bruno, John Dee, Christian Rosencreutz, and Robert Fludd. The search for harmony was the driving force behind many of the deep thinkers of the fifteenth, sixteenth and seventeenth centuries, men in turbulent public life as well as philosophers. The parallel between the archetypal yearnings for harmony and the researches of the alchemists gives added significance to the internal search for *coniunctio* of depressed patients. It happens to give me personally much interest and encouragement when I find the main lines of observations, thoughts, and intuitions being followed in several arts and sciences. At the same time the differences between them must be taken into account, analogies must not be overworked and there is also the danger of falling into the simplistic view that "history repeats itself."

The reconciling symbols have to be the alive ones for each of us. A particular patient may have no inclination whatsoever to make a living connection with the mythologies, or the periods of history or the particular arts which appeal to his analyst. Detailed descriptions of the clinical use of amplification would perhaps help those analysts who are chary of introducing their own cultural associations, who fear they might prevent the development of the patient's own imagery, or interfere with its potential flow. I do not think I have helped patients forward significantly when I have tried amplifying openly. It is rather, I find, that the implicit offering of a concentrated extract (so to speak) of my attempted inner harmonization, and of the work done so far on splitting and other defenses, will be what the depressed patient who was once the child of a depressed mother will feed off and make his own. It is the psychology of conjunction which has to be understoood and appreciated.

Summary

The hypothesis is offered that patients whose mothers were depressed during their infancy and childhood may be enabled to emerge from their own long-term depressions (or other consequences of early emotional difficulties) if in the therapy they are able to make use of their analyst's having achieved a reasonably viable sense of self, based on the internal *coniunctio of parental* imagoes. Transference and countertransference manifestations of the workings of malign imagoes and of the gradual emergence of benign and uniting symbols in fantasies and dreams are given in relation to the therapies of six patients.

It is suggested, implicitly, that current observations and studies of narcissistic deprivation, splitting defenses, shadow material and hungry and envious attacks can be usefully furthered if they are related to Jung's exploration of the theme of *coniunctio* as having been the main psychological importance of alchemy.

References

Fordham, M. 1974. Defenses of the Self. *Journal of Analytical Psychology* 19:2.

Gordon, R. 1980. Narcissism and the Self: Who am I That I Love? *Journal of Analytical Psychology* 25:3.

Hubback, J. 1969. The Symbolic Attitude in Psychotherapy. *Journal of Analytical Psychology* 14:1 (Chapter 1 of this book).

————. 1972. Envy and the Shadow. *Journal of Analytical Psychology* 17:2 (Chapter 8 of this book).

Humbert, E. 1980. The Self and Narcissism. *Journal of Analytical Psychology* 25:3.

Jacoby, M. 1981. Reflections on Heinz Kohut's Concept of Narcissism. *Journal of Analytical Psychology* 26:1.

Jung, C. G. 1912. *Symbols of Transformation*. In *Collected Works*, 5.

————. 1936. Concerning the Archetypes with Special Reference to the Anima Concept. In *Collected Works*, 9/i.

————. 1938. *Psychology and Religion*. In *Collected Works*, 11.

————. 1946. The Psychology of the Transference. In *Collected Works*, 16.

————. 1956. *Mysterium Coniunctionis*. In *Collected Works*, 14.

Kalsched, E. 1980. Narcissism and the Search for Interiority. *Quadrant* 13:2.

Ledermann, R. 1982. Narcissistic Disorder and its Treatment. *Journal of Analytical Psychology* 27:4.

Schwartz-Salant, N. 1982. *Narcissism and Character Transformation*. Toronto: Inner City Books.

Chapter 10

Reflections on the Psychology of Women

The sex of anyone who writes about feminine psychology has been thought relevant for a long time. Jung expressed that opinion when, as a man, he wrote:

> The elementary fact that a person always thinks another's psychology is identical with his own effectively prevents a correct understanding of feminine psychology (1927, p. 116).

The same observation was made by the woman psychoanalyst Karen Horney:

> It is only right and reasonable that [men analysts] should evolve more easily a masculine psychology and understand more of the development of men than of women (1926, p. 324).

She opened, in that paper, a new phase in the long discussion that has been going on ever since in the publications of psychoanalysts, on the central problem of the extent to which anatomical differences and genital development affect the psychology of men and women. She rather mildly remarked that her

> intention in this paper was to indicate a possible source of error arising out of the sex of the observer, and by so doing to take a step forward toward the goal that we are all striving to reach: to get beyond the subjectivity of the masculine or the feminine standpoint and to obtain a picture of the mental development of woman that will be more true to the facts of her nature—with its specific qualities and its differences from that of man—than any we have hitherto achieved (p. 239).

Originally published in *The Journal of Analytical Psychology* 23 (1978), pp. 175–85.

Books and papers by analytical psychologists on matters connected with feminine psychology have also appeared over the years; I will mention by name only a few which seem to me most characteristic of the breadth of study that has been done: Emma Jung's (1957) *Animus and anima*, Ester Harding's (1935) *Women's Mysteries*, Neumann's (1955) *The Great Mother*, and June Singer's (1977) *Androgyny*.

The topics of the father and the mother archetypes, of the anima and the animus, of intersexual envies, of feminine masochism and masculine sadism, of bisexuality, of homosexuality, of gender identity, of the creativity of men and women, of destructive forces, and of spirituality, have all been discussed extensively and valuably. Taking into account the different approaches which are revealed in the papers collected in *Psychoanalysis and women* (Miller 1973) and in the collection, *Female sexuality* (Blum 1977), and my personal reading of many of the writings of analytical psychologists on femininity, I think there are three major and complementary themes, or problems (1) is anatomy destiny? (2) can there by a scientifically valid discussion of clinical material which leaves aside social and cultural factors? and, (3) what really is the nature of woman?

This paper is a description of one woman analyst's tentative exploration of those allied themes, in the context of a present-day practice which includes no patients who are extraordinary, either clinically or in the eyes of society.

Cultural and Social Considerations

One of the most important strands in the twentieth-century women's emancipation movement has always been to work towards a fuller recognition by society of women's multiple and varied potentialities. The early struggle for the franchise stressed what now seems so obvious, that with education they could become citizens with rights as well as duties and responsibilities. Political emancipation was followed by a new phase, when those who worked for society's full acceptance of women's potential had to pause, as it were, so that those women who bore children and brought up families could have their physical difference from men understood psychologically. That stage was at first seen by "progressives" as reactionary, and it took nearly a generation for it to become clear that equality between the sexes in some material areas, such as the political, was best developed as equivalence in other areas and at certain stages of life—especially the reproductive. We have perhaps now reached the time when the gains of the previous phases can make the next step less difficult, namely the elucidation of what are the psychological similarities and what are the differences between the sexes.

Note added to the earlier text:
On the theme of equivalence *versus* equality, I could refer to my book, *Wives Who Went to College* (Hubback 1957), which described and commented on my research into the lives, occupations and views of almost 1200 married university women and 420 socially similar nongraduates. The final chapter was entitled "Wife, Mother, and Self," and it contains in outline much that forms the basis of my present views. The book preceded the work of the Women's Liberation Movement writers. It was less of a fighting book than any of theirs: I was using (in now old-fashioned terms) the pen rather than the sword. Since then also there has been a large number of analytical books and papers on the animus and on the psychology of women, including ones in which the personality traits in modern girls and women can have light thrown on them by studying ancient goddesses.

It seems to me to have always been implicit, whenever individuation was being discussed, that it was being considered for both women and men. Yet is it identical? If we accept the truism that in analysis we work towards individuation, we have to take into account that that involves integrating the manifestations of the maximum possible number of archetypal representations in order to achieve a good cooperation between ego and self. Two thoughts arise; one is that the animus and the anima correspond the one to the other, but differ somewhat; and the second thought is that collective attitudes in society about men and women are partly unconscious and it is the open challenging of them that is leading to changes. Those are precisely the changes which are syntonic with the work of individual analysis.

When listening, when interacting (within the limits set by the analytical structure), and interpreting with the intention of facilitating development and individuation, when evaluating the dynamics of the transference and the countertransference—at all those times I find it is well worth having at the back of my mind some knowledge of literature, history, art, mythology, anthropology and the human sciences in general; they are there in a kind of reservoir. Information and associations from those fields yield analogies which go some way, and on occasions go a long way, towards understanding what is happening in the present (Hubback 1973). To an analytical psychologist the principal use of such anal-

ogies from the past, and from other places in the world, is in determining which archetypal relationship is currently being aroused and
experienced in the transference, with reference to other past and present
life events and internal imagoes. When there is a physical shiver in the
patient who is speaking of her mother who committed suicide, or when
my blood runs cold at the intensity of the paranoid fantasies being revealed, or when genital arousal occurs in me, unconsciously intended by
the young man patient who is the son in the transference—on such varied occasions memories of the vicissitudes of the House of Atreus and the
agony of the King-at-arms in "La belle dame sans merci" add to my certainty that the parental and the sexual archetypes are in action. But I
doubt whether a patient who has a homosexual "marriage" and who
wears a wedding ring, would benefit if I were drawn into weighing up
current sociological and cultural factors as compared with purely psychological ones.

It is most valuable, in my opinion, for the analyst to know the facts
about the twentieth-century women's movements in various parts of the
world and to appreciate the general climate of opinion. Yet those contemporary facts need to be known and understood no less in treating
men than in treating women, as men are deeply affected also. They are
as important in observing the form that the male patient's anima problem takes, and the changes it undergoes during analysis, as in tracing the
development of animus formations in women. Behind and within the
current cultural forms lie the much more basic features of the nature of a
woman, and the nature of a man's relation to her. During the analyses
of many women I find a great anxiety is revealed about whether the
twentieth-century enlargement of life and of opportunities—on the face
of it "good"—is not bringing into play some deep danger which may
threaten something which they know belongs intrinsically to them: and
they are afraid of the attacking and counterattacking forces in themselves.

That "something" is their sense of their own nature, which is made up
partly of their femaleness, their sexuality (whether that is as yet unful-
filled, or has been distorted, or is part of a satisfactory relationship), and
partly of feminine gender identity. Both those constituents of being a
woman are complicated.

There will be no attempt in this paper to describe or discuss the various aspects of sexuality which can be found (at least where "5940 white
females" in the USA are concerned) in Sexual Behavior in the Human Female (Kinsey et al. 1953), and in Human Sexual Response (Masters &
Johnson, 1966). The large scale of both those research reports gives re-

sults which are in a different category from any in which a practitioner of analytical psychology such as myself can partake. An analyst is in a position to offer individual material which she thinks illustrates tellingly several important themes in the matter of gender and feminine identity, where evaluations, feelings, and the more purely psychological factors operate. There is no possibility of quantification, but presentation and discussion will be attempted.

I hope that what has been said so far makes it clear that the clinical illustrations given later in this paper have been extracted from the analyses of women who are living in the current cultural climate, which is sufficiently well-known not to need description—and there is no question of disregarding it. But my observations lead me to think that that liberalizing climate has not done away with the fundamental intrapsychic conflicts which, if they remain unconscious, not only affect but sadly vitiate interpersonal relations. It is possible that the conflicts clustering round the early mother-infant interactions, those connected with the child's first achievement of unit status, those of rivalry with the parent of the same sex and all the incestuous and oedipal struggles, the envies of siblings and of sexual partners, are becoming fairly easy for the contemporary analyst and patient to reach and to experience in the transference, and the countertransference, thanks to the emancipation of women from many inhibitions in their material, their emotional, and their instinctual lives. That should mean that the analysis of a woman stands a better chance now of facilitating individuation than it used to. There is no way of satisfactorily assessing such matters, so opinions and estimates remain subjective.

Psychological Considerations

Gender identity in a woman who is biologically female is achieved in the setting of childhood environment and depends very largely on the psychological attitudes of the adults in the child's life. It is those adult attitudes and the extent to which there are depressed or disturbed people about, which effectively produce the feeling-tone of whatever actual vicissitudes occur—illnesses, separations and deaths in particular—and contribute in an essential manner to the type and quality of gender identity. My first clinical theme is extracted from the analyses of two women patients who were brought up exclusively by women. I have changed their names.

Geraldine's mother developed pulmonary tuberculosis before the baby was born, and from earliest infancy she was looked after by her maternal grandmother, who kept her father at bay. When the mother had to be hospitalized Geraldine was allowed infrequent visits to her, but these ceased when she was about five without any explanation being given. She was encouraged to write letters to her regularly, but cannot remember being puzzled about receiving no answers. Several years later she discovered that her mother had died at the time when she was no longer allowed to visit her. The grandmother was in some ways a good figure in her life, but she was also someone who kept her very young and who overprotected her from pain and mourning. By the time Geraldine came to analysis her inability to relate emotionally or sexually to a man was very firmly established. My patient believed the grandmother saw her daughter's death as caused by the man making her bear a child when she had tuberculosis, so Geraldine's father was seen as being kept out of her emotional life by the grandmother's hate rather than by any material circumstance. That hatred of the father contributed to the fear Geraldine revealed during analysis, that she had been *bad* for her mother, had caused her illness and her death, for which silence was the punishment. When she was hating and wishing to punish me she was effectively silent by simply not coming to the next session. There was no experience of childhood incest fantasies and no liberating of the locked-in heterosexuality. In her relationships with women she invariably tried to be the powerful and phallic mother-partner, yet envied them being more "womanly" than she was.

Xenia had even less experience than Geraldine of an actual man during childhood. Her mother brought her as a baby to live in her own mother's house. The grandmother (who was a widow) was the effective mother, and the real mother seems to have been experienced internally as a criticized "father" for whom Xenia developed no affection whatever. Her grandmother's incapacitating illness, and her mother's later life confirmed Xenia in her belief of having to look after herself. Where her case differed from that of Geraldine lay in the fact that there was a "father" (in the form of her real mother) to hate, rather than an absence, for whom no such emotion can be felt. Her strong physical aversion for her "father" led her in the transference to experience me at times as the father with whom she was terrified of coming into contact, for fear of incest; at other times I seemed to her to be the longed-for and idealized symbiotic mother, and if there occurred anything to upset her then, she believed a disaster was imminent.

Discussion of the Cases of Geraldine and Xenia

Where two of the questions posed earlier are concerned, whether anatomy is destiny and wherein lies the nature of a woman, the cases of

Geraldine and Xenia are of some use. As neither had a father in infancy and childhood (the one emotionally, and the other actually as well as emotionally), they were living entirely in the woman's world in all its primitivity and intensity. Both had the dual-mother to contend with, to add to the difficulties caused by the lack of a male. There was a certain amount of masculinity to which to relate, although it was concealed within the mothers and grandmothers, and that resulted in the development of mainly unhelpful, negative, animus formations. There was very little possibility of experiencing the positive version of the animus, which could then have been internalized. That feature was even less satisfactory in Geraldine's life experience than in Xenia's and my impression is that Geraldine's homosexual life in adulthood, in contrast to Xenia leading a heterosexual life, was due to the more serious malformation of animus structures in Geraldine. In her sexual life she could not relate positively to the animus.

Xenia had a more comfortable sense of herself as a woman than had Geraldine. Although she knew rationally that her birth had very materially altered her mother's life she seemed to be free from undue anxiety about having been *bad* for her mother when she was an infant. She was emotionally able to have children, whereas Geraldine was not. Her internal woman-imago was not so excessively persecutory as Geraldine's; she was able to progress from the stage of experiencing the elemental mother archetype in projection to the second and developed, creative, great mother (Neumann 1955). Her capacity to relate to the physically protective mother archetype was there before analysis started, which meant that in the transference she could rely on a well-articulated use of me, as representing womanhood at various stages.

In contrast, Geraldine's internal woman-imago was virginal. Xenia feared an incestuous contact with me-father, but I felt she really was female and feminine precisely in having that fear. Geraldine took no account of such a fear, or taboo. Interplay between her and me was, at various times, that of the close mother and daughter who exclude all male and masculine elements, or that of two sisters who are (mysteriously to me) not yet rivals for any man whatever.

Anatomy was, to a considerable extent, destiny for both those women patients. They each at first identified with the parent (the grandmother in Xenia's case) of the same sex as themselves who was not living in visible relationship with a member of the other sex. Their experience of the single-sex family determined the kind of grown-up woman each became. Whereas Geraldine remained—which perhaps means she was destined to remain?—in the primitive homosexual world of preheterosexual women, Xenia moved on to the next stage and was able to live in rela-

tion to her husband, to children of both sexes and to a wide circle of
friends. Her destiny was to suffer serious depressive moods; the dynamics
of depressive self-attacks had, in themselves less to do with her anatomical femaleness than with masculine and feminine archetypal structures.
Taking those structures to be what a Jungian means by "the nature" of
anyone, I think it was less her nature as a woman that was attacked during depressions than her sense of self. With Geraldine, in contrast, I
think it was the other way round.

Femininity, Creativeness, and Destructiveness

[Throughout this section the author is using the term "creativeness" in the sense of "the ability to create." It becomes the ability
to link and to symbolize. The term "creativity" is used as meaning
"the activity of creating." Creativeness is expressed in the various
forms that creativity takes.]

The attempt to throw light on what is the nature of woman includes
considering the problem of whether the forces of creativeness and destructiveness operate in men and women equally, or with different energy charges, or in different areas of life. Looking for two suitable clinical
cases with which to explore those themes has proved difficult, possibly
because the subject is so vast and I am trying to discuss only the aspect of
it which is comparative and relevant. Should on the one hand a mother,
and on the other an artistic man be described, which would probably
"show" that the female physically makes children and the male com-
poses, paints or writes—and perhaps each is envious of the other's creativeness? An alternative criterion would be to select and contrast one or
several dreams of a patient I experience as typically male and masculine,
with some dreamed by a woman patient. No one else but myself would
be able to say whether I had selected in a fair manner. But as I am trying
to solve the problem of evidence without opting for "mere" subjective
impressions and generalizations, it has to be admitted that I find it in-
soluble.

There is no difficulty whatever in adducing a particular dream to demonstrate that the dreamer had been creative in the simplest sense of having brought something new into existence—the dream also is unique
and could only have been dreamed by that particular person at that
time. Similarly, the small child who suddenly connects two previously
separate objects to ideas and produces a new one, has the experience of
creativeness which is essentially the same as when the sperm fertilizes

the ovum and a new person results. The difference is that the child is pleased and that is observable. Neither of the above examples (the dreamer and the child) has to be male or female to be creative.

Among my patients, one man and one woman have been conspicuous producers of dreams. Each is in fact a creative person in personal and professional ways; that is, they are both parents and both psychologically skilled at discerning connections, links of all kinds, symbols of integration and the primary patterns which have an ordering effect in the inner life. Their range of action differs, but I would be hard put to decide whether the most fundamental element in that woman's creativeness is that she is a woman who has borne and raised several children, and that the comparable element in the man is not that he has fathered children but that he is artistically developed. The extreme form of that way of approaching the problem of creativeness is to point out that in all history there are many more men geniuses than women; to which some people find it easy to retort that the subjection of women has been the operative cause of that result, so that they have been confined to expressing their creativeness in the production of children and in personal relationships. Genius in the dictionary sense of "extraordinary capacity for imaginative creation, original thought, invention or discovery" is infrequent in men and extremely infrequent in women. I submit that ordinary creativeness, in its essentials and irrespective of social and cultural factors, is found in women just as much as in men. It is in the manner of expressing, or acting on, creativeness that there is a great difference.

Creativeness as an ability and a function can fruitfully be discussed by analysts insofar as we study and (with some patients) modify and increase, the capacity to connect and integrate. With a patient of whichever sex who reestablishes lost connections with split-off portions of the psyche, the analyst has successfully mobilized the integrative way of functioning. I cannot as an analyst find any evidence showing that in women creativeness is principally biological in its nature and in men is of a different kind. The function that is creativeness operates in men and in women. The ways it operates are often very different. It is most satisfactory to leave the discussion of creative actions and productions to such other specialists as the art philosopher (Langer 1951, 1953) and the polymath (Koestler 1964). The analyst's contribution comes from experience of the unconscious areas of the mind. The capacity to perceive possible links, to dream in such a way as demonstrates the symbolic, bridge-building, function in a man or a woman's inner world, to integrate within the ego features which were previously out of reach in the self or in its constituent archetypal images—those are the manifestations of creativeness that as analysts we liberate in the patient who is not too defensively protected against newness, change, and development.

Destructive impulses work in the opposite direction from the creative ones, and they are conceptualized as having much in common. It is usual for any integrative and creative experience to be felt as good and exciting, and the "going to pieces" one to be bad and terrifying. A patient whom I will call Helen, who believes that she wore down the patience of her previous analyst and that several months in a psychiatric hospital with twenty ECTs were the resultant punishment, is beginning to tolerate her fearful experiences of fragmentation when she is reminded of her own creations, the images she has made during and between sessions. When I can, in that way, give them back to her, which convinces her that she has actually made them and that I have appreciated them (which confirms their existence), she discovers that the destructive going-to-pieces is followed by a coming together.

Lisa, another woman patient, is frightened about being "such a fighter"—she has associations which are meant to prove to me that fighting is about aggression and that is *bad*, about being an overpowerful woman, enviously emasculating her husband, bossing her children, destroying the happiness of family life, and trying to deploy her omnipotence in her analysis. When she comes to see that those associations all illustrate the negative ways of action of an intrinsically neutral force or energy, she finds she can go over to understand that most of the time she is fighting for an improvement in her self-feeling, and that such fighting against other people as she still does can gradually be subordinated to the renewal and recreation of a very valuable woman.

Lisa describes the combination of ecstasy and terror in a good intercouse: "If he goes on a moment longer I shall explode!" and "I'm going to die, I'm dying." Making love and the terror of disintegration go together. Rosemary Gordon (1978) has explored death and creativity in a recent publication.

The Animus Archetype

The contrasexual archetype as concepts, and also their dynamics, have been studied by many analysts since the first tentative formulation of them by Jung in 1916, in *The structure of the unconscious* (1934). It was a work he revised several times and the definitive version appeared in 1934; the anima was further described in *Psychological types* (1921) and the animus was also given some attention there—this present paper contains no recapitulation of any of those findings, which are well documented. It is now acceptable, I think, to point out that Jung's description of the animus was conditioned and bounded by his culture and his period, as well as by his sex, which he himself acknowledged, as referred to above (p. 135). The psychology of what he, and also Emma Jung, wrote about the animus is still valid, even if the sociological aspect and coloration now seem dated, perhaps most particularly to women (Singer 1977). The perspective today presumably contains the bias caused by current attitudes. The imagery by which the archetype is experienced is invariably both of its own time and yet somehow beyond time and even repetitive.

Wishing to confine myself to observations made during clinical encounters with the images of the powerful animus and to eschew the generalizations which are all too easy to reiterate, there are two principal things to say.

The first is that a major indication of the nature of the animus is offered when a patient is displaying omnipotence and, so to speak, bringing up big guns to prove her point, trying hard to argue and fight, trying to demolish me by tearing to pieces (as happened recently for example) something she has discovered I have written (my "creation"). She is aping the denigratory and destructive male who is envious of me having had a "child." That situation occurred during a phase in analysis when she felt angry and sore that her efforts to get me to say that I loved her were being frustrated, and she was unable to appreciate the symbolic quality in the analysis which I believed could potentially develop. The desire for greater masculine-type power, and the inability to appreciate her own feminine kind of it, are components of the psyche of the animus-possessed woman. The working through of that stage in analysis is inherently interesting for a woman analyst who is constantly needing to watch out for indications of persistent (or renewed) animus difficulties in herself.

The second observation I wish to make about the workings of the contrasexual archetypes, and the analysis of them, is that the animus-ridden woman patient and the ordinarily masculine man patient both use denial as their most favored defense against ontological anxiety, or anxiety stemming from the self. Correspondingly, the anima-gripped man and the feminine woman most often use self-attacking depression as a defense: he feels attacked by a force stemming from his inferior side and goes "down" to try to meet it, and she, when doubting her personal identity and worth, falls into depression also. In clinical work with any patients like the four different ones referred to here, the analysis of the attack yields favorable results, especially when the transference projections

offer themselves as aides to the analyst. The attacking which is an essential feature of sadistic fantasies, and the being-attacked which is the
hallmark of masochistic ones, can be understood, tolerated and worked
through when the aggressive component in both denial and depression is
acknowledged.

During the analysis of either anima or animus manifestations, the analyst who feels comfortable enough about having integrated his or her
own contrasexual characteristics reasonably well is able to set going the
growth of a similar internal trust in the patient. The harshness of the
animus-woman on the one hand, and the flabbiness of the anima-man
on the other, become firmness which is valid for both.

As well as that process which shows the similarity between men's and
women's difficulties, I would like to point to a difference between men
and women which I think stems from a basic and natural source. The
nearer someone is to the feminine end of the spectrum of psychsexuality,
the more she is capable of the mother-type behaviour of being available
when wanted: "the other" to her very easily becomes "the infant," and
she is drawn towards trying to meet its needs. The nearer someone is
to the masculine end of the spectrum, the more readily he finds it in
himself to distinguish between the occasions when he can respond, and
those when it is impossible. He knows how to absent himself and confidently leave her.

Summary

This paper is an attempt to separate the psychological factors from all
others in the discussion of what is the nature of woman. Cultural and social considerations are given the place which the author thinks suitable
for modern analytical therapy. There follows a section where two clinical
cases are presented and discussed, women whose fathers played almost no
part in their upbringing, in order to illustrate typical difficulties in establishing a hetero-sexual adult life. Creativeness is discussed, distinguishing
between that as the intrapsychic ability to link and symbolize, which
members of both sexes can do, and the expression or activity of creating,
in which differences are evident. A final section touches on some animus and anima manifestations and the author sees those archetypal
structures as the most productive area for studying the psychological nature of women and of men, and their ways of relating to each other.

References

Blum, H. P. ed. 1977. *Female Sexuality: Contemporary Psychoanalytic Views*. New
York: International Universities Press.

Gordon, R. 1978. *Dying and Creating: A Search for Meaning.* London: Society of Analytical Psychology.

Harding, M. E. 1935. *Women's Mysteries.* London: Longman.

Horney, K. 1926. The Flight from Womanhood: the Masculinity Complex as Viewed by Men and by Women. *International Journal of Psycho-Analysis* 7.

Hubback, J. 1957. *Wives Who Went to College.* London: Heinemann.

———. 1973. Uses and Abuses of Analogy. *Journal of Analytical Psychology* 18:2 (Chapter 6 of this book).

Jung, C. G. 1921. *Psychological Types.* In *Collected Works,* 6.

———. 1927. Woman in Europe. In *Collected Works,* 10.

———. 1934. The Relations Between the Ego and the Unconscious. In *Collected Works,* 7.

Kinsey, A.C., Pomeroy, W.B., Martin, C.E., Gebhard, P.H. 1953. *Sexual Behavior in the Human Female.* Philadelphia & London: Saunders.

Koestler, A. 1964. *The Act of Creation.* London: Hutchinson.

Langer, S. 1951. *Philosophy in a New Key.* London: Oxford University Press; New York: Mentor.

———. 1953. *Feeling and Form.* London: Routledge & Kegan Paul.

Masters, W.H. & Johnson, V.E. 1966. *Human Sexual Response.* Boston: Little, Brown.

Miller, J.B. ed. 1973. *Psychoanalysis and Women.* Harmondsworth: Penguin.

Neumann, E. 1955. *The Great Mother.* London: Routledge & Kegan Paul.

Singer, J. 1977. *Androgyny: Towards a New Theory of Sexuality.* London: Routledge & Kegan Paul; New York: Doubleday, 1976.

Chapter 11

The Assassination of Robert Kennedy: Patients' and Analysts' Reactions

The impact of the news of the assassination of Robert Kennedy on June 5, 1968, and of his death the following day, was the subject of a small *ad hoc* piece of research among analytical psychologists practicing, and at work, in London at the time. From the unpredictable nature of the event it is evident that the method adopted could not be planned in advance: it grew spontaneously from the positive responses of all the analysts with whom I was able to get in touch on June 6 and 7. These contacts were by telephone, and the greater number of those who had any appropriate material to contribute did so in writing shortly thereafter.

The response to the initial individual suggestion was a collective one. This brief paper makes use, with acknowledgements, of their experiences as well as of mine, but they are not responsible for such deductions or interpretations as follow, because it was not possible to do enough work on the matter for a joint report to be produced. The inquiry elicited material bearing on individual and collective reactions to the act of violence, and on some aspects of countertransference. It might turn out to be a pilot project for similar inquiries into the impact of unpredictable events on analyses, not necessarily requiring a large numer of participants or elaborate research techniques.

The idea arose in my mind from noticing how much the analytic hours with two very different patients were affected by the news of the attack on June 5, and another one on June 6, and I found myself irresistibly wondering whether other analysts' experiences had been similar and whether, within the necessary limits of confidentiality, they would be willing to record and to communicate them, either partially or fully.

The analytic sessions involved were limited to those taking place on three days only—June 5, 6 and 7. There was at the time no thought of publication. The central intention was to discover any analytic facts oc-

Originally published in *The Journal of Analytical Psychology* 15 (1970).

curing on those days which might have been exceptional in character, while they were still very fresh, and to try to compare experiences in order to see what emerged.

Although there were no foregone conclusions, there were in my mind from the outset a number of bases from which thoughts sprang, and these were apparently personal only. Their general or collective quality and aspects only emerged after contact with several other analysts had thrown light on them. Owing to childhood, university, and later experiences, I am interested in historical and international affairs—as are millions of other people, of course. Here already were individual and general, or collective, facts. Patients' violent acts, or fantasies, intentions, thoughts, wishes, or fears are daily matters for their analysts, and their own aggressive impulses are also essential factors to take into account, all being miniature examples of rampant violence in the world outside. Analysts usually try to recognize their affects and to avoid uninvestigated countertransference phenomena. So it seemed to me from the outset of this inquiry that the analyst's part, in the manner that the assassination affected any analytic session, was certain to be relevant, even if it were difficult to analyze satisfactorily the anxieties and defenses involved. The aim, which in the circumstances was only partially achieved, was to study particular experiences to see what matters of general validity emerged, with the assumption that these would have a significant bearing on analysts' countertransference problems and on the relationship, within an analysis, between individual and collective unconscious factors.

Collective Psychology

Where collective psychology is concerned, the first thing to record is that the greater number of those analysts approached, who had had patients mentioning the assassination even if only minimally, were willing to follow up the suggestion of studying the matter. Even if they did not find themselves, for whatever reason, able to take part in a joint inquiry, or if they had found that all their patients were currently so engrossed in their own personal problems as not to make any reference to the assassination, they welcomed the idea in principle. Defensiveness on the part of those approached was therefore not noticeable, and I think it is possible to ascribe this to a collaborative reaction to a collectively experienced act of violence, although the event took place in a foreign country. It is also to be surmised that they saw it as only a little more than an extension of a single analyst's study of analytic material and the subsequent communication of it to colleagues.

A further collective feature is that the assassination was an event of which virtually everybody could be assumed to have heard by at any rate June 6, and they were bound to know that others also did, except in the case of patients living very withdrawn lives. Apart from the themes of violent attack and death, this common knowledge of it was an aspect which made it particularly suitable for a collective inquiry. Any patient who was aware of it having happened would probably assume the analyst also did. Patients' particular reactions to this fact of sharing something with their analyst would be as variable as the number of patients, and, according to the current ego state and capacity for reality testing, might include a wide spectrum of accuracy about the analyst's supposed reactions and the likelihood of his or her divulging them.

In telephone conversations with the analysts who participated in the inquiry, it was apparent that most of them felt that other violent public events which had cumulatively and obviously preceded Robert Kennedy's assassination, whether in time only or possibly in cause also—the killing of President Kennedy and of Martin Luther King, the Arab-Israeli War of June 1967—would be assumed to be known to patients, and this led several of us to comment on how few had mentioned it in comparison with what they had expected. "I thought, my God, aren't you going to mention it?" was the way this was expressed.

Retrospectively, this can be seen to be an expectation held somewhat irrespective of the particular patient, and to be the analyst's own affective reaction and the examination of it belongs more accurately under the heading of countertransference than in connection with collective psychology. Some patients were thought by their analysts to have avoided mentioning the assassination, either consciously or unconsciously, as a result of their sophistication as analysands and it is possible that, if that were so, it occurred in response to the patient's fantasied view of the analyst only wanting to hear individual material. There was an instance, in my experience, of a patient not mentioning, at the time of its occurring, an event of such outstanding collective significance because of (as yet unanalysed) wish to be superior to the common run of people.

Another reaction of a collective kind was for analysts to welcome the possibility of discussion with colleagues as we felt so alone with the amount of violence which the news of the assassination had released in one or more of our patients. I include this among aspects of the collectivity because I believe it to be the concentrated individual version of the communal experience of suddenly being shaken into a new, frightening, lonely psychic area by the fact of a man being murdered in the view of so many people who were powerless to save him. The analyst has to try to hold the patient, whether we interpret currently-experienced violent feelings as stemming from raging hate, raging hunger, or in any other way which we feel to be suitable; part of this psychic action on our part will be to accept or to encourage the projection as it is on any particular occasion.

In the accounts of several of the relevant sessions, it appeared that patients projected various conflicting psychic aspects and experienced a succession of rather confused identifications. The images of the helpless victim, of the attacked father, of the impotent onlookers, all featured. Analysts knew from their own insight that these representations put the patient potentially into touch with very early states, at the same time as themselves experiencing a painful if sophisticated version of the sense of smallness, which is felt by members of a profession who can hardly do anything about violence on a large scale, as they confine themselves to working with a few individuals. But total aloofness was hardly possible, and in this they were responding to their patients' needs in the same way as Jung (1946, p.177) described when he wrote:

> We are living in times of great disruption: political passions . . . internal upheavals . . . This critical state of things has such a tremendous influence on the psychic life of the individual that the doctor must follow its effects with more than usual attention. The storm of events does not sweep down upon him only from the great world outside; he feels the violence of its impact even in the quiet of his consulting room.

and "Were psychopathic symptoms ever more conspicuous than in the contemporary political scene?" (p.178).

Individual Psychology

The material elicited from the participating analysts covered a wide field of predictable individual psychology, which could be listed and described under various headings, but this material is of such an obvious nature that it does not seem pertinent to go into it. It is more interesting to focus the discussion, first, on the question of whether the course of any particular hour was significantly affected by the news of the assassination, and, second, the close parallel question of whether the violence and the associations with it had any particular quality of content or mutative effect on the patient, or on the analyst. Without going into clin-

ical detail it is best just to record the opinion expressed by several analysts at the time that the assassination did have a perceptible catalyzing
effect on a small number of analyses. But from my own personal experience of the continued analysis of three patients, one or more of whose
sessions that week were clearly affected by it, I did not find its effect persisted. It had perhaps more lasting effect on me than on them, in that it
alerted me to a certain countertransference problem which I had not yet
sufficiently analyzed.

Most of the analysts who collaborated thought that some kinds of patient rather than others were affected, temporarily showing this in their
analyses, but showing affect in the way the analyst felt was characteristic
for the patient and for his type, or his current psychological stage. It was
noticed that in the more mature neurotic patients, ambivalent and
oedipal feelings were evoked; the whole Kennedy family situation was
the setting, the murdered fathers, the two widows, the many orphans,
rather than the sudden violent and internal destructive features which
were more common with patients who were functioning at a more infantile level of development.

Another important group of patients was thought to have found the
assassination of use in their analysis as it enabled them to reach areas of
their personalities which they had previously found inadmissible to consciousness. It made it possible for some of them to realize that they also
had murderous impulses; they were able to admit this if they were at a
level of development where they were largely free from persecutory anxieties and prepared to acknowledge a temporary and partial identification
with the murderer. It was difficult, several analysts felt, to rely on this
effect with certainty, but the descriptive clinical details on which their
views were based did give some substance to it. Sensitivities of various
kinds, sadness or compassion, an ability to admit to internal destructive
fantasies or to idealizing processes, even if not strikingly produced then
for the first time, were in several instances rather more pronounced or
helped forward than was usual.

Yet the impression which emerges as a result of studying the accounts
carefully at the time, and then again after an interval, is that a great or
specific influence cannot be ascribed to the news of the assassination, although in particular instances defenses which had previously been clung
to were broken down rather than solidified. It made a general contribution in analysis toward a more effective working-through of ambivalence
and further steps were taken by some patients toward completing mourning processes and experiencing grief which they had previously denied.

These impressions correspond closely with observations from two independent American sources. "Much of the behavior of neurotic patients in response to the death of President Kennedy represented a displacement of feelings that they were not able to express towards their own ambivalently loved and incompletely mourned deceased parents" (Kirschner 1964, p.128), and "an intimate relationship was found between mourning anxiety and fear of separation" in the psychotherapy of a group of emotionally disturbed girls at the time of the assassination (O'Toole 1966, p.755).

Countertransference

The original impetus to the inquiry came from my own personal experience of countertransference in a very split session with a patient, which was followed by much thinking on my part and much anxiety on his before the next session, during which it was then possible to analyze what had occurred on the evening before; the second session was both significant and I believe mutative, in that desolate loneliness, inappropriate protectiveness towards me, and intense hunger were actually felt during the time on the couch and his need for instant responses was fully actualized rather than being talked about, as it had been previously.

Unlike some other analysts who subsequently communicated their experiences to me and whose virtuosity I admired, I had been unable to eliminate my own shattered feelings during the session on June 5. The patient arrived, very shocked from hearing the news of the assassination on his car radio, only minutes after I had seen the evening newspaper headline. The particular problem I encountered then was of being largely unable to interpret his behavior and what he was saying in terms of his own personal life, which it seemed to me at the time I should be doing.

On examining my associations later I came to the conclusion that I had been afraid that he would attack me for being callous, if I interpreted his personal reactions and seemed to him to be taking no account of the assassination itself; I imagined that if he had been angry with me for such callousness, I would agree with him and grow confused as to who most urgently needed analyzing. It was only with an evening's reflection that I was able to disentangle the defensive confusions, the protective behavior and the patient's subsequent anxiety. He associated more freely the next day and his analysis proceeded. I have described these events in outline in order to give an illustration of the way in which an analyst's personal limitations and predilections can interfere with the patient and temporarily increase his splitting defenses; in this instance I told him directly on the second day what I thought had happened on the day before, what I considered my part in it had been, and why his anxiety had increased; this resulted in his violent impulses becoming analyzable and his anxiety about the danger of attacking was reduced.

In exceptional circumstances, which these felt to be at the time, the analyst can either defensively conceal the affect he or she experiences, or can do so validly, by which I mean a minimizing or suppression of feelings, through experience that this is in the patient's best interests. If the patient directly observes and remarks on the analyst being affected by the same public event as he or she is affected, the analyst can interpret the perception and the consequent interaction, and concentrate on the current transference projections, the individual background and the underlying psychopathology.

Summary

An account is given of an inquiry, conducted in June 1968 among analytical psychologists in London, into patients' and analysts' reactions to the news of the assassination of Senator Robert Kennedy. A brief outline of method is followed by descriptions of collective and individual aspects of the material which emerged. An attempt is made to evaluate the effect of the news on some analyses; it was established to have been perceptible, but probably transitory. An example is given of countertransference in which the patient's anxiety over his aggressive impulses led to the analyst reacting overprotectively, thereby temporarily increasing the anxiety rather than analyzing it.

Acknowledgments

My thanks are due to many members of the Society of Analytical Psychology for their help in carrying out this inquiry, chief among whom are: Dr. M. Fordham, Dr. R. Hoffman, Dr. K. Lambert, Mrs. A. Lyons, Dr. D. Ogden, Dr. A. Plaut and Mrs. E. Seligman.

References

Jung, C. G. 1946. Preface to Essays on Contemporary Events. In *Collected Works*, 10.

Kirschner, D. 1964. Some Reactions of Patients in Psychotherapy to the Death of the President. *Psychoanalytic Review* 51:4.

O'Toole, J. K. 1966. The Reactions of a Group of Emotionally Disturbed Adolescent Girls to the Assassination. *Psychiatric Quarterly* 40:4.

Chapter 12

Development and Similarities, 1935-1980

There is something about the beginning of a new decade that leads to looking back to the past as well as to looking forward to the future. Both Freud and Jung found the very distant past, archaeology, a gripping subject. Freud's consulting room contained many Egyptian and Greek statuettes, and it is said that he even used to place one on the dining table and gaze at it in preference to conversation with his family. Jung hesitated between archaeology and medicine when he first entered the university. The desire to understand our past is one of the important strands in the reparative wishes that can inform a therapist's motivation. Much of the past is with us in the present, and one aim in studying history is to further the understanding of conflict, the psychology of the attackers and of the attacked.

1980 is 45 years, or nearly half a century, after Jung gave what came to be known as the Tavistock Lectures, to some 200 doctors assembled under the auspices of that Clinic—they were psychiatrists, psychotherapists, analysts (mainly medical ones then) and general practitioners. As well as the lectures, the discussions which followed were reported verbatim, and the whole was published under the title of *Analytical Psychology, Its Theory and Practice* (June 1935). Someone picking up the book now could perhaps assume that it constituted a definitive statement by Jung and that it is a description of present theory and practice. But between 1935 and Jung's death in 1961, much happened in the world and he himself did much more very sophisticated work. Added to that, during the years since the lectures, thousands of hours of analysis have been lived, reflected upon and thought about. Those are the hours from which I hope to distill something in this paper, but that does not mean

Adapted and expanded version of a lecture given in January 1980 under the auspices of the Society of Analytical Psychology. Originally published in *The Journal of Analytical Psychology* 25 (1980), pp. 219–36.

that the milestone quality of those pre-World War II lectures should be disregarded.

I am focusing at the moment on some of what Jung said at that particular time, to a mixed, but not a popular, audience. They were experienced people in this field and well-informed. I am using what he said as a stepping-off ground for describing, *selectively*, what has happened since and what I think is going on now. I have had to select rather ruthlessly from many developments, and from much that is the same. I shall say something about the splits among Jung's followers, about some of his own ways of analyzing that we do not now follow closely, about our greater freedom from anxiety about using the transference. I want to draw attention to the kinds of research that analysts can do, and why we do not do enough. Work on the theory of the self can only be hinted at in the space available. Much has been written about it, showing how valuable Jung is to us. To do justice to it I shall give illustrations from day-to-day work. Jung is to be admired and greatly respected, not adulated, and we need to be able to live in the present and to go forward from where he left off. Indeed it is easy to quote him as saying he did not want those who came after him to call themselves Jungians, so we have his authority for developments and even changes (1973, p.405). But, if some of my generation of analytical psychologists put forward somewhat different views on some of his concepts, and use methods different from those he favored, we can give our reasons for doing so, and we can hope to show the effectiveness of our ideas and practices. They are open to discussion, it hardly needs saying.

Differentiation

Jung's Tavistock Lectures constitute a very personal statement of where he stood in 1935, when he was aged 60, which is why it seems a good idea to start this new decade with an examination of what we are doing, which includes, I hope, a receptivity to what others are doing. In 1935 Jung was in a strong position to declare what were the concepts and practices of analytical psychology: they were his. Varieties of ways of being an analytical psychologist had not yet developed. There are now many centers of teaching and practice, which are only loosely affiliated in the international organization. There are even two in each of the (geographically) small countries, Italy and England. Training groups are influenced by, first, a combination of the individual personalities of the senior analysts dominant in them (some of whom worked with Jung); second, by the extent to which recently qualified analysts have identified

with them or reacted against them; third, by the collective cultural characteristics of the places in which they grow; and last, by the forces in the
collective unconscious of the violent times in which we live. We may
mourn the loss of original, ovumlike, unity (even if we do not call it the
world egg, as the ancient Egyptians did), and we may long for an idealized *unus mundus*, or the walled Garden of Eden, or infant-mother to-
getherness, but we will not be able to bring the actual early days back.

The Jungian societies are not the only ones which have split and di-
versified over the last forty to fifty years. The psychoanalyst Pearl King
has recently discussed splits in the psychoanalytic world in developmental terms, seeing the differences between adaptive and maladaptive ones
(1978). She showed how there are the "don't want to know" kinds of
splits, which are defensive against various anxieties about identity; and
there are the "don't agree" kinds, which are ones where healthy differentiations and ego growth are taking place. She discussed the psychological
disadvantages there are when societies do *not* split in spite of groups or
factions having developed. The mere maintenance of "peace" can be a
dangerous clinging-on to a no longer appropriate *status quo*—it is worth
remembering that the full term is *status quo ante*: where we were before.
Moreover, in the theory of intrapsychic splitting, the pathological kind
is to try to keep the bad right out; but the mechanism can be used
developmentally. When there is a drop in fear and anxiety, there can be
an appreciation of diversity.

The splits that have taken place in our training groups can be seen as
examples of the theory of typology a well as in developmental terms, as
King has shown. It will be remembered that Jung's type theory grew from
his need to examine the personality differences between him and Freud,
as he could not restrict himself to seeing the break as only the result of
an unresolved oedipal conflict. Another kind of split has also developed
over the middle years of the century; that is, between the Jungians practicing clinically and those whose major interest is in the cultural aspects.
I regret that it is not possible in modern life to find the libido to pursue
both to a high standard. By "modern life" I mean the combination of
economic factors and social ones which affect analysts along with other
people: they supplement the psychological ones that we analyze, such as
greed, which has to be faced as a neurotic remnant of childhood, and
can show itself in a vain desire for the intellectual omnipotence of a
latter-day renaissance scholar or an eighteenth-century polymath. There
has to be some sacrifice of peripheral tastes, in the professional area of
life, and I remember that there was a particular stage when I realized I
had come to a crossroads: the choice for the way forward was between

developing on the cultural side or becoming a clinical Jungian. The result of the decision is evident, seeing that I am writing about analytical psychology from the viewpoint of the consulting room.

Theory and Practice

In the discussion of clinical work in depth psychology, we can only offer our personal truth; statistics, with their kind of information, are impossible. Where evaluations of therapy are concerned, and descriptions for other people's information, three groups can be mentioned: the interested public, supervisors, and colleagues. To people who have no personal experience of any kind of therapy it is difficult to convey the almost limitless subtleties of objectivity and subjectivity which are, so to speak, the flesh and blood of each session and of each long-term analysis. Nor are those easy for a trainee therapist to convey to his supervisor; some feel that by reporting verbally on their patient to a third person they are affecting the transference. The immediacy of interaction may be damaged; essential spontaneity can be lost, like the bloom on a fingered plum. The actual words spoken often appear, when printed, quite other than what they really were, when alive. Yet the difficulties inherent in reporting have to be faced if we are to have seminal meetings with colleagues and take forward the practice of analytical psychology. Considerations of that kind were perhaps behind Plaut's two papers, "'What do you actually do?' Problems in communicating" (1966), and "'What do we actually do?' Learning from experience" (1971). The present paper is only one person's short selection of themes from a mass of material which already runs to thousands of pages. The hours spent in meetings produce a gradual accumulation of impressions about what other analysts think, feel, believe, and do, or do not do.

In the Tavistock Lectures Jung spoke about the basic concepts concerning "the structure of the unconscious mind and its contents" and "the *methods* used in the *investigation* of contents originating in the unconscious psychic processes" (1935, p.6). He proposed discussing, first, the word-association method which he had by that time discarded as a diagnostic technique with patients, though he still used it with criminal cases (p.48); second, dream analysis; and third, active imagination. In the event there was no time for a more-than-cursory description of that, because the audience wanted him in the last lecture to talk about transference, and he did. He displayed much affective involvement in that topic and its problems: he made contradictory statements which reveal the painful ambivalence with which he experienced transference projections from his patients, and the struggles he had with countertransference, which at that time had not yet been as widely studied as it has been since. He implicitly associated countertransference and intuition. He likened intuition to "a sort of miraculous faculty" (p.14). Neither intuition nor countertransference are seen as miraculous now, and we know from repeated experience what he already knew, in a less defined way, that it is via intuition that we discern our previously undetected countertransference interactions with patients, and that we can then study them, using the other functions, sensing, thinking, and feeling. Jung pointed out that it is easy "to mix up feeling with intuition" (p.14); by the word feeling he meant evaluating—but the word *feeling* has stuck. And it has been noticed that he himself used "the terms 'feeling,' 'emotion,' 'affect,' and 'affectivity' in overlapping and sometimes contradictory ways, owing in part to the fluidity of affective life" (Willeford 1976). In the popular mind and usage, *feeling* is still confused with *emotion*.

Jung urged us to differentiate carefully when we use what should be scientific, i.e., standardized or verifiable, terms. One trouble is that many of those terms are also ordinary words in common use, and the accuracy of our communications is bedeviled by sloppy, ignorant, or imprecise use of such terms. The term *self* is one of the flagrant and contemporary examples of that trouble, being a day-to-day word and also a technical one—it was at first thought to be primarily a Jungian term, we knew how we used it and the meaning we gave to it, but now many psychoanalysts have taken it up and they are increasingly studying the concepts connected with it.

The persistent fantasies of members of each school of depth psychology about what goes on in the others are often wide of the mark. Analytical psychologists are less casual, or mystical, and psychoanalysts are less run by rules and techniques than their respective opposites believe them to be. Much work is being attempted here in London with people whose "normal" processes are very seriously disturbed and with patients in a far wider range of ages and educational levels than Jung in his later years specialized in analyzing. Members of this Society are, I think, increasingly known for clinical stringency, even though, rather unfortunately, that may result in it being imagined that the current disuse of Jung's specialties of amplification and of active imagination means that we are poor on that side, or have become crypto-Freudians.

Amplification

In amplification the analyst offers associations, which in the past were frequently found in mythology, designed to draw attention to the collective and archetypal features which the patient's dreams or fantasies demonstrate. I think the climate has shifted away from our being able to assume that our patients are anything but very vague indeed about ancient myths, whether Greek, Egyptian, or from other early cultures; some are hazy or even ignorant of the Bible, but familiar with fairy and folk tales and with contemporary myths and cult heroes from many parts of the world, carrying major archetypal components.

How much amplification is offered by modern analysts is difficult to know. It may have fallen into comparative disuse, seeing that members of the London Society publish few papers that mention it. But examination of what has been written over the last twenty years or so does reveal that analysts occasionally introduce their own amplifying associations. I can cite Mary Williams's "Before and After the Flood" (1974, p.57). Plaut told me that he brought in Red Riding Hood while a patient was speaking about a dream, to show him that "he [the patient] was the (anorexic) girl and I [Plaut] the greedy wolf-grandmother. I may say that he does not swallow interpretations gladly, but he felt silent, which is unusual, after this one." I asked several other analysts whether they use amplification. One said she uses it only occasionally, in the form of reference to fairy stories but not myths, for example when she feels that a therapeutic alleviation of guilt will result. Another, when asked the same question, answered, no. Then she qualified that by remembering a recent occasion when a patient's dream had led her to amplify the image with a very general remark about its mythological meaning. She feels there is a danger that amplification might be a demonstration of cleverness and that it could cause an intellectual distancing from the immediacy of the patient-analyst interaction.

It seems probable that amplification has attracted to itself a certain opprobrium not only for the reasons just given, but also because a trend has arisen for the way in which a patient is acting, reacting, or fantasizing, to be given greater weight than the form taken by his images, actions or thoughts. Recently, while I worked on this paper, three different patients felt I responded too slowly to the doorbell. Each of them pictured me dead, inside the house, themselves paradoxically imprisoned outside in the street. Each time, I thought the "killing" was the primary feature of their experience, and the fantasied cause of death of lesser importance. On neither occasion did I feel that amplification would forward the work of finding out more about the parricidal/matricidal fantasy.

It is immensely valuable for the analyst to have, and to have time to enjoy and to add to, his own fund of cultural riches, historical, literary, artistic, musical, and so on. He can in any case practice in his continued self-analysis. But patients can be oppressed by those riches, or excessively envy them—though such reactions can be analyzed at the time when they are most acute. A particular patient comes to mind, saturnine and desperately envious: suddenly one day he shouted that my bookcase was horrible, he was going to jump up and hurl all those books out through the window, the large volumes of Jung's *Collected Works* would shatter the panes into smithereens in the street below. And the oils on the walls, for another patient, once became almost unbearable: he was going to slash them all. Both those patients' analyses were, at the times of those incidents, deeply concerned with the primal self and early distortions of self-experiences. And I find myself wondering whether an additional reason for amplification having somewhat fallen into disuse might be that there is now a high proportion of people coming to analysis who need the analyst to tolerate the resurgence of early rage and despair, for whom amplification could be experienced as an inappropriate overfeeding, motivated by the analyst's anxiety. Understanding the patient's emotions and productions, and his use of them, is, in such cases, considered more important than adding to them. So there has come to be a preference for the analyst to leave associations to the patient, and with most of them sufficient integratable material emerges that is extrapersonal and that carries archetypal significance. We try to discern whether or when it is archetypal even if it is not overtly given in terms of myths, or fairy tales, which classical Jungians write about; we try to find the right way to link the patient to the collective significance of his personal emotions and feelings, without denigrating their force for him and without talking about archetypes. I do not find that I have to "explain," as Jung says he did, that a dream or a fantasy shows the patient "that his case is not particular and personal, but that his psychology is approaching a level which is universally human" (1935, pp. 104–5). As the analysis progresses, he (or she) sees that without my saying so, and benefits by being the one to discover it.

Active Imagination

Jung advocated a positive effort to instigate active imagination. He said it was an essential stage in any complete analysis, and that means for anyone who can live with the demands that it makes and is not going to be precipitated into a psychotic episode. He used it as the final stage of his therapy of the transference, and said "it is an essential part of the process of individuation" (p. 166). The patient has to differentiate the personal factors in the relationship to the analyst from the impersonal ones: his recognition in consciousness of what the analyst does for him is not part of the transference, rather it is factual and realistic. That "real" relationship is what is meant by the term "rapport," which is not the same as transference.

Jung described how, during the stage of active imagination, when "the impersonal images are given shape," when the individual "is able to objectify them and relate to them," he will emerge from his neuroticism, no longer be in conflict with himself, be "in touch with that vital psychological function . . . (which is) . . . a sort of center within the psyche of the individual, but not within the ego" (p.167). Readers of *Memories, Dreams, Reflections* will recognize there an abstraction from, and a definition of, the extraordinary imaginative activity which enabled him to come through his mourning for the loss of his relationship with Freud. It led to the formulation of the transcendent function and the integrative power of the self (Hubback 1966).

A number of papers and chapters in books have appeared over the years which have added to Jung's discovery of active imagination and formulations about it. The most notable have been: "Active Imagination and Imaginative Activity" (Fordham 1956), "Problems of Active Imagination" (Fordham 1958), "Transference as a Form of Active Imagination" (Davidson 1966), "Reflections of Not Being Able to Imagine" (Plaut 1966), and "A Possible Root of Active Imagination" (Fordham 1977).

The "vital psychological function" that Jung found emerged during the active imagination stage of therapy used to be, he said, "taken care of by religion" (1935, p. 167). Such figures as, for example, Christ, were objectifications done *for* people, ready-made; but imaginative projections from the individual psyche which were then possible (for religious people) and which could correspond to such figures as those Jung's own active imagination conjured up, are "no longer possible for the modern enlightened mind" (p.166). In active imagination Jung was offering "enlightenment" of a different sort. But the nature of the function is of the same kind: it is linking.

Research

The dialectical movement between research and clinical therapeutic work is going on constantly, if not always satisfactorily. Although the subject of what are the therapeutic, or mutative factors in analytical psychotherapy is constantly being considered, it is difficult to formulate the lines along which more exact research would be possible. For example, on the specific point of trying to discover whether a particular analysand would achieve psychic health more lastingly if the analyst suggested active imagination, than if he or she did not, we cannot reach certainty. I can merely, at the moment, cite my personal approach to that problem and my own views. With some analysands, nothing that could be called active imagination ever develops, even though they reach the stage when termination begins to be considered and when, therefore, according to the 1935 brand of Jungian technique, it would be suitable, or perhaps essential, so that individuation might be achieved. Other patients find they can use the opportunity analysis offers them, the enabling atmosphere, the contained quality of the relationship, the chance of reflecting in both its passive and its active forms, to foster imaginative use of their own material combined with images from other sources. Michael Fordham has suggested that Jung in effect provided his patients "with parallels which can be compared with a mother's story-telling techniques. He probably did so when the imagery became highly autonomous with a view to making a framework in which his patients could feel safer" (1977, p.327). I find myself wondering whether the now older technique Jung used—based as it was on what he himself had discovered as his way of getting to his individuality and his potential—fits less well now that we do not conceptualize individuation as a once-only achievement. An analysis that enables the patient to use his or her maximum imaginative capacities usually results in a series of individuation experiences. Each deep stirring phase produces, as it were, seeds for the next one. We go on asking: what brings about change for a particular person, and for different types of people? When we make time to step back from daily pressures we can ask fundamental questions. We need more facts, time, and perhaps above all a combination of confidence and energy to sift and sort them out; then we would have some more general answers, no doubt temporary ones, but ones which would lead on to the next series of questions.

Since 1935 a great deal of unsystematized research has in fact been going on and at intervals senior members of the Society throw out ideas about themes which they suggest could be explored. But we are all such individualists that their promptings are not very successful. When something is "in the air," there is a chance of progress. For example, the theory of the self is currently under a lot of scrutiny, and there is renewed interest in structuralism and symbolism. Here are two instances of senior analysts suggesting specific topics. In 1958, Michael Fordham called for research into active imagination and allied topics when he pointed out that: "No study seems to have been made distinguishing . . . processed psychotic splitting from hallucination and delusion formation, hysterical dramatizations, and even obsessional reverie" (1958). In 1977 he wrote: "Little progress has been made in furthering the understanding [of active imagination] for which I called in 1958" (1977). He then did say that two members as well as himself *had* published relevant material, Plaut and Davidson. On another occasion, in his valedictory editorial in 1979, Plaut wrote: "I hope that future papers in this Journal will touch on the relationship between the following questions, all of which have a bearing on the selection of patients and the well-being of analysts. 'Who (or what) are you?' . . . 'What do you (fervently) believe in?'" (1979).

I think we analytical psychologists, apart from the rarely exceptional ones, work best with our private notions of the only kind of research that is really compatible with respecting the patient's psyche as much as our own; that research takes the form of listening, and later doing the sorting, discriminating, evaluating, and thinking. At those stages our personal characteristics, states, and predilections always affect the material. Provided we bear that in mind, what any of us discovers and formulates is usable by others, often verifiable and usually fertilizing. As examples of that, I could cite many papers published in the *Journal* in which the authors state that such and such a topic has attracted their attention because over recent months several of their patients had spoken of it or been affected by it. Here are a few that give the numbers of patients concerned: "About three years ago it struck me that time plays a very special rôle in some analyses, and I started to make notes after sessions in which time, or the discussion of time—in this or that aspect—had been prominent. My paper has grown out of these notes on nine patients" (Paulsen 1967). "My own interest in eating disorders was triggered off when I found myself working simultaneously with four patients whose ostensible central preoccupation was with food" (Seligman 1976). "Having had three patients who produced flood dreams at crisis points in their treatment, I have had the opportunity to study the significance of flooding in each case, and the factors prevailing before and after the flood" (Williams 1974). The next is an example giving no exact number of patients: "I . . . discovered, almost to my surprise, that, whatever the age and whatever the symptom picture, sooner or later concern with death becomes a feature in nearly every analysis" (Gordon 1977). Here is one of an organized project: "This paper is a report on the results of a research group working for the last three years in Berlin on the subject of transference and countertransference . . . Blomeyer and I reported on the results of the first twenty-five cases in the archetypal dream series. . . . " (Dieckmann 1976).

It is frequent for the authors of papers that contain clinical material to offer perhaps two or three examples from analyses which illustrate the concepts they are discussing without including all the patients they have treated who bear out that theme. Other papers that are entirely theoretical can be trusted to have a background of research. The kind of research that is difficult to do is based on the clinical experience of two or, even more difficult, several analysts. In the life of the Journal (launched in 1955 with Fordham as editor for the next sixteen years) there have been only four clinical papers by more than one author: "Psychodynamics of Therapy in a Residential Group" (Champernowne and Lewis 1966), "The Use of Fantasy Enactment in the Treatment of an Emergent Autistic Child" (Allan and MacDonald 1975), "The Real Mother, Ego-self Relations and Personal Identity" (Newton and Redfearn 1977), and "A Mythic Search for Identity in a Female to Male Transsexual" (Fleming and Ruck 1979).

What I am saying does not, perhaps, amount to more than being an instance of the difficulty in moving from particular data to general hypotheses and concepts, in such an essentially human science as this one. The thinking behind L. Stein's paper "Analytical Psychology, a Modern Science?" (1958) is still at work like a leaven which keeps on offering food for thought on the topic of our work being art, craft (technique) and science—not either or. And that applies even more to the contents of Jung's *Collected Works*. In some way which eludes clear definition, I think, and feel, and hope, that ways of researching might somehow develop, which would result in improving our training and daily work. The problem may lie in the intrinsic nature of the psychology of the unconscious, that the psyche develops slowly, and that clarity and formulations have an alien quality which it may not be possible, or wise, to try to incorporate. Moreover, as in other disciplines, the general practitioners simply carry on working and the exceptional ones do research as well. The two abilities are somewhat different. The researchers probably have another kind of libido, not simply more of it.

Modifications

Having mentioned those perennial subjects of study and of controversy, transference and countertransference, I would like to attend further to something I said earlier about concepts and methods of Jung's that these days we find less satisfactory than he did, or that we have modified. The major thing is that we have worked through the ambivalence about the transference and its uses that he showed in 1935. He told his audience that he developed amplification as a therapeutic method to be used at

the appropriate time in the therapy because of being "terribly worried by
the problem of transference" (1935, p.136). Forty-five years later, if we
are honest, I think we should say that we certainly are at times unable to
work satisfactorily with a patient because of some feature of the unconscious transference, what he or she is getting right into us, that defeats
our ability to understand and elucidate. I think of one of my patients, for
example, with whom for many months it seemed that I had to—as he
put it—"get it wrong." It emerged later, I think, that the trouble was
that there were two simultaneous and powerful but contradictory transference projections: at one level I was re-presenting him with a lifelong
difficulty with one of his parents, which had been particularly acute, but
denied by everybody concerned, throughout childhood and adolescence;
with that projection he was constantly (though as yet unconsciously) attacking my therapeutic potential. On another level, which would perhaps with time and further analysis become the arena for growth and
maturation, I was having projected on to me the image of the parent
who survives attacks, who nurtures, who is concerned and interested. It
was through the patient projecting that second kind of parenting, and
then reintrojecting the potential for it which was also his, that the analysis emerged from a difficult stage. I would not deny that during that
stage I was undoubtedly worried by "getting it wrong," but not to the
"terribly worried" extent that Jung seems to say.

"A specific form of the more general process of projection" (Jung
1935, p.136) is how he succinctly defines transference. It is "never a vol-
untary act" (ibid.), it is automatic, spontaneous. The full extent of it
may be unrecognized. "The emotion of the projected contents . . . es-
tablishes a dynamic relationship between the subject and the object"
(p.138). "Emotions are contagious" (ibid.). It is the doctor's "duty to accept the emotions of the patient and to mirror them. That is the reason
why I reject the idea of putting the patient upon a sofa and sitting behind him. I put my patients in front of me and talk to them as one natural human being to another, and I expose myself completely and react
with no restrictions" (ibid., p.155). My experience is that when the
primitive projections of persecuting, splitting, denying, and idealizing
have become delusional, they can be more effectively taken back and
worked through if I as an analyst am not physically visible during the
main part of the session, but all the same am fully available psychologically, which is what I think my job is. The direct quality of the attack by
the patient is experienced and can well be made absolutely clear in my
tone of voice ("You *are* hitting hard today!" or "Swipe! You're trying to
knock me out!"). The fact that I am an actual person is both true yet

minimized in the interest of elucidating unconsciousness. The eyes channel only one of the senses; and using them may delay the development of a more psychological "sensing" of the holistic functioning of the analyst.

Jung said that he talked to his patients "as one natural human being to another." Of course there is a lot of naturalness, and perceptive patients get to know the analyst's psychology pretty well, I think, over the years, as ego development takes place. But psychotherapy (and I use that word to show I am referring to the whole process) is not really "natural." It is a unique situation, very specialized indeed; it is "ordinary life" under a magnifying glass, or even at times under a microscope. It selects the aspects of the therapist that are necessary, though some days of course it needs his wholeness, his sense of self. So I offer the couch to any patient who shows signs of being able to accept and experience as deep and as emotional analysis as I believe he and I will be capable of sustaining. Weeks or even months may go by before it becomes clear how much each patient can tolerate and then benefit from. Of those people I am seeing at present almost all use the couch. One of those who sits on a chair wants therapy for only delimited difficulties; another is probably right to be firm on the subject, as he believes he tipped over into an actual psychosis when "put" (Jung's word, p. 139) on the couch in a previous therapeutic encounter. That kind of thing is a matter of varying opinions or judgments about what precipitated the psychosis, but he is not unlike the "elderly woman of about fifty-eight" who Jung describes on pp. 139–140, and slightly like the woman, who was a borderline case, who features on pp. 100–101. With those who use the couch there can be stages when the transference becomes delusional (as mentioned earlier), when the dreams, fantasies, and anxieties are reproducing very early infancy terrors and confusions and the defenses against them, but I do not abandon the couch at such stages. For the patient to use eyes on coming into the room, and again on getting ready to leave, keeps and restores the sense of the present and the ability to take up exterior life again in the world outside.

Jung's statements, to the effect that the analyst must "keep in touch with his unconscious objectively" (p.141), must know his vulnerable spots and not fall into "a condition of personal contamination through mutual unconsciousness" (p. 141) are still just as important as when he made them. Training analysis, which it is well known Jung was the first to advocate, has lengthened considerably over the years and the subject of how we should train analysts is constantly under review. The impossibility of being categorical about the length of it is obvious: linear time is measured in months and years, but maturity, quality, and value are not.

There could perhaps be a rough and ready check-list for personality features for the analyst which might be thought to add up to that desirable state called maturity, and I suppose we all keep our own list somewhere around in our minds, and usually know when we fall short of it ourselves. Yet a consensus of opinion on someone's maturity is very often not reached, seeing that personal likes and dislikes cannot be eliminated. On the whole, longer as compared with shorter analyses seem to lead to a decrease of projective animosities in groups and among colleagues, as well as to more effective professional work.

Transference

One feature of maturity in the analyst is presumably the ability to distinguish between the various manifestations of love. What kind of "love" or "being in love" is going on in any particular session? On the subject of the overloving transference, Jung's view in 1935 was that "anything can be made a matter for projection, and the erotic transference is just one of the many forms of transference. There are many other contents in the human unconscious that are also of a highly emotional nature, and they can project themselves just as well as sexuality" (p.141). He says that "inexperienced analysts make the mistake of taking it for love" (p. 143). One of the young therapists whose work I am surpervising still takes her patient's hate as personal: she has too low an opinion of herself. But then "love" and "hate" are extraordinarily general words, as indefinite sometimes as the powerful "good" and "bad" that patients bandy about when they are in regression. Jung's research on the opposites comes to mind, and the primitive quality of those absolutes is sometimes with us in its full force. It is not necessarily adult genital love that is activated in good-enough analysis; it is the dualistic, Janus-like, emotion of *going out toward* and of *going out against* that we are dealing with from whatever stage of life it stemmed. Once a patient discovers he can survive the loss of an early infancy transference to the analyst and is moving towards developing concern and regard, he can in his life outside analysis tolerate moving from being "in love" with someone towards a more maturely-based loving. If that is happening, suitably, then an apparently adult erotic transference can be experienced in its various psychological stages and not concretely. In one passage of the fifth lecture Jung refers to energy having been "wasted" (p. 143) in the transference. That now seems an unfortunate word to use, as if the patient had not really needed to project his unconscious affects before he could see them objectively and then have them successfully returned to him by good enough interpretations. The analyst has held, or looked after, those contents while the patient could not yet make use of them if they were positive, or admit and integrate them if they were shadow elements. A patient who splits off, forgets, or loses bits of himself, may have to have them offered back time and again until he accepts full responsibility for himself.

Among Jung's 1935 hostile remarks about transference are: "We do not need transference"; "transference or no transference, that has nothing to do with the cure"; "if there is no transference, so much the better. You get the material just the same . . . you get all the material you could wish for from dreams"; "Leave people where they are. It does not matter whether they love the analyst or not" (p.152). Those passages seem to be all referring to what is loosely called "positive transference," but an analysis is not by any means adequate if the analyst fails to uncover and interpret the negative one as well. The most dramatic of Jung's antitransference remarks in that lecture is: "A transference is always a hindrance; it is never an advantage. You cure in spite of transference, not because of it" (p.151). I think I have probably said enough to show that current experience here in London goes differently from that. One factor in the therapies where I think I have been unsuccessful—when the patient has broken off suddenly or left very dissatisfied—has been that I did not become conscious enough of the countertransference and consequently could not enable the patient to experience and to integrate the transference projections. I was presumably not finding the true nature of the psychic activity which was occurring. If the patient does not become conscious, in the partially rarefied and safe conditions of therapy, that dynamic interactions, and at time poisonous attacks, are at work, he is unlikely to develop the necessary insight and libido to detoxify his relationships with people in the rest of his life.

The views on transference that feature prominently in the Tavistock Lectures are easily available in the book entitled *Analytical Psychology, Its Theory and Practice*, and, as stated earlier in this paper, they could be taken as definitive if the reader did not know they were modified by Jung in the following years. His altered and extended views are to be found in the more difficult "Psychology of the Transference," published on its own in book form in Zürich in 1946. In English it is combined with other, much simpler, chapters in Volume 16 of the *Collected Works*. He examined precisely what the title points to; the model which he used was a particular alchemical work which fascinatingly and elegantly images much of what goes on between analyst and analysand, irrespective of their actual ages and sexes. That and the extraordinary composition, *The Seven Sermons to The Dead*, were the two strange documents I came upon

during my training, and by which I was captivated. Plaut has commented
to me on "the fascination which the illustrations [in the *Rosarium philosophorum*] exert on successive generations of trainees." In the foreword
Jung said this work was "not intended for the beginner who would first
have to be instructed in such matters . . . I am afraid my description will
not be easy reading for those who do not possess some knowledge of my
earlier work" (1948, p.165). In the section on the Conjunction, writing
of the need for more knowledge on the whole theme, he states: "I have
carried my researches back to those earlier times. . . . I have learned
much for my own practice, especially as regards understanding the formi-
dable fascination of the contents in question" (p. 255). In a footnote to
the Introduction he states "the *coniunctio* motif owes its fascination primarily to its archetypal·character" (p. 168). The incest archetype in its
various forms throws light on L. Stein's view of the etymology of "fascination"; he said it came from the late Roman underworld slang use of
the word "fasces" for the male genitals.

　　"The Psychology of the Transference" is about the analysis of the self:
the primal self which in this Society, Fordham, Redfearn and others
have done so much to investigate, the self in individuation, and the self
as collective symbol. We can talk of the subjective and the objective
self, and, consequently, of the subjective, objective, and archetypal
transferences; of individuation as a lifelong process experienced in successive episodes, or (as Jung usually did) individuation as "the integration of the self . . . a fundamental problem which arises in the second
half of life" (1948, p.264). However, he went on to say: "Dream symbols
having all the characteristics of mandalas may occur long beforehand
. . . isolated incidents of this kind can easily be overlooked. . . . " (*ibid.*,
p. 264).

　　At intervals in the life of an analyst, a restudying of Jung's use of the
alchemical model of the *Rosarium Philosophorum* can keep one in touch
with a source of renewal and a possibility of increasing one's understanding of patients and of oneself. Much of what is being done now owes a
considerable debt to Jung's post-1935 revaluation of transference, its
"central significance in psychotherapy" (p. 319), and "one of the most
important syndromes in the process of individuation" (p. 321).

　　Literally scores of papers have been published on transference and
countertransference since the first (Moody 1955). I looked through all
the back copies when I was planning what to write, and decided it would
be impossible to give the names of all the important contributors. Of a
total of 294 full papers published since then, 140 have treated the subject of transference, and its correlate, countertransference, as the main

theme or an essential subsidiary. There is a very great deal of empirical evidence to show that, with a wide variety of patients, confident use of the transference projections and constant work on countertransference are the special tools that are of most use to us and to our patients. More research needs doing on it, and could only be valuable; we certainly do not know all about it.

Individuation Versus Selfishness

The main advance that we are probably ready for is in studies of what Jung called "patients who are shut away in autoerotic insulation and have a thick coat or armour, or a thick wall and moat around them" (1935, p.146). Those phrases are of course descriptive and pictorial ones; anyone in the field knows what kind of theoretical areas are being referred to, and that Fairbairn, Guntrip, and Bettelheim have written about them as well as Jungians. At present a strong tide of interest is flowing in studies of the self, in observations of the early defenses against primitive anxieties (which may be manifested in people of any age, but which were established at the stage of infancy and reinforced on later occasions), and careful thought is being put into studies of narcissism as well as the Jungian term, the self. Both these words and concepts come under fire from ill-informed commentators on modern depth psychology. Resistance to analyzing unconsciousness frequently takes the form of criticizing psychotherapists for having supposedly contributed to a dangerous increase, in the modern world, of narcissism and self-engrossed individualism. That is a naive point of view, which involves forgetting the psychologically sound Christian recommendation to "love thy neighbour *as* thyself." The term *narcissism*, when correctly used, should refer to an early way of functioning, before the object, "the other," or "thy neighbor," has been effectively perceived. The term *self*, when correctly used in our particular specialty, does not refer to a way of functioning, but to the wholeness of the psyche, conscious and unconscious. So the two terms and concepts should be kept separate. We need them both, and it would be valuable if we could reach a wide audience to whom to demonstrate that both are neutral, scientific terms. Selfishness and egotism are in a different category.

Jung throughout his professional life was in effect often a moralist in the broad sense, and even openly censorious of patients whose selfish attitudes he could not stand, and I think that the present generation of analysts here is motivated by a basically ethical outlook on life. Individuation is only effective if it operates in both directions, towards the sub-

ject's internal confidence and towards respect of the object. Individuation is about both the self, and the self in relation to the other.

Summary

The theme of this paper is that the practice of analytical psychology has
developed and altered to some extent in England since Jung's Tavistock
Lectures, delivered in London in 1935, but the change and alteration are
not fundamental.

Among the many possible aspects of theory and practice a selection
had to be made. The paper touches on the differentiations in Jungian
training groups that has occurred as numbers of members have grown in
different countries. It discusses the use and relative disuse of amplification, and certain views on active imagination; it raises the issue of what
kinds of research are pursued and whether more research could be
activated.

The subjects of transference and countertransference are gone into in
more detail, comparing Jung's statements on them made in 1935 with
what he wrote in *Psychology of the transference* (1946), and describing
some current views held by the author and others who have published in
recent years. There is a certain amount of clinical material in the paper.
Attention is drawn to the current interest in the self, and the author has
aimed throughout the paper to emphasize development on the basis of
fundamental agreement with Jung's work, and the need for continual
rereading in conjunction with clinical observation and reflection.

References

Allan, J. A. B. and MacDonald, R.T. (1975). The Use of Fantasy Enactment in
the Treatment of an Emerging Autistic Child. *The Journal of Analytical Psychology* 20/1.

Champernowne, H. I. and Lewis, E. (1966). Psychodynamics of Therapy in a
Residential Group. *The Journal of Analytical Psychology* 11/2.

Davidson, D. 1966. Transference as a Form of Active Imagination. *The Journal
of Analytical Psychology* 11/2.

Dieckmann, H. 1976. Transference And Countertransference: Results of a Berlin Research Group. *The Journal of Analytical Psychology* 21/1.

Fleming, M. and Ruck, C. 1979. A Mythic Search for Identity in a Female to
Male Transsexual. *The Journal of Analytical Psychology* 24/4.

Fordham, M. 1956. Active Imagination and Imaginative Activity. *The Journal of
Analytical Psychology* 1/2.

———. 1958. Problems of Active Imagination. In *The Objective Psyche*. London: Routledge & Kegan Paul.

———. 1967. Active Imagination—Deintegration or Disintegration? *Journal of Analytical Psychology* 12:1.

———. 1977. A Possible Root of Active Imagination. *Journal of Analytical Psychology* 22:4.

Gordon, R. 1977. Death and Creativity in the Light of Jungian Theory and Practice. *Journal of Analytical Psychology* 22:2.

Hubback, J. 1966. VII Sermones ad Mortuos. *Journal of Analytical Psychology* 11:2 (Chapter 7 of this book).

Jung, C. G. 1935. The Tavistock Lectures. In *Collected Works*, 18.

———. 1946. The Psychology of the Transference. In *Collected Works*, 16.

———. 1973. C. G. *Jung Letters*. London: Routledge & Kegan Paul.

King, P. 1978. Crise d'identité—scissions ou compromis. In E.D. Joseph and D. Widlöcher eds. *L'identité du psychanalyste*. Paris: Presses universitaires de France.

Moody, R. 1955. On the Function of Countertransference. *Journal of Analytical Psychology* 1:1.

Newton, K. and Redfearn, J. (1977). The Real Mother, Ego-self Relations and Personal Identity. *Journal of Analytical Psychology* 22:4.

Paulsen, L. 1967. The Unimaginable Touch of Time. *Journal of Analytical Psychology* 12:1.

Plaut, A. 1966. Reflections on Not Being Able to Imagine. *Journal of Analytical Psychology* 11:2.

———. 1970. "What do you actually do?" Problems in Communicating. *Journal of Analytical Psychology* 15:1.

———. 1971a. "What do we actually do?" Learning from Experience. *Journal of Analytical Psychology* 16:2.

———. 1971b. Imagination in the Process of Discovery. *Journal of Analytical Psychology* 15:1.

Seligman, E. 1976. A Psychological Study of Anorexia Nervosa. *Journal of Analytical Psychology* 21:2.

Stein, L. 1958. Analytical Psychology: A "Modern" Science. *Journal of Analytical Psychology* 3:1.

Willeford, W. 1976. The Primacy of Feeling. *Journal of Analytical Psychology* 21:2.

Williams, M. 1974. Before and After the Flood. *Journal of Analytical Psychology* 19:1.

Chapter 13

Body Language and the Self: The Search for Psychic Truth

Every one of us who presents a professional paper to colleagues is at the same time presenting his or her own personal self as it was felt to be when writing the paper. My hope, as writer, is that I know the state of my personal self as well as possible and am still researching into it, and that I do not write and communicate from a ground in which there is still a great deal of personal unconsciousness. Each time a paper is composed it is a voyage of self-exploration, even if it has the appearance of being a search for the best way of understanding and treating patients of such and such a kind, or research into psychological theory. A description and discussion of our work, combined with a continuation of self-analysis behind the scenes, may be of benefit to future therapist-patient encounters and interactions.

The theme of this paper falls into three stages. First, the reality of the analyst includes body factors of all sorts, as well as psychic ones. The analyst's personality is housed in the material body, which has its characteristics, sex, idiosyncrasies, and vicissitudes. I think a great many body factors of the analyst as well as of the patient come into the texture and life of the therapy, into the transference and the countertransference, and not only at the beginning, even though in the long run the psychic ones are probably the most potent for change.

In using the term "body language", therefore, I am referring to far more than the patient's facial expression, gestures, and other immediate messages, or concealments of meanings. It is usual for the therapist to take note of general demeanor. The perhaps fleeting look in the eyes, of which it often turns out the patient was unconscious, or had not known that it was perceptible, may ask: Is the analyst well? Such a question may indicate self-concern as well as concern for the other. Similarly, the swift or furtive glance all around the room to see if anything has changed or if

Originally published in *The Body in Analysis*, N. Schwartz-Salant and M. Stein, eds. Wilmette, Ill.: Chiron Clinical Series, 1986.

some danger lurks in the corners; the difficulty in making eye contact; the particular moment at which he or she opens or closes eyes or fists; and no doubt countless other behaviors are ways of speaking without words. Those matters are important, but I wish here to take their occurrence for granted and to explore body language in the broader and perhaps deeper dimension of transference/countertransference. This small study, within which the patient's body language and that of the analyst will be considered, is meant to be linked with contemporary Jungian and psychoanalytic studies of the self. It reflects the difficulty that many an analyst has in relating the archetypal self of the collective unconscious —which is basically a concept and an abstraction—with his or her personal experience of the self, without falling into the grip of the extremes, inflation and denigration.

The second part of the theme is that, along with what might be called the benign aspects of the analyst and the setting, which have evidently a positive nature and effect, body factors must be taken to include those shadow features which manifest in bodily or other material form. The regrettable shadow features I intend to examine are, first, the analyst's occasional illnesses. Are they only physical, or have they also a psychic and synchronistic meaning which may add unbearably (or so the patient feels) to his or her anxieties, which were being analyzed before the intrusion from the analyst's shadow, and which compound together, perhaps at an especially difficult time? Following that, I shall describe a particular violent event that took place when burglars broke into my home, where I work, during a session with a patient.

The last part of this paper aims to open up the discussion of how those temporarily bad or unfortunate experiences can be integrated with the patient's search for psychic health, for the truth about himself or herself and about the larger self as manifested within, and for improved relationships with others. Those features of the analytic experience are subsumed in the quest for individuation, or an approximation to that potential.

The term "personal self" has been adopted advisedly. A great deal of ink has flowed on the subject of the self. This contribution is an attempt to explore one part of the subject, to describe and comment on some examples of the experienced body basis of the self. While we are still alive we can only know and do anything at all by means of the self, that mysterious factor that holds matter and spirit together, links them and enables them to related. We are neither disembodied psyches nor mindless bodies. "The self" has become a marvelously catchall term that means basically the factor of me, the me-ness of the person I am. It is experienced as the essence of me. Not only has each of us a "me-ness," but also each of us potentially senses that whoever we are talking to has his or her own me-ness. I think it is correct to assume that the personal essence of me is both individual and shared with every other individual in the world. The sharing adds the dimension of relatedness, without which the concept of the self does not make sense for living human beings. Even at the stage when it is an autistic or narcissistic self (at, and soon after, birth) it relates to itself and thereby it has potentially the first, repeatable, expandable, and applicable experience of relating, which becomes relationship with the object, provided that development is fostered by adequate parents and other figures in the environment.

Some people find that the idea of God helps them to be sure they have their own me-ness and to know that every other individual also has that. For example, one of the earliest Christians, St Paul, wrote: "Know ye not that your body is the temple of the Holy Ghost which is in you, which ye have of God, and ye are not your own?" (I Corinthians 6:19). That is an assertion of the belief that something very remarkable—Holy Ghost, spirit, or self—lives in the body. Other people do not like bringing any god into the matter; they find the boundary of the human dimension suits them better than the difficult combination of boundlessness and comprehensiveness that there is in the deity.

Healthy newborn infants look very self-contained, or even self-sufficient, but in normal development they do not stay isolated either physically or emotionally. Their self-containedness rapidly becomes something much more complicated as they progressively spend more time awake, and they probably only feel integrated again when they are asleep. And as they—we—get going in life, we have the all-in-one integrated experience less and less often; but always it is a possibility. When it comes, it is very powerful indeed, and we can get caught in its power and mistakenly believe we are powerful; or we can fear that it is utterly big and we are utterly small. The language about the self and myself and yourself has to be a translation from the psychic actuality of being it or being in it, first into body language of all kinds, from infancy to the grave, then into spoken language, which involves a further translation. That reminds me of a line in an early poem by T. S. Eliot: "I've gotta use words when I talk to you" (1936, p. 131).

The Analyst's Body and the Patient's

After studying at least a small amount of the huge literature on soma and psyche, it seemed to me worthwhile to devote myself first to certain general features of patients' and analysts' bodies. The analyst's physical life affects the patient, the transference, and the countertransference, and attention to this topic leads to larger theoretical issues.

We are creatures of the senses. Our patients can affect us consciously and unconsciously by their looks, their beauty or their ugliness, and we affect them since we also are actual people as well as being receivers of projections. I remember a woman with a face that looked to me like that of a horse; I could not stand more than a few sessions with her as I came to hate her, and I wondered if it was only for that particular body feature. She was not a kind of female Chiron (with the centaur's body parts reversed) but unfortunately seemed to me to be a concretized horsewoman, and I found no facilitating image to help me out of this fantasy which dehumanized her in my eyes. At the sixth session she told me her boyfriend was odious, so I knew there was too much hate for analytic *agape* to develop (Lambert 1981) and we parted company.

Another woman was very tall but she did not remind me of any animal, and she had a beautifully proportioned body to go with her height. She said she hated her largeness; her father had been large and domineering; and she added that her eldest brother was huge. In a few weeks it emerged that her problem was that she felt possessed, a state similar to that of being in the possession of an evil force. However, early in her therapy this did not appear in the transference/countertransference, nor did I experience her as overwhelming me or as trying unconsciously to deprive me of what I needed in order to be her therapist. I think her boundaries were healthy, so that the possession, or archetypal image of the overpowerful father, could be worked with.

Body Language and the Self

Patients for their part are affected by the sense impression they get of their therapists. One of my patients was, early in her analysis, convinced that my hair was just the same color as her mother's had been. She suffered from an unconscious and dangerous identification with a deeply depressed mother, and that was one of her main impediments to change. The extent to which I reminded her of her actual mother got in the way of thoroughly working through some of the fusion periods in the analysis, in which she was omnipotently using me as an idealized good mother whom she wanted desperately to be a total contrast to her bad internal mother.

My impression is that more male analysts have spoken and written about the attractiveness, or the opposite, of female patients than have female analysts about male patients (Stein & Alexander 1959). And I do not know whether the subject of the objective good looks or ugliness of the analyst, as compared with the transference projections, has been given any attention. Presumably the use of the couch, which maximizes the transference as compared with the impact of sense perceptions, results in the actual face and body of the analyst being relatively unimportant, particularly once the analytic relationship is thoroughly engaged. The French phrase *joli-laid* (pretty and ugly) which is, perhaps surprisingly, applied to men more often than to women, could be applicable to some analysts. But the presence of that composite characteristic is fairly rapidly superseded by transference fantasies, so its actuality is only a relative factor in analysis.

I am writing about body factors evident in the first place to the senses, but carrying a large component of psychic meaning. It is a combination of the analyst's body as it actually is and of "the living body" that affects the transference. In *Spirit and Life*, Jung wrote of the need both to separate conceptually the material body proper from "the living being", and to integrate in our thinking the fact that the body is "a material system ready for life and making life possible with the proviso that for all its readiness it could not live without the addition of this 'living body'" (1926, par. 605).

The sense impressions that the analyst and the patient have of each other are immediately changed into images, which either of them (but more likely the patient) may express at the time that that happens; or they may keep them inside, the analyst probably consciously suppressing the expression of them, and the patient either doing the same, or repressing them. They may then later reappear in imagery or even with a symbolic quality to them, when they will be available for transformation. If they have attracted to themselves archetypal images that are waiting for a form, then changes can occur within the transference/countertransference, which can be brought to light. The material and the concrete become symbolic.

At her first meeting with me, a certain woman patient "thought" —i.e., fantasized—that I looked like a lioness. Without revealing the reason, she said she did not want to come again, and fled back to the colleague who had referred her to me. Fortunately she was encouraged to return and talk about it. I thought, but did not say, that in the psychic circumstances her flight was understandable. She gradually managed to allow me to become, for her, human, and her fantasy became analyzable.

Jung considered that

. . . the psyche consists essentially of images. It is a series of images in the truest sense, not an accidental juxtaposition or sequence, but a structure that is throughout full of meaning and purpose; it is a "picturing of vital activities." And just as the material of the body that is ready for life has need of the psyche in order to be capable of life, so the psyche presupposes the living body in order that its images may live (1926, par. 617).

I think a close analogy to, or an illustration of, the foregoing remarks of Jung is to be found in many aspects of therapeutic work with patients. The patient often brings physical pains to the session and needs the psychic response of the analyst, who will most likely be able to find both the meaning and the purpose, by way of what is happening in the transference and the countertransference, and to relate it to earlier life events or old familial constellations. For example, a patient arrived looking pale and clutched his abdomen as he sat down and huddled into the chair. He said it was indigestion caused by eating too much popcorn the evening before. He did not mention it again and I made no comment. As the session developed it became possible to see that the "indigestion" was an internal experience "caused" by an excess of something otherwise good, and the bad from outside met some inner malfunctioning which, in the analysis, carried the significance of a negative archetypal image. It would not have been possible to interpret the opening remark without all that happened in the session, by which time the similarity had emerged between the genesis of the physical pain and of his very difficult current life pains, which he considered were being caused by other people but which he also knew went back to childhood interactions and attitudes he had developed during those stressful years.

I can refer back to Jung:

> There is, in a certain sense, nothing that is directly experienced except the mind itself. Everything is mediated through the mind, translated, filtered, allegorized, twisted, even falsified by it. We are so enveloped in a cloud of changing and endlessly shifting images that we might well exclaim with a well-known sceptic: "Nothing is absolutely true—and even that is not quite true" (1926, par. 623).

The reader will remember that one of my intentions in this paper, expressed in the title, is to search for psychic truth.

Psyche-Soma

Up to now I have been offering some examples of the sense aspect of the body-psyche theme, stressing the interconnections and interactions of the two in analysis and therapy. Another aspect is contained in the large field of illness classified as psychosomatic. Here again the literature is voluminous and growing every year. In it the medical doctor speaks with authority of a different kind from that which someone can offer who came to analytical psychology from the arts side of learning. It is increasingly noticeable, at any rate where I work, that many general practitioners — basically physicians — are more willing than they were some years ago to discuss the origin and the meaning of the illnesses suffered by people who are both their patients and mine. The old mana-based medical superiority is on the decrease, but the present "psychosomatic fashion", in C. A. Meier's words, is not simply a reaction against medical materialism but a modern version of a view of illness held by many ancient Greek physicians (1962). Already then the conundrum of whether the truth is that bodily ills are independent of psychic states, or that affects bring about those ills, was carefully considered. It is the view of analytical psychologists that unconscious complexes produce symptomatic actions and accident proneness, and somatic symptoms that can result in genuine organic damage. A simplistic psychosomatic approach or interpretation may lead to the apparent remission of the symptoms, but if serious organic disturbance has become independent of the psychodynamics, the view of the matter as psychogenic will no longer be effective enough and physical treatment will be necessary. The Freudian concept of conversion, according to which the psyche produces the physical symptom, is perhaps better known than Alfred Adler's theory of the links between neuroticism and unacceptable organ inferiority, whether that is actual or fantasied. The somatic factor was usefully acknowledged in Adler's view, without being considered to be necessarily causal on its own; it often brought it within range of treatment which could result in the patient's undertaking further and deeper therapy, exploring more areas of the unconscious.

As well as referring cursorily to psychosomatic illnesses, it is worth mentioning Leopold Stein's paper, of major importance in the study of psychesoma, "Introducing Not-Self" (1967). He "postulates a psychosomatic unity superordinated to the body and the mind" (p. 110). He points out that etymologically, the very early pre-Latin word *fendere* means to beat, to protect, and to beat back, which leads him to write that "the hostile attitude bound up with destructiveness, and thus for beating back and slaying, presupposes the ability of the self to recognize not-self," although "defense is often tacitly regarded as a mechanism characteristic of the reasonable ego" (p. 103). Also, he writes that from what little is known of "the etymology of most of the words standing for the concept of the self as we or as ordinary folk understand it . . . we can glean two motifs . . . , one, that of omnipotence; another that of belonging to a clan" (p. 101).

Stein's "psychosomatic unity" is of particular interest when manifestations of transference/countertransference are being examined, particularly in the context of synchronicity. The patient's defense system and the analyst's are each at work, both in their own areas and in interaction. The analyst's perhaps defensive shadow—uncaringness—his or her not-understanding which the patient may be at one and the same time imagining and instigating, because it suits the patient to make out that the analyst is a cold fish—those shadow factors may well be connected with phases in the analysis when the analyst is not liking the patient, since the patient is literally being unlikable as a result of his or her persecutory attacks. Yet the problem is a shadow one. The shadow of the "good" analyst is the uncaring one, who cannot but look forward to the end of the difficult session, or even to the resolution of the long phase in the analysis when he or she does not know what is happening, after which the analyst "feels himself or herself" again—no longer ill, or ill at ease. The working through of these events or stages may be quite painful.

The Analyst's Illnesses

These views on interactions between patients and analysts are offered as a background to the attempt to find out how useful the concept of synchronicity can be in throwing light on the situation when there is a psychosomatic relationship between two people: patients' reactions to the analyst's physical illness. It would be more correct to call that simply "the analyst's illness" and not to beg the question in advance of whether it is a physical or a psychic illness.

It is easy enough, if facile and unprovable, for an analyst beset with a harsh super ego, or with judgmental parent-imagoes, to believe that succumbing to a flu virus, for example, means that he or she does not want to see such and such a patient for a few days—perhaps a patient who has not yet worked through some psychopathology from which the analyst also suffers. An actual flu infection can occur to an analyst whose range of patients at any one time includes more than one whose transference projections are particularly apposite. The flu then temporarily rescues the analyst who, assuming he or she takes some days off work, can probably gather enough strength to withstand what is being experienced as persecution, by means of analyzing a not-yet-healed wound, or as an obstinate personality defect. It could be that flu hits the analyst just as he or she needs, yet once more, to pay serious attention to a recurrent tendency to a narcissistic but unconscious omnipotence. If the illness is interpreted as flu getting power over the analyst, he or she is thereby offered the opportunity to deepen the ongoing personal analysis.

I think such a mild physical illness can operate valuably if the analyst can perceive whence comes the internal mental attack. It is not coming from the patient, who is probably needing an uninterrupted series of sessions to attack *within the transference*. This does not disturb the physically well analyst unduly if he or she is skilled at seeing when attacks are happening; the analyst probably finds it more difficult if he or she is succumbing to a virus attack. It is the analyst's job to discern the subtle and the devious aggressions; then the true psychic target can be interpreted.

I am of course not alone in thinking that the psychogenic factor in the analyst's illness can and must be worked on. However, as in all matters of a psychosomatic nature, the difficulty lies in finding out convincingly what led to the choice of illness, particularly if the analyst has not suffered from it before, as that is not always obvious. The questions that any illness raises for the analyst are: what is the analogy offered, what is the meaning, and what is the symbol?

Illness and the Self

There are many medically more serious illnesses than flu that an analyst may get, and many that result in far longer interruptions of analytical therapy. I am writing here of intensive therapies where the patient comes three, four, or five times a week, anxiety is not shunned or otherwise bypassed, and deep structures are affected. For such patients with not yet firm enough boundaries, even a short gap caused by the analyst's illness may bring on extremist fantasies of abandonment—the patient is being abandoned—or of death—the analyst is going to die. The impact of a rather longer gap can be almost impossible to tolerate.

Two psychoanalysts, Dewald (1982) and Abend (1982), have recently published papers closely connected with this theme, in which each of them describes transference and countertransference considerations that arose as results of serious illness in the analyst. My contribution to this subject is to relate how, some time ago, after a series of minor interruptions that built up a mood of emotional irritation and fear in a certain patient who was struggling to tolerate and work through anxiety about a lump in one of her breasts (her mother had had a mastectomy), I had unfortunately to stop work for two weeks owing to having developed shingles, *herpes zoster*.

I had been unaware that a rash on my right arm was shingles. When acute pain attacked my shoulder I thought it was a renewal of an earlier arthritic condition and I had consulted my doctor about it. I only casually told him about the skin condition, which he then diagnosed. The shingles was, medically, very minor, but the pain was fiendish.

What resulted psychologically was an experience of almost total loss of interest in almost everything and everybody, of a nature and quality quite different from run-of-the-mill tiredness or depression. Some people would call it loss of soul. The patient who was so anxious about her breast lump had to go into the hospital just then, and my complete inability to do more than listen to her on the telephone and to remind her that if she felt even worse she could go to her doctor, had a long-lasting bad effect on her. Her lump was not malignant, and my recovery duly took place. But her reproaches about how deeply I had hurt her recurred at intervals over several months. The pain in her psyche seemed to dig right into her feeling of herself. She felt I had hit her, as well as abandoned her to her fate. Her reaction seemed to me to indicate that she had regressed to a very early state — in developmental terms it even had a preparanoid quality — and the very young infant girl in her desperately needed me to care for her and to nurse her back to health.

During the days when I had almost completely lost interest in everything and when I could not apply any thinking capacity to how things were, what was happening had nothing to do with "being interested" in the usual or thinking sense of the words. All I did was to be, for nearly two weeks. And I was greatly helped by a friend and colleague who quickly and simply said, "you are having a self experience." I had not been consciously afraid of losing my self, or my soul, and I had not reached the stage where I might have feared losing my life. The I-feeling was still there and by simply waiting, the greater self and the smaller me were both restored and became viable again.

Retrospectively, it could be thought that, where I was concerned, I had an absolute need for the loss of soul experience, and the fact that it cut across my patient's need for me to be fully available to her had to be lived with and lived through. That view of the matter cannot be satisfactorily validated if the rational angle is predominant; it smacks of justifying the occurrence of the events by saying they "had" to happen. Yet that view can also lead on to seeing that she had another need which the synchronicity helped: the need to discover my limits, to find out that overprotracted intensive care can become unhelpful *participation mystique*. And that is not relationship. There was a need not to have *coniunctio* at that turning point, and for her idealization to decrease. That

way lay development for her and emergence from the power of early infancy fantasies, archetypal ones.

When I resumed analysis with the patient who feared cancer, I did not
interpret much, nor did I communicate to her directly anything of my
own experience. As the weeks went by her belief in herself as an alive
person who was valued and who was going to continue living was restored. It seems to me virtually impossible to decipher the truth about
the synchronous quality for her and for me of the weeks lived through in
that summer. As her analyst—previously trusted, but less and less idealized as her attacks of envy were worked through—I felt sure that she was
getting the benefit of somehow absorbing through her psychological
pores the discovery that the fear of loss of life can be faced. The body
events came into relation with their psychic counterparts, and the psychic experiences seemed to need body form for their impact to reach
deep enough. It has appeared to me to be a series of events in her life
and in mine in which the immensity of the self dimension was presented
first in a very malign form; then, thanks to the synchronicity, it was possible for the action of the self gradually to become benign and available
as libido for going on in life.

It is somewhat invidious to select one quotation from among so many
possible ones about cancer (or the fear of cancer) and the psyche, but
this one is especially valuable. I think it illustrates some of what occurred in the foregoing case, in the transference/countertransference:

> The phenomenology of cancer is full of images of guilt and retribu-
> tion ("What have I done to deserve this?") and promises to one's
> self and others that, should there be a recovery, sacrifices will be
> made, and there will be a *change of ways*, life will be lived properly
> (Lockhart 1983, p.63; italics added).

I did not feel pathologically guilty about what I had done to the patient,
and the whole episode certainly led to an increase in consciousness ("a
change of ways") for me as well as for her. Then in another passage
Lockhart wrote:

> Cancer as an image in dreams or as a reality in the body signifies
> something wrong in one's relation to life, and so cancer is both
> a warning and an opportunity to seek out the paths of unlived
> life—in whatever period of time one has remaining (p. 63).

It seemed to me that while I had merely had shingles and she had had a
breast lump, both of us had some more "unlived life" to live, though my
period of remaining was most likely going to be shorter than hers.

A Violent Incident

The second clinical event that illustrates the interactions of body and psyche in analytical therapy is one that occurred some years ago. At intervals colleagues have suggested I should try to write about it. I would like now to offer the bare outlines of the violent episode of the burglars in order to link the material incident with the forward-reaching concepts of analytical psychology. What it has in common psychologically with the first case is that there was considerable danger (though of a different kind) and fear. An additional factor of uncertainty was introduced the next day when a psychoanalyst who lives in the same road as I, gloomily predicted that I "would lose the patient," i.e., it would be the death of the therapy. I took that to be his (unsolicited) interpretation that I had killed it. I certainly hoped he would be proved wrong, although I could see it was a possible forecast to make.

The body side of the incident is that two men broke into my house through the front door, upstairs from where I was seeing a patient (who I will call B) in my consulting room, which is at garden level. Instead of using my ego and calling the police when I heard two sets of footsteps in the room above, which I was certain could only belong to intruders, I put not only myself but also my patient at risk by acting on the basis of instinct. I went upstairs to investigate.

The intruders were surprised, and the nearest of the two hit out when he saw that they were going to be frustrated in their intention of burgling undetected. They had believed they had the house to themselves. There followed a fight in which both B and I—he was a tough male psychiatrist—were injured. We were lucky that the burglars were not armed. My first reaction had been anger, hence the fight. When the battle began to turn against B and me, and the intruders demanded that he should hand over whatever cash he had on him and that we should both lie down on the floor, fear replaced anger. I think I had never before in my life punched and kicked anyone with such anger, nor have I ever been quite so physically afraid as I was in the second stage of the affair. Both were simply instinctual and body reactions. However, B did not hand over any money, nor was either of us willing to lie down on the floor, and (or was it "so"?) the intruders departed.

Discussion

This very physical event was in every sense a violent intrusion into B's analysis, and it was unique in its nature and range. As a psychiatrist working partly in the community, B had often had to handle aggressive people physically, so to some extent he knew that there is no hard and fast distinction between body and psyche in psychiatry. But I have had no comparable experience with patients; analysis is very different in that respect and B had always kept his aggression verbal, or covert.

The first psychological reaction of both me and B was that we had had a shared experience, a bad one, and one that had perhaps dangerously broken through the usual boundaries. The actuality of "being in the same boat" could never again be denied. It was henceforth a bond in which action had featured. The question arises as to whether some previously inexpressible factor had been acted out, inadvertently, and certainly against our wills (Hubback 1984). It was not sexual acting out, at least not in any obvious way, but I wondered whether there was some obscure sexual quality, using the term sexual in the broadest possible sense. Throughout the analysis there were the two parental transference projections, so the acting out would have been both of male homosexuality and of mother-son incest.

B and I each took a week to recover. When sessions resumed, his main communication was of great self-reproach. The intruders had managed to do what he never had, to break in and really go at me. He felt he had never attacked in such a way as really to hurt me, and that was irrespective of a deeper need not to knock me so hard that I was eliminated. The parent/analyst is required to survive all onslaughts.

His deep anxiety about passivity surfaced in a way that an analysis of five-and-a-half years' duration had not made possible until then. I felt awe about how he and I were talking about the material version of the sort of thing that some—and perhaps many—analysts say quite glibly: "You wanted to kill your mother," or your father, as it might be.

Flesh-and-blood homicide might have happened in my house, though not by B, and there was B saying that in hitting me, the intruders had shown that they had something he had not. That "something" was phallic bravery, expressed with arm and fist. He had not yet been the hero who literally fights the dragon-mother.

The boundary between talk about physical events and psychological-symbolic ones was temporarily lost. It was restored in the course of the following months, yet I think it took a long time for B to get over what amounted to a deep envy, experienced at an instinctual level, of the two men who had done with their physical fists what he had never done by symbolic punching. So the intruders had acted out for him. What was ultimately important was that they had physically hit him as well as me, and that his negative hero had at last the possibility of turning into a positive one. B had not, in the youthful years, been able to free himself from certain depressing features in family life. His experiences with each of his parents had been unsatisfactory at that stage. In relating to them in middle and late adolescence, the positive hero had not been in evidence. He had found himself unable to go forward constructively, but had become increasingly depressed, in a way that many young people do when the passage through that archetypal stage is not well negotiated. It can be more like the death of the three hundred Spartans at Thermopylae than the achievement of the young runner from Marathon to Athens.

Where I was concerned, I felt far from heroic. I had punched the nearest intruder almost as much as (if less effectively than) I had been punched, and I had kicked, hoping to kick where it would hurt a man. But that was foolish, as it made him angrier. I had never in consciousness wanted to attack B in a big way, but I realized retrospectively that there had been times, early in his analysis, when I had felt like shaking him. It is possible that I had not released in the transference enough of the pent-up attack from which he was suffering, and that my desire to shake him (that is a fairly mild form of attack, compared with breaking someone's nose, which is what the intruders did to him) was an indication of far more aggression than I had been prepared to acknowledge in myself.

My main anxiety about my part in the events was that by acting from primitive instinct when my cave was entered by wild animals, I had caused B, for whom I was responsible, to be at physical risk. I was well aware of his having a wife and several children. So, where I was concerned, the intruders had acted out my shadow: the fear or the risk of increasing a patient's illness. The bad analyst, being the representative of the bad parent, can do a great deal of harm—can spoil the patient's chance to return to health, or, where narcissistic disturbances are concerned, can forever prevent the discovery that healing, growth, and change do exist. I was partly haunted by the remark of my psychoanalyst friend, and partly found it a challenge. B had been harmed. Was his analyst, who had inadvertently played such a part in the harm, going to be able to work through with him the emotions that had been aroused?

The factor of having acted on instinct was one that at the time exercised me strongly, perhaps excessively. It was not much use to me that everybody said it was natural not to have considered using my telephone to call for help. I was worried about that particular point; analysis is a nonnatural experience (unless I split hairs with a minute investigation of "nature" and "natural," which will be reserved for another time), and the open enacting of either aggressive or erotic instincts does not take place

in what should be the symbolic *hieros gamos* of the therapeutic relationship. *Agape* is what we strive for. Just as we do no more than read
Mysterium Coniunctionis and pore with fascination over the illustrations
in the *Rosarium Philosophorum*, so should neither the erotic nor the aggressive instincts be acted out in analysis. Damage is damage, whichever
unbridled instinct it comes from.

   The next challenge, however, was to emerge from what had gone before. One of the most valuable features of analytical psychology is, I
think, the dual concept of the personal and the archetypal shadow. For
B, his passivity and inability to move forward into the hero phase of developmental life was a shadow problem. The equivalent, or parallel, personal shadow for me at that moment was impulsiveness. I had not then,
developmentally, nor indeed have not now, reached the stage of life
when the archetype of the wise old woman can perhaps be constellated.
It remains to be seen whether B will ever be as free from passivity, or I as
free from impulsiveness, as each of us would like. In his outer life he is
active and effective; in mine there is these days a welcome indication of
slowing down. I know that even moderately wise old women do not dash
about like youngsters; they have to be wary of broomsticks that would seduce them from reflectiveness. The psychological point here is that because of the intruder incident, a deeper understanding became possible of
day-to-day shadow and body-and-psyche shadow. The instinctual and
the psychic poles of the archetype had both been in evidence. And developmental energy was released by being, inadvertently, channelled
through the electrical currents of the shared experience and the transfer-
ence/countertransference.

   Most of the interactions and intrapsychic events in analysis are not
known to anyone but the two people concerned. Many drop into obliv-
ion, and it is best if the *vas bene clausum* is indeed kept well closed, even
if that is a counsel of perfection. Where long-term deepening of understanding is concerned, combined with the possibility of continuing
change of perception of, and attitude toward, psychological events, one
outcome of the intruder incident was that since it could not be concealed, it was available for detailed examination.

   Over time the main focus of interest, where I am concerned, goes toward drawing attention to the fact that even the most sustained attempts
to analyze omnipotence are never quite effective enough; the fantasy of
omnipotence is such an early feature of the human psyche. Throughout
my time of being an analytical psychologist I have been interested in
finding out how to be effective in analyzing that fantasy. I am concerned
with the problem of how the analyst can maintain his or her knowledge

of both established and of new theory and technique, combined with constant vigilance over the danger of omnipotence. The search for psychic truth is, I suggest, at the core of the work, the effort toward consciousness of as many factors as possible from which to build a profile of what actually happens in the body or in the soul. While there cannot be certainty of truth or absoluteness, it always has to be sought.

Conclusion

It is ambitious to direct attention to the search for psychological truth; it even has a grandiose ring to it. All the same, it seems to me that to bear in mind the very broad issues of our work as psychotherapists and analysts, as well as the details, helps us to keep a sense of proportion. "The search for psychic truth" refers to both the research and the therapy aspects of analysis. The need to relate them to each other can only be met effectively if more and more factors are brought in; the main ones in most of our current research are theories of the self and transference/-countertransference.

We can also usefully place those words and terms in the reverse positions, since one of the main courses to pursue is the analyst's subjectivity interacting with that of the patient and generating archetypal forces. In other disciplines (for example, physics, anthropology, and history), as well as in our own, the standpoint, the attitude, and the person of the observer are now being taken into account most valuably. Much if not most of analytical therapy hinges on trying to find out the real psychic happenings and to set them in a framework and model of the psyche that improves the likelihood of taking a few more steps toward a true understanding of interactions or the lack of them. By taking the body fully into account we are, I think, demonstrating an intention of keeping analytical psychology as sane as possible.

References

Abend, S.A. 1982. Serious Illness in the Analyst: Countertransference Considerations. *Journal of the American Psychoanalytical Association* 30.

Dewald, P.A. 1982. Serious Illness in the Analyst: Transference, Countertransference and Reality Responses. *Journal of the American Psychoanalytical Association* 30.

Eliot, T.S. 1936. *Collected Poems*. London: Faber & Faber.

Hubback, J. 1984. Acting Out. *Journal of Analytical Psychology* 29 (Chapter 5 of this book).

Jung, C. G. 1960. Spirit and Life. In Collected Works, 8.

Lambert, K. 1981. Individuation and the Personality of the Analyst. In: Analysis, Repair and Individuation. London: Academic Press.

Lockhart, R.L. 1983. Cancer in Myth and Dream. In Words as Eggs: Psyche in Language and Clinic. Dallas: Spring Publications.

Meier, C.A. 1963. Psychosomatic Medicine from the Jungian Point of View. Journal of Analytical Psychology 8:2.

Stein, L. 1955. Loathsome Women. Journal of Analytical Psychology 1:1.

———. 1967. Introducing Not-Self. Journal of Analytical Psychology 8:2.

Chapter 14

Change as a Process in the Self: What Is the Mutative Factor?

Most professional analysts and psychotherapists have by now read a great many of the books and papers on the subject of the self, even if each of us admits (whether privately or publicly) that there are many we have not read—yet—and that we could benefit by rereading those we do know in order to improve the integration of them in our lives and work. But here I wish not to acknowledge the written word so much as to offer readers something different to keep at the back of their minds, to treat as a sort of frontispiece illustration.

A man who was in analysis with me quite a while ago, told me of something very important in his early life, which had been on a rocky and austere island. He was extremely unhappy throughout almost all of his childhood. He had many memories of grimness, both in the natural and in the human environment. Some time during those early years he had fashioned for himself a ball of peat and he kept it in a small gap in one of the dry-stone walls on the edge of the moor. He used to go at intervals to see that his ball of almost black peat was still there, secret, safe, waiting for him. Sometimes he picked it up to handle and hold it. At other times he simply saw that it was there.

It is in the nature of analytical therapy that patients entrust the pictures of their secret selves to their analysts, provided there is basic confidence. The man who made the ball of peat fortunately had that, although it was very often hidden in the blackness of intense hate of me, his analyst. The opening of one of his dreams was: "It was the dead of night, I was alone on the rocky outer side of the island, it was raining hard." It can be seen—through the dark and the rain—that the blackness of the peat is intrinsic to the whole story; the ball was a miniature globe, small enough for a boy's hands; the wall it was kept in was made from the rocks embedded and strewn all over the soil of a harsh island,

---

Originally published in *The Journal of Analytical Psychology*, 32:3 (1987), pp. 241–55.

windswept in a stormy northern sea. But it must be remembered that peat consists of (I quote from the dictionary), "vegetable matter decomposed by water and partly carbonized by chemical changes." Remember also that it is used as fuel for warmth and for cooking. For that particular man there could hardly be a more valuable symbol for the self than his ball of peat. His analysis was stressful for me and often agonizing for him. He threw vicious hate at me on many occasions, but towards the end he drew pictures and wrote poems and played to me on his Jew's harp, telling me that it is an instrument used all over the world and that in the South Seas beetles are tied to the central spring so that the vibrations include the beetles' sounds.

I am giving these details so that the reader can, I hope, get the feel of the richness of this man's imagery connected with the central symbol of his secret self. Liberating the dynamism of the self and directing it creatively were the forces for change in his analysis.

Theories and Reflections on Theories

It was Jung who pioneered the study of the self in depth psychology: he wrote about it extensively and intensively. So there was already a great deal to read, about the empirical bases of his studies, and the concepts which he abstracted from them, without going outside the pure Jungian field. Before we had by any means fully absorbed Jung's researches, we found ourselves overtaken by a new wave of productions on the subject, written by analytical psychologists of major importance in this field. Then quite a number of Freudian psychoanalysts took it up, some in a big way: the study group which grew up around Kohut in Chicago is now said to be some fifty strong and self psychology is an important element in psychoanalysis, particularly in the USA.

So it is not wise to consider the self and allied concepts without reference to at least some of the writings of the following: Klein, Winnicott, Erikson, Jacobson, Hartmann, Kohut, Kernberg, Bion. Among the analytical psychologists who have made major contributions in recent years there are Fordham, Redfearn, Gordon, Humbert, Lambert, Schwartz-Salant, Zinkin. And there are in fact many others who would feature in a comprehensive bibliography of writers on the concept of the self.

The ways in which the term self has been used, both in the recent past and currently, have to be studied. So there are various concepts, and factors, and theoretical approaches which have to be taken into account in any reasonably thorough consideration of the matter. Then we have to experiment with applying that body of knowledge when we study what we do as psychotherapists. The self is both the experiential core and the basic theoretical concept in analytical psychology; but it is also the essential dynamic factor which gives meaning and life to the process of ego development, to relationship to others, and to individuation.

Curiosity about what is mutative, as a result of the dynamic factor, and about where and when dynamism and change begin to operate, is behind the work of analysis and therapy. Analysis tries to get to the roots, the origins, and the elements; therapy attends to bringing about healing and improvement. Behind such well-known platitudes is the continuous work of regular sessions where basic research takes place. What happens in the sessions is the raw material and, where the analyst is concerned, reflection is necessary for him or her to make full use of observations and experiences. Fortunately, many patients take great strides forward in their lives without having been the focus of such re-search—like children who get on well with unanxious parents and a bit of healthy neglect. So I do not claim that I do impressive "research" with respect to each of my patients.

Interpreting is one of the things we do to try to bring about change. In searching to describe how we do that appropriately and well, in order to tap mutative possibilities, we must distinguish between two different kinds of interpretation.

First, there are the relatively unanalytic ones, which comment on what is happening, as it seems to the analyst, or which highlight some feature of what the patient has just said. By being enabled to reflect in that way the patient may, semi-independently, gain insight and move forward to integrate a previously unconscious factor, which might any-way not have been very deeply unconscious. Such interpretations are usually accepted easily, provided resistances have been previously well analyzed. The therapist on such an occasion does not need to draw on his or her own deep structures; the use of the therapeutic ego will be all that is required at that point and it will be effective. But of course (if all is well) the therapist's ego is structurally in contact with the less evident self out of which it emerged. His or her ego can be seen as an entity which is, all in all, rather like the patient I spoke about, who used to go to the ball of peat secretly hidden among the stones, to keep in touch with it—which for him "was" the self.

In the other kind of interpretation the analyst can, I think tell that something very inner is at work. It may be described first by its attri-butes—such as inner, or deep, or penetrating—there is a quality, a sense, of approaching the core of the patient's present ill-health and fu-ture health. The hallmark of such an interpretation is the truth of it, to which the patient testifies in whatever is his or her characteristic way. A hallmark, stamped on an object made of precious metal, gold or silver, is reliable and trusted. It is authoritative in a positive way (not authoritarian). And behind the attributes and the imagery which I cannot help using—about inner, and depth, and the hallmark—is the psychological nature of this kind of interpretation. The analyst has confidently relaxed ego controls and defensiveness, believing without much, or indeed any, conscious deliberation that his or her sense of self is reliable. What is happening is that the analyst is in a safe regression and is using the self to link creatively with the self in the patient. That is the mutative factor: the psychic action of linking, which is comparable to the physical act of creation, or generation. The act is fertile: there is life in it.

There is an old saying, which used to be semiconcealed in a Latin tag, that after coitus every man is sad. I have written of fertile interpretations and that is imagery from sexual intercourse. Every physical act of coitus does not fertilize an ovum, but I am speaking in analogies, and sessions where the self of the analyst has generated change in the patient do draw on our inner resources. Analysts get sad at times and tired, as well as patients. Tiredness can be an indicator that a major linkage has been effected. And each one needs a personal equivalent of the ball of peat— we need to know for sure that it is there, we need accessibility to the self.

As well as the analogy of coitus, there is the other body manifestation of the experience of a self interpretation which women analysts can get, I suppose, more directly than male ones can—it is the sensation that it was *as though* there had been a literal breast-feeding, that other kind of intercourse. Male analysts have spoken and written about experiencing genital arousal during a session (but not acting on it); that of course can apply to female ones as well. But the activation of the physical breast has, I have found, happened when the self is linking with the self of the patient. It could be surmised that what happens at such times is that the concurrence of both a primal self experience and a body one show that the patient has regressed to a presymbolic psychic stage, and that a similar regression is possible for, and happening in, the analyst; she can simultaneously step forward in psychic time and understand what is happening—not getting either engulfed or caught in a form of projective identification. It is neither a frightening regression, nor one with negative effects. While consciousness in the analyst remains strong and reliable, such concurrent experiences are not dangerous to the patient, or to the analysis and the therapy, which the patient has implicitly entrusted to the more developed ego of the analyst. It is an ego (all being well) that has integrated earlier regressive experiences and which can tolerate to and fro movements in the psyche, with the attendant but not excessive anxieties.

Aspects of the Nature of the Self

When we study the large and growing literature about the self, we find that much of it stems from an attempt to delineate the nature of it, to discover what it is and what anyone means when using the term. It is wiser to describe than to define it. Definitions constrain it into a perhaps too narrow shape, and then its potential dynamism cannot be given its due. In searching for the source of psychological change, the question is: how do these dynamic symbols arise? The nature of the self has to be studied while we are on the way to the question of change.

Some writers have held that (I quote Rosemary Gordon), "Jung gave us the concept of the 'self' to describe that part of the psyche that is concerned with the experience of wholeness and with the production of images and symbols of wholeness" (1978, p.30). She also wrote: "The self can . . . be thought of as the source of those mental drives and forces that seek and strive for wholeness" (p.31). Those quotations refer to two models: the structural one, in which the term self refers to the wholeness of the psyche, its combined conscious and unconscious areas; and the experiential one, which accounts for symbols which show the self as being the source of drives which seek on some occasions fusion and on others wholeness. We can observe that sometimes those drives operate regressively, when, for instance, a patient has a fantasy of getting right into the analyst's body: the patient's body and psyche will then, it is fantasied, be kept whole and together inside the analyst-mother, or even meet and fuse into the analyst's whole being. The dynamic symbols can also operate in a forward-going movement, a developmental one, when the patient finds that previously separated-off parts of himself or herself are brought in to cooperate with his or her main feeling of personhood. Though real and developed multiplicity is then experienced as integration and may be described as a renewal of original oneness or unity, it would be incorrect to think of the number one and the quality of oneness as invariably preceding two and further numbers. It is, I think, just as possible to conceptualize the unity and selfhood of the individual as having started from two—sperm and ovum—and going forward towards becoming one, the new person. Hence the symbolic use of rebirth in all mystery religions and in Christianity. After each integrating experience of the self in the course of a searching and painful analytical therapy, the patient, who has on successive occasions fully given himself or herself to what was happening, then finds there is a new sense of unity, at the same time as being able to use inner diversity.

Dynamic Aspects of the Self

When the self is studied as a source of dynamism we can see much truth in the various ways that different analysts have written about it. It would be logical of me to move from making use of those passages in Rosemary Gordon's book, *Dying and Creating*, to remind you of Fordham's contributions. And I will come to them shortly. But on the way it is fair to bring in some others who have reflected deeply on these subtleties, since many analysts have revealed implicitly in their writings that they know from personal experience that when a patient is moving into a necessary therapeutic regression the analyst's ego strength is flexible enough for him or her to be in touch with the personal, internal, earliest level. Balint collected several of the terms that different psychoanalysts have used about these states and analytic interactions. He listed: Anna Freud, the need-satisfying object; Hartmann, the average expectable environment; Bion, the container and the contained; Margaret Little, basic unity; Masud Khan, the protective shield; Spitz, the mediator of the environment; Mahler, the extrauterine matrix; Balint, the harmonious interpenetrating mix-up (1968).

Winnicott is studied by many analytical psychologists and indeed he described the self very often: the search for the self, the sense of having an identity or the sense of being, the fear of the loss of self, and the false self. He put at least part of his view clearly if aphoristically at the end of the chapter on "Creativity and its origins" in *Playing & Reality*: "Now I want to say: 'After being—doing and being done to. But first, being'" (1971). In his writings it is clear that the interplay of being and doing happens between people, by means of people; there have to be other selves for the self in an infant (or in any of us) to move from only being, to doing as well as being.

How does that movement arise?

Does any of the "doing"—that is, activity—arise in the self irrespective of other people's selves? For Winnicott the way of describing the basics of being and doing, and being done to, was to conceptualize the original existence, at birth anyway, of a core which could already be called the ego. He wrote that the infant has an ego, which is "unformed, weak, easily disrupted" (1965, p.234). He held the view that it would form, strengthen, and develop integratively provided the famous good-enough mother gave it "ego support . . . with her whole self" (p.234). He also pointed out that the experience of *being* (which is the essence of the entity we call the self), "is passed from one generation to another, via the female element of men and women and of male and female infants . . . it is a matter of the female elements in both males and females" (1971, p.80).

I find Winnicott's writings valuable both from the point of view of the now well-known concepts that can be extracted from them but also, and perhaps even more, because his feeling for how infants, mothers and other people *are* when they interact and interplay—or fail to—corresponds closely to how I feel them and would describe them at times when I do not want to conceptualize or apply my intellect. I want to assume that that part of me is there, but it had better not monopolize the situation. Winnicott's concept of "female elements in both males and females" can be associated with Jung's concept of the syzygy, the animus and anima, which is in some ways more sophisticated. Winnicott's way of looking at the male and female elements can be applied to adulthood, and though for his part Jung did not think of anima and animus in terms of early infancy those contrasexual archetypes can be located very early, if we want.

The main point I wish to stress in alluding to Winnicott in connection with my interest in whether we can trace the mutative factor into the self, is that he was principally studying the interactions between the infant and the mother, and between patients and analysts. It looks as though, if he had been asked where, when, and how, change and development are activated, he might have answered: "In what happens to the one and to the other, between the two."

I will take a short step back in time from that speculation. In 1919 Victor Tausk published a paper entitled, "On the Origin of the Influencing Machine in Schizophrenia (1950). According to Edith Jacobson in her book, *The Self and the Object World* (1965), it was Tausk in that paper who introduced into psychoanalytic literature the term "identity." That fact alerts us to the need for any study of the nature and dynamics of the self to include attempts to answer the following series of questions about identity: "What am I? Who am I? Am I alone? Who else is there? What does the other do to me? What do I do to the other? How do we influence each other?" Those are questions about influence, though not necessarily about pathological versions of it, as I suppose Tausk was writing about. Jacobson pointed out that we have to have a term for the "earliest infantile period," the one in which Fordham locates the primary self. She opted for primary narcissism (p.15), then she added that we have to account for the energic differentiation which happens *when the object starts to be perceived* (italics added). That leads to the well-worn subject of what is an energic drive? or, what several drives are there? She wrote that the term, self, refers "to the whole person of an individual, including his body and his body parts as well as his psychic organization and its parts." That presumably means that she included the drives. She also wrote of a "primal psychophysiological self-containing undifferentiated drive energy" (1965, p.14).

Jacobson's thinking comes near to Fordham's conceptualizations, although I do not think that her work has influenced English analytical psychologists as much as has that other less classical psychoanalyst, Kohut. He had had a wide appeal because he wrote in a clear way where clinical realities are concerned. I am not sure that I can get from his works quite enough help in the search for the mutative factor though I like his hyphenated 'body-mind-self' (1971, p.152), and I appreciate the way he saw introjection and projection functioning within "a total cohesive self" (*ibid.*). In another place he wrote about how "the living self . . . become[s] the organizing center of the ego's activities," which is a pointer to the sort of energy within the self to which I wish to draw attention. In his book entitled *The Restoration of the Self* (1977) there occurs the phrase which has pleased several Jungian writers, the self is "the center of the psychological universe." In another passage he wrote that man's ultimate goal might be "the realization, through his actions, of the blueprint for his life that had been laid down in his nuclear self" (p.133) and that the self is "a center of initiative" (p.245). However, at the end of that book he wrote: "My investigation contains hundreds of pages dealing with the psychology of the self—yet it never assigns an inflexible meaning to the term self, it never explains how the essence of the self should be defined. But I admit this fact without contrition or shame. The self . . . is not knowable in its essence" (1977, pp.310–311). Perhaps what Kohut refers to in writing of the self as a "center of initiative" is something very close to what I am seeking, the dynamic factor which sets change going, as it seems to me most likely to be found in the self.

Deintegration and the Mutative Factor

Many adult people seeking analytical therapy in Britain these days are suffering from the results of deep disturbances which started in infancy, or even earlier, so that increasingly analysts have had to work on the basic structural defects, the sickness of the primary self. Inevitably much attention has been given, on behalf of those patients, to the analytic problems surrounding regression to infancy states, so that Fordham's work on the primary self is of central importance. The research for which he is perhaps best known was on children and babies, and it is mainly from work on infancy that deintegration was launched into the corpus of theories in analytical psychology. For those of us who work with adults it has proved very valuable: the concept throws light on many experiences with them when they are in, and emerging from, regressive primitive states.

Since putting forward many years ago the idea that the self functions not only integratively but that it can deintegrate, Fordham has written about this often. His latest book contains a number of elucidations which draw together his early thesis and his developments of it (1985). In the search for how change is set going, reference can be made to his thinking, in order to test out its applicability to day by day clinical work. He writes about, first, "the infant's individuality, continuity of being and adaptive capacity" (p.31); second, "the self is no longer conceived of as a static structure, instead the steady state represents one phase in a dynamic sequence: integration is followed by deintegration, which in turn leads to a new integrate. The sequence is conceived to repeat throughout life and lies at the root of maturational development" (p.102); and third, "the states arising from deintegration are often unadapted in the first place, since they arise when a new development is required under the stress of internal or external dynamisms" (p.119).

Time and again Fordham stressed the normal healthy infant's inborn capacity to adapt to the mother, and to activate her to adapt to her infant. The infant's adaptation is not mere acquiescence with the environmental demands and realities; Fordham sees it as including in a more important way an infant's capacity to bring influence to bear on outer reality, and to master that area of it in which he finds himself. The infant is making sense gradually of the inner and outer world. If we view the self in its primal state (as compared with the clasical Jungian later-in-life-individuated-self) we see it as a body-psyche integrate. Jung conceptualized libido as consisting of energy bound up in such an integrate; libido in the primary self is neutral; it contains both a loving and creative driving possibility and an attacking and destructive one. The concept of deintegration takes both into account.

In patients whose interactions with their analyst are at times steady and benevolent, and a few sessions later are fraught with envious attacks, we can detect within the *fact* of the deintegrative process the different *qualities* or *characteristics* of the two contrasted driving energies, loving calmly and attacking fiercely. The regression is to early infancy

within the transference and—if the analytic container is strong enough
—only within the sessions. The swings from calmness to attack have to
be tolerated. In such phases of an analysis the analyst has to use the
model of the unanxious mother who tolerates her infant's swings from
steadiness to agitation, and combine that with the analytic understanding that agitation and attack are the forms in which the process of deintegration manifests itself. Since patients often describe themselves as
feeling that they are "going to pieces," or "falling apart" under the impact of more stress than they think they can bear, analysts know they
have to work in such a way as to enable that fear to be lived with while
the patient experiences change and development as in fact acceptable.
The loss of the previous steady state can be integrated when the patient
deepens his or her understanding that these fearful times do not have to
be gone through alone: the presence of the other dispels the fundamental
terror of abandonment, which is perhaps the ultimate loss ("My God, my
God, why hast thou forsaken me?").

An essential aspect of the states and phases being discussed here is
that the analyst and the patient are each still aware of being the people
they are, of the continuity of the sessions and of the changes that the
process entails. Their distinctiveness as individuals is maintained; fusion,
if it occurs, in the course of the kind of experiences I am describing, is
not facilitating. Much like the way the infant gradually discovers (as
Jacobson wrote) that it is in contact with someone different from itself as
well as distinct, so the patient benefits by the analyst not being drawn
into an identification. Full empathy on the part of the analyst and emotional contact of a very deep kind do not entail loss of the essential
boundaries. The ends of the sessions may be very painful and difficult for
both people, but they make possible the acceptance of developmental
differentiation. There is, I think, a close parallel between what is observable in a very elementary form in the young infant's discovery that the
mother is different from itself, and what is experienced countless times
during the working through in painful analytical therapy.

Clinical Example

My hypothesis is that movement leading to change occurs in the following way. In the interests of initial clarity I am omitting the feelings and
emotions which will emerge in the subsequent clinical account. In each
of the analyses in which I have found these things happening, the affect
has been very deeply felt.

The patient has (over the months and probably years) trusted himself or herself, and trusted the analyst, enough to work through and to drop many defenses and accepted psychic intimacy with the analyst, who knows there are strong forces at work. The patient may appear to be in a state which can be described as one of internal unity, and it is also one of regression to preambivalence. Although in some senses he or she is in pain, no effort to emerge seems to be possible. Stress occurs when the analyst detects some signal which shows that the patient is almost ready to emerge from this state of unity—it will have become a lonely one. If the schizoid feature is paramount, the patient may even seem to want the quietness of retreat to death. The signal may be in a dream, or several dreams, or something said. The analyst, if true to the task as caretaker and receiver of the transference projection of motherhood, responds and offers something; on some occasions it might be only a single remark—but it is felt as intrusive—that is what causes stress of some sort. Then perhaps there is a fantasy or another dream or a gesture which when analyzed bring to consciousness a developmental change. It is revealed that "the other" exists and is being responded to.

Where there had been unity (even though it was a pathological one) there is now diversity. The creative interaction between patient and analyst was preceded by readiness for change. Since archetypes are inborn potentialities, that readiness has an archetypal quality and it is an intrinsic element in the original healthy self which must, if at all possible, be believed to be there, and reached.

I would like to describe a phase of the analysis of the patient who features at the beginning of this chapter, which substantiates my hypothesis (see also Chapter 8, "Envy and the shadow").

G, as I will call him, and I were both finding his analysis very stressful and difficult. He had been coming for six years. There were days when I was not sure if I would be able to go on. G had become unemployed— he had never had work which was up to his potential—and the schizoid factor seemed to be becoming ever more pronounced.

I thought, as indeed had been evident all through the analysis, that unless the deep splits could be healed there was not much hope of improvement in his life. It was midwinter—as it was so often in his black dreams. One particularly cold day G arrived twenty minutes late and said he did not want to go on coming, he would rather stay where he was and desist from the apparently endless effort involved in analysis. I can now see from perusing the notes I took at the time that in the countertransference I was seriously caught up in the depressive reaction he was causing in me and the consequent deep tiredness, both of which were strongly tinged with hopelessness. Somehow—responding to his absolute need to find a parent that he could use developmentally?—I took up the whole issue of how frightened he was both of going on and of stopping. Then he became very blocked and gave me a most baleful look as he left, hunching up his shoulders which seemed to demonstrate that his paranoid fears were paramount, that he was all alone and that only he could look after himself. He was evidently alone in a bad, cold, place. I wondered if he was abaondoning me.

The next day, having arrived punctually (an initial good sign), a potential change from bad aloneness towards less bad relationship was just perceptible. He told me that he was afraid he had been trying to do his own analysis, trying to exclude me: he gets too little and too much from me. He had—during the session—a fantasy of his eyes, his nose and his mouth excreting black dirt unless he controls those holes very strenuously; he cannot let in anything I say since the holes have to be kept shut. Then he said: "I see! I was trying to blackmail you into telling me not to go on coming." While blackmail was evidently meant to sound exclusively bad, it was just perceptible that it might be an improvement on not wanting to continue the analysis, which would have been a deathlike state, not one symbolically comparable to the infant's steady restful sleep after a satisfactory feed. So it seemed to me that I should continue to try to function as his analyst, accepting and acting on the hint that "blackmail" contained.

In the succeeding weeks attacks of various kinds continued in reaction to what he, correctly, perceived as my efforts to be allowed in to him. He complained that I would not let him be. I was, naturally, anxious about whether it was either right or wise not to give up. One day I risked interpreting the painful sessions as being reproductions in the present of the dangers early in his life. He had been given the same name as that of two uncles each of whom had drowned and he had needed to be actively kept alive; I said he felt I was being too hard on him, as perhaps the infant in him feels he is being rubbed to keep his circulation going, but the rubbing is rough. Looking back, I think it was right to keep in with his frequent use of body imagery, since he and I were in the area of the body-psyche integrate, although unfortunately for G it was not one felt to have been good. I still had to see whether that could change.

There followed two blessed sessions in which he moved from sitting at the end of the couch in a stiff and hostile way to lying down again, relaxing physically, lying sideways, with his legs bent, his hands and arms both directed towards me. His usual position on the couch was lying very straight—he was tall and lanky—and I had some time before told him that he looked as though he were laid out in his coffin. Now there were easy silences and he told me he felt comfortable for the first time in many months. He said he felt my face was now certainly *mine*; previously it has been *a* face, and at times even only an eye. The evil eye, presumably.

The weekend gap led to a renewal of tense and angry attacks, but he was able to accept that his anger had been brought about by frustration; he would have liked to continue in the comfortable relaxation. Once G could appreciate that feeling angry and attacking were not being interpreted as negative reactions but that they were evidence of hunger, he was able to tackle the anxiety that he was "too much" for me. He did not discover that he nearly had been, and he was able to find out a great deal, over the next few weeks, about the destructive character of that hunger when it turns into dangerous envy. The schizoid cutting off came within reach of being interpreted via the transference and countertransference projections; he discovered that I was not going to be the one to cut the analysis short. Could my desire to be like a mother whose capacity to respond to him was activated by him, the infant, be brought into line with the psychic reality of his early deprivations and be of use to him?

Retrospectively, I think the issue was whether the positive mutative energy inherent in the self was going to be generated between him and me, so that emergence from the early integrate was going to be possible. In his case, all the appearances were that that integrate had not been experienced comfortably. But I do not think he would have emerged (as he did) if there had not been the fundamentally healthy possibility of him evoking responsiveness in me.

In some sessions he complained, 'You're sitting there, I'm lying here'. He would like, he said, to cuddle warmly, rocking to and fro, while a quiet voice spoke to him. He dreamed that I had fleas in my hair, which I had caught from him. Then various fantasies developed designed to convey he felt I was keeping him at a distance. He probably took the flea dream literally. He also said I was not interested in him—he was far from the mark!—and he wanted me to be. Then he divulged that he "had always felt it was a law that he should not get the things he wants." He talked about the sensation as of ants in his legs, a kind of wriggling liveliness which he longed to respond to but forbade himself. He accepted that trying to deny my interest in him was a form of denying his natural needs. And after a while he allowed himself excited pleasure. It was the pleasure of change.

This series of sessions during the midwinter weeks culminated (after several set-backs which always took place over the weekend) in him discussing whether he could make some marmalade and bring me a pot of it. He found he could. He decided he was not only a giver of black shit. The events of that winter were followed by a considerable period of working through, with similar though less extreme regressions and dangers.

In sum, I had had to make an impact on G at the time when he was at risk of regressing irretrievably to a primitive state of psychosomatic unity. But I could only do that when I trusted to the very small possibility that "blackmail" stemming from him was an unconscious but active reaching out from the self in him to the self in me. The adaptive capacity in me sensed that same factor in him. I think it has been worth examining my records of an analysis which took place, as I wrote at the beginning of this chapter, quite a while ago. It has been possible, I submit, to set those experiences side by side with the hypothesis of the dynamic, mutative, factor in the self, and to see their relevance. The concept of the ordinary healthy baby's inborn capacity to adjust to the mother and to activate her to adapt to him was in effect applied in the case of a far from healthy man, although I did not think of it that way at the time.

Conclusion

There is still an ultimate question, much less easily solved than the riddle of the Sphinx, as to what the mutative factor is, where it is to be found, and how it can be activated. I cannot claim to offer an irrefutable answer. Within depth psychology the question is probably analogous to the problem which activates the microbiologist's research into the beginning of life. But I believe it is true to say that the possibility of change lies *in* the self and that it moves from the possible to the actual when two selves meet. We observe archetypal activity, not archetypes in their essence. We take part in change, it is integral to us as alive and active beings.

References

Balint, M. 1968. *The Basic Fault.* London: Tavistock.

Fordham, M. 1985. *Explorations into the Self.* Library of Analytical Psychology, Vol. 7. London: Karnac Books.

Gordon, R. 1978. *Dying and Creating.* Library of Analytical Psychology, Vol. 4. London: Karnac Books.

Jacobson, E. 1965. *The Self and the Object World.* London: Hogarth.

Kohut, H. 1971. *The Analysis of the Self*. New York: International Universities Press.

———. 1977. *The Restoration of the Self*. New York: International Universities Press.

Tausk, V. 1919. On the Origin of the "Influencing Machine" in Schizophrenia, in Fliess, R., ed. *The Psychoanalytic Reader*. London: Hogarth (1950).

Winnicott, D.W. 1965. *The Maturational Processes and the Facilitating Environment*. London: Hogarth.

———. 1971. *Playing and Reality*. London: Tavistock.

Subject Index

Author Index